So many of us are disillusioned, despairing [...] hollow God-talk we hear today. Yet we can't quell our soul's ache for an encounter with divine love. St. Teresa knew this despair, this ache—and Laurel Mathewson knows it too. These pages, from the heart of a pastor with the pen of a poet, carry us through deep, mysterious waters and into the Mercy that will never let us go.

—Winn Collier
Director, The Eugene Peterson Center for Christian Imagination,
Western Theological Seminary, Holland, MI
Author, *Love Big, Be Well* and *A Burning in My Bones: The Biography of Eugene Peterson*

There seems to be an invitation afoot to unfurl our hand, unclench our fist, release the stormy first draft of how we see God, how we think about religion and spirituality. Through the depth of Laurel's hike, her wrestle, her honesty, and the intimacy of her conversation with St. Teresa of Ávila, we are invited to re-member, re-story and wonder anew. *An Intimate Good* is the book I want to read when I'm wrestling with my faith. This is a book I want more of.

—Felicia Murrell
Author, *And: The Restorative Power of Love in an Either/Or World*

I was deeply moved by *An Intimate Good*. Laurel Mathewson is a fantastic guide to St. Teresa of Ávila's masterpiece *The Interior Castle*. The writing is engaging, accessible, and deeply sincere. And yet this book is more than a companion to reading Teresa of Ávila—it's also a powerful personal memoir of Mathewson's own journey of experiencing the close presence of God through the gift of prayer and contemplation. I would highly recommend this book to anyone who wants to understand why Teresa of Ávila's writings on prayer have been celebrated for hundreds of years and the integral connection between a life of contemplation and a life of action.

—Rev. Adam Russell Taylor
Author, *A More Perfect Union: A New Vision for Building the Beloved Community*
President, Sojourners

Christian mystical experience in the American context includes shimmering testimonies from Ann Lee, Nat Turner, Rufus Jones, Howard Thurmond, Thomas Merton, Kathleen Norris, and more. Now add the surprising experiences of Laurel Mathewson—a thoroughly postmodern priest, wife, and mother in Southern California—who falls in love with sixteenth-century Spanish saint Teresa of Ávila. Mathewson's voice is so refreshing one is tempted to guzzle her words—but sip and savor. The voyage of a single soul is more precious than all else. Mathewson invites readers on a candid journey through spiritual wreckage that anyone serious about knowing God will confront. With St. Teresa of Ávila guiding Mathewson, and Mathewson guiding us, we can learn to breathe in the darkness.

—**Rose Marie Berger**
Author, *Bending the Arch: Poems*
Senior Editor, *Sojourners* magazine (sojo.net)

Long recognized as a classic text on the mystical way, *The Interior Castle* of Teresa of Ávila can seem remote and impenetrable to the contemporary reader. Not so for this author, who engages Teresa as an experienced guide and teacher. By chronicling her own spiritual journey with a disarming candor that reflects Teresa's own transparency, Laurel Mathewson opens the way for readers to find their own story embedded in those "dwelling places" with God whose contours Teresa knows so well. This is, above all, a *helpful* book for spiritual seekers no matter their starting point along the inner path.

—**The Reverend Julia M. Gatta, PhD**
Bishop Frank A. Juhan Professor of Pastoral Theology
The School of Theology, The University of the South, Sewanee, TN

An Intimate Good gracefully merges St. Teresa of Ávila's timeless wisdom with Laurel Mathewson's thought-provoking insights, creating a profoundly inspiring guide for skeptical and deconstructing Christians. This beautifully crafted book offers a trustworthy roadmap through the vast terrains of the spiritual journey, encouraging transformative self-discovery and a deeper connection with the Divine. A captivating exploration that leaves an indelible mark on the heart, *An Intimate Good* is a must-read for those seeking a more meaningful understanding of their faith.

—**Rev. Brandan Robertson**
Pastor and Author, *Dry Bones and Holy Wars: A Call for Social and Spiritual Renewal*

Laurel Mathewson offers an intimate and contemporary inquiry into Teresa of Ávila's life and spiritual journey. Many who seek a deeper knowing have heard of the saint of Ávila, yet relatively few have walked Teresa's way for years and years, journeying closer and deeper into the heart of God. Those who abide in the journey will, at turns, discover frustration, enlightenment, muteness, surprise, boredom, ecstasy, doubt, confirmation, and more. The author describes her own experience of persistently walking alongside Teresa, supported and accompanied by the divine presence. Readers of this book will meet wonder, joy, the desert, and a deeper and more expansive knowing of God and self. Teresa's journey is both contemporary and ancient, and her wisdom a bountiful gift for our season.

—**Katharine Jefferts Schori**
Former Presiding Bishop and Primate of the Episcopal Church of the United States

AN

INTIMATE
GOOD

A SKEPTICAL CHRISTIAN MYSTIC IN CONVERSATION WITH TERESA OF ÁVILA

LAUREL
MATHEWSON

WHITAKER
HOUSE

AN INTIMATE GOOD:
A Skeptical Christian Mystic in Conversation with Teresa of Ávila

laurelmathewson.com

ISBN: 979-8-88769-090-2
eBook ISBN 979-8-88769-091-9
Printed in the United States of America
© 2024 by Laurel Mathewson

Whitaker House
1030 Hunt Valley Circle
New Kensington, PA 15068
www.whitakerhouse.com

Library of Congress Cataloging-in-Publication Data
LC record available at https://lccn.loc.gov/2023051625
LC ebook record available at https://lccn.loc.gov/2023051626

1 2 3 4 5 6 7 8 9 10 11   ⊔⊔   31 30 29 28 27 26 25 24

To Christ Jesus:
   "Behold, I did not restrain my lips;
   And that, O LORD, you know."
                              —Psalm 40:10

and

To my mother, Elizabeth,
   who first taught me
   that truth is more valuable than comfort
   and that to be cherished and well-loved marks us indelibly.

NOTE FROM THE AUTHOR

I employ the term *mystic* in the title of this book and in reference to myself in a particular and limited way. As derived from the work of Evelyn Underhill, I define "mysticism" as *the experience of the love of God.* Underhill used the witness of the mystics themselves to develop this definition.[1] Underhill, Teresa of Ávila, and basic Christian theology and anthropology would all assert that *every* human being has a capacity for knowing God—and receiving that same love in various forms and through different avenues.

O secrets of God!

I would never tire of trying to explain them to you

    if I thought I could do so somewhat successfully.

Thus I will say a thousand foolish things

    so that I might even once succeed,

    and we may give great praise to the Lord.

                    —Teresa of Ávila, *The Interior Castle*

CONTENTS

FOREWORD

Laurel Mathewson's book begins in a conversation with her young daughter about "the stories of God." Why, asks her six-year-old, don't more people have these stories, know them, care about them, or "believe"? It ends with a family discussion—now including her husband Colin and their young son—about the same subject. In the middle is Laurel's story about God in her life, which has culminated, so far, in a calling to ordination in the Episcopal Church and co-pastoring, with Colin, at St. Luke's, a multicultural and refugee-centered urban church in San Diego, California.

That story includes a year (2006–2007) during which both Laurel and Colin served as interns with Sojourners. When Laurel invited me to write this foreword, she wondered if I would remember her and her husband. Of course, I did, and readily agreed to read the book and say a few words about this conversation between a "skeptical Christian mystic" and a prayerful saint who lived four hundred years ago: Teresa of Ávila. It sounded interesting—and it is.

To understand God's story, it is important for all of us to understand our story with God—our faith journey, with all its twists and turns, starts and stops, ups and downs, pain and sorrow, love and joy. I often contrast the religion that for some is about *certainty* but for many of us is rather about *reflection*. On the certainty versus reflection front, this personal journal or memoir is on the reflection side, and focused on another word that has been crucial for the author: *trust*.

It's hard for many people to trust religion these days, and attendance in churches across the country, including in Laurel's mainline denomination, is declining. Even the language to be found in this book, full of religious terms, is off-putting for many people. Given these realities, I tried something.

The famous Smithsonian Folklife Festival, always held during the summer on the Mall in Washington, DC, decided to focus its 2023 event on a subject they had never highlighted before: religion. That choice evoked many responses and clearly prompted some concerns and even provoked backlash because of what religion has sometimes meant in this nation and in people's personal life experiences. I was asked to participate in an opening session with my friend and colleague Brad Braxton, an African American theologian and the new president of Chicago Theological Seminary.

In my opening remarks, I told the crowd that they were about to hear words, terms, and texts that were considered "religious," and I predicted—no, guaranteed—that many in the audience, even most, would react to that language with feelings of disappointment, pain, rejection, hurt, betrayal, abuse, and even assault. There wasn't time to go around and hear all of the underlying experiences before we began, but I wanted to acknowledge them, respect them, and bring them into this discussion with a moment of silence and reflection. I found, as I had in other very "secular" settings, that just acknowledging those very common feelings—which we find among both the nonreligious and religious—would help calm the moment and perhaps make us all more open to listening. Afterward, many people shared how they had felt welcomed into the conversation.

I will offer the same acknowledgment here. This book does contain lots of religious words, terms, Scriptures, sculptures, prayers, and books of reflections about the true meaning of faith. But Laurel does not use them uncritically or without purpose. Rather, she digs into her faith tradition for tools to build a more just and restorative spiritual framework.

I found it intriguing the way Laurel discovered in Saint Teresa of Ávila an ancient partner with whom to engage in dialogue. For all the importance of our dialogues with contemporary mentors and friends, a dialogue with a past believer—such as the one we witness in this book between two women of faith in patriarchal societal and religious structures separated by over four centuries—is a fascinating conversation. That is because questions of faith and practice are not new but very old. After reading this book, I might even suggest that you follow Laurel's course here: find an ancient saint of the faith who may inspire and help instruct you in the ways of prayer and action.

This book speaks about how the love and closeness of God we experience is intended to move out into the world. Laurel says she is very interested in the relationship between Christians committed to social justice and those more drawn to individual expressions of faith. But she is not interested in a mere balance; rather, Laurel explores a deeper integration of faith focused on changing the world with faith drawn to changing personal lives. How about both? What is the deeper connection between spirituality and justice? Or, what is the spirituality of justice?

Saint Teresa was a reformer as well as a contemplative; she did not want to segregate her faith and spirituality from the "complexities of real relationships in a dysfunctional world." Turning prayer into active love was what she lived for, a path "exemplified by Jesus." Unconnected "mystical spirituality" she found "foreign in many ways," which leads Laurel to refer to Saint Teresa as a "grounded mystic." Saint Teresa believed that "the movement of God to an individual must be extended into the world." Throughout this book, Laurel cites many quotes from Saint Teresa—in fact, many more than I had ever read before. One of my favorites is this: "Perfection as well as its rewards does not consist in spiritual delights but in greater love and in deeds done with greater justice and truth."

This book also refers to a retreat during Laurel and Colin's time at Sojourners, led by Vincent Harding, where he said, "If you allow yourself to really hunger and thirst for what is right and just in this world, you will be filled." You can read Laurel's very personal back-and-forth with Vincent, expressing her deep grief after the tragic loss of her mother. While being deeply sensitive to her despair and hopelessness, Vincent responded:

> I think that one of the ways I would just begin to respond to the cry that you are expressing is [to say] that I have lived my life... among just such a magnificent set of witnesses to love and compassion that I know that in spite of what I run into in certain dry periods, I know that the universe is full of that kind of love and compassion; everywhere I go there are people who manifest that. And so I know that that is not in short supply.
>
> And part of what's involved is simply being willing to let my hunger and thirst be known...and out of that comes a response, almost automatically, in ways that would have to be called miraculous sometimes. But crazy folks who are involved with things like quantum physics tell us that that's the way the universe works. When we let certain energies flow out of us, they attract certain energies that are almost waiting for that call and response. And all I'm trying to say, Laurel, is that the encouragement towards hope that you are crying out for is already present, and is going to be surprising you around one corner or another, or even around this circle. And the great challenge is not to be afraid to expect it.

Vincent went on:

> As I understand it, one of our major purposes for being human is to engage the grief and the joy of other humans. And, indeed, it seems to me that we can't even be fully human without exercising that gift that human beings share with one another.... And what I find all through the accounts of the biblical experience is testimony to this whole idea that we exist to help mediate the loving presence of God—to each other, through each other, with each other, in each other—and that, in a deep sense, we're not meant to grieve alone, nor are we meant to rejoice alone, that the connecting web is one that, in a sense, it's like a cord that needs to be plucked for us to really know both the depth of the grieving and the possibilities of the healing.

We were created to be with and for each other. When we miss that, we miss the point of our creation—and that's why we feel so miserable sometimes.

I remember that retreat and Laurel's painful place and questions. You should read the whole exchange, which she recounts in detail. It is another example of the importance of mentors like the now departed Vincent Harding—one of my dearest—and the ancient voices from the past that can show us the way in the present and for the future.

Near the end of her book, Laurel says that "humans have a tendency to become spirituality junkies, seeking the high and wanting to find ways to avoid the hike." This is the story of Laurel's hike, and I am sure she and Saint Teresa will be valuable companions for your own.

—*Rev. Jim Wallis*
Archbishop Desmond Tutu Chair in Faith and Justice,
Georgetown University
Founder, Sojourners

PROLOGUE

October 15, 2017
The Feast Day of Saint Teresa of Ávila

It is early evening and already dark. I'm approaching the San Diego skyline, heading south on I-5, when my typically taciturn six-year-old daughter pipes up from the back seat. "Why don't most people go to church?" she asks. "Because a lot of people don't go to church," she adds, in case this is news to me. Obviously mentally running through her list of school friends, who were a recent topic of conversation, she concludes, "Most of the people I know don't."

I fumble, pause, surprised that this reality is already apparent to her. I thought we had a couple more years.

"Well, some people go to church," I say, "but they don't go that often, or they haven't found a church that they feel is a good fit." The delusional and optimistic church employee in me is speaking now. I am dodging the truth.

"Yeah, but some people don't go at all because they don't even believe."

"Whoa," I think. "'They don't even believe'? What is that shorthand for in her young brain? Is it 'believe in God' like 'believe in Santa Claus'?" I suppress my questions about the nature of her belief so the conversation can continue. I am thinking of my sister, my brother, and so many friends who believe in some benevolent force or higher power—some who would even call that force or power "God"—but who never go to church; I want to be fair:

"Some people believe, but they don't go to church," I say. "They don't find it helpful. We are trying to help people connect with God and one another at church, but sometimes we don't do a very good job."

This feels closer to honest, but still…I know I digress. I am sidestepping.

She circles back around to the insistent truth that she doesn't want me to miss: "But a lot of people don't even believe. They just don't believe."

You can't dodge the truth easily with a six-year-old.

"Yeah," I say, "but sometimes they have never really heard the stories of God."

I don't know exactly where I am going with this. Defending these little unbelievers from her potential judgment? And "stories of God"? Was that really the best way to put it? Nevertheless, it feels honest. I do think our culture is awash in generic Christian words, but these words are like strange-looking tchotchkes from another generation. We know little about them except that they were prized by our grandparents.

But my daughter gets excited: "I know! I've heard the stories of God *so many times*, but some people haven't even heard them." I wince a little at her overconfidence, but she is on a roll, and I say nothing as she continues.

"It's like they don't even know what they don't believe, you know? Which doesn't make any sense! Like, I can say I don't believe in orange whales, but they don't even know what they don't believe; they can't even describe it."

She begins to try to problem-solve. I don't think she likes Sunday morning church very much herself, which is maybe why she asks, "What if everyone just had church in their home every night, like we used to do with compline?" She has been hinting that she misses this intimate ritual of candles and set prayers in the living room. We gave it up when her younger brother came along.

Then she almost seems to talk herself out of this proposal, perhaps realizing that a home group, by itself, would be too small to fully express the stories of God. "Because then you might only hear the same two stories again and again, one on one night and then the other, and back and forth and back and forth, but you need to *push through*, not just go back and forth with the same two stories." She is getting really animated now: "You can't just stay with the same stories again and again; they need to *push through*!" I don't know where she is getting this phrase. Is it from school? Do they talk about "pushing through" to new understandings or something?

Yet I am struck by her insight. "You are right," I say. "God is very complicated, very difficult to know about and understand. We cannot know God from just our own experiences or one or two stories."

We need help. We need a lot of people to tell us what they know about God. I think about the hundreds—maybe thousands—of stories that have given me food for mind and soul during my relatively short journey on earth.

I think about how there is so much I want to share with my daughter—and her friends—but the car ride would never be long enough.

I hear a question from Scripture echoing in my head as we pass through Balboa Park and on toward home:

How then shall they call on the One in whom they have not trusted? And how shall they trust in the One they have not heard of? And how shall they hear without someone proclaiming?[2]

Most Bible translations use the word *believe* in this verse, but I prefer *trust*. Because for most of my early adulthood, I didn't believe the central claims of Christianity, in a head sense. For a long time, I was basically an agnostic, or an enlightenment-styled deist. But with a few short exceptions, I have tried, all these years, to trust that God is real and good and loving. I have tried, often failing, to *live* as though the claims are true. In time, God graciously, insistently confirmed for me the wildest claims, the ones I had the most trouble believing: That God is close. That the name and person of

Jesus have cosmic significance. That the One who made us knows us better than we know ourselves, and loves us more than we could ask or imagine.

I want my children to call on this One who loves beyond belief—and I want the same for my daughter's friends who don't believe. At six, my oldest already knows it is weird to believe. I want her to know why the label of weirdness is more than worth it to me, why I hope that friends who are leery of religious-talk will push through to a place of listening. Yet *"how shall they hear without someone proclaiming?"* The Lord knows I am a reluctant evangelist; talking about faith is not normal in my family of origin, and I like to be thought of as normal and well-adjusted as much as the next person. But some things are just too marvelous to keep to oneself, reputation be damned.

There are lots of "stories of God" out there, and mine is but one. My story will be as inadequate to the task of portraying the goodness of the One we can trust in as the words "stories of God" are in their attempt to describe what it is we humans are doing when we talk about our knowledge, our personal experiences, of God. But I take comfort and courage in the fact that such an effort is not something new; it is not just a sub-fad of the memoir genre. It is older, even, than the work of a sixteenth-century Spanish saint whose own stories of God have illuminated and clarified mine.

Saint Teresa, I will write. Pray for me.

July 29, 2022
Santa Maria della Vittoria, Rome

On a late afternoon in July, when the streets of Rome are full of heat and light and cars and people, my husband and I make our way to a quieter, cooler place: the church of Santa Maria della Vittoria, where the doors have just reopened after the afternoon break. I had visited this ornate baroque building twelve years earlier, but I am still disoriented as the heavy, dark doors close behind me.

My first visit in 2010 had been singular in purpose, the same purpose as so many visitors to "La Vittoria": to view the next in a long parade of beautiful and historically important churches that were on my sightseeing list. I remember entering the church on a rainy May morning and looking at its most famous sculpture—*Ecstasy of Saint Teresa* by Gian Lorenzo Bernini—with recognition and curiosity. Recognition, because, one time in prayer, I had known something like what Teresa is depicted as experiencing (angel notwithstanding) but had never talked about it. Curiosity, because I didn't know anything else about Saint Teresa of Ávila except her name. I had tried to read her work *The Interior Castle* in college but had found it frustrating—full of strange images and foreign. I didn't make it far before giving up on the book and wondering dismissively about its designation as a "masterpiece" on prayer.

Yet when I looked upon the Bernini sculpture, I was intrigued. When I connected Teresa with the seemingly impenetrable tome I'd cast off after two chapters, I took note. "Maybe someday I'll give it another look," I thought. But then, I didn't—I went off to seminary, and I got busy reading other things. Teresa remained frozen in my mind as Bernini had rendered her: semi-reclined, eyes closed, mouth half open, her right hand palm up, with a single finger curled evocatively toward the sky.

It wasn't until March 2017—about six months before my conversation with my daughter in the car on I-5—that Teresa's ideas and person began to come alive for me, beginning with, but moving beyond, this image of ecstasy. In the wake of some very new and surprising experiences in my own prayer life, I felt God inclined my head to her anew: "Turn to Teresa," I heard. "She will guide you." And so began the next leg in my life of faith, in which this sixteenth-century saint and her teachings, particularly in *The Interior Castle*, became my trusted, venerable, and well-traveled companion on the journey.

Now I have come back to Santa Maria della Vittoria to look again upon this iconic depiction of Teresa that I had first seen before I knew her. However, I do not make a beeline to the Bernini sculpture, as so many visitors do. Having gotten to know Teresa through her own voice, to do so seems voyeuristic. So, I first take time to pray in a side chapel, trying to re-collect myself to God's presence and open my heart and mind to what this visit might reveal. Eventually, I continue into the nave of the church, looking at each side chapel with intent. I ponder a statue of Joseph, Mary's husband, receiving a comforting touch from an angel while he sleeps, addressing his distress at Mary's scandalous pregnancy.

Finally, I turn around and see that other, more famous angel by Teresa's side. Yet, this time around, I am not captivated or even particularly intrigued by the central sculpture itself. Instead, I notice what is all around it: the flaming heart set into the small gates to the chapel, an image that reflects the "real" center of Teresa's work, if not Bernini's: the human heart inflamed with and by love, the human heart burning with passion from and for God. I think of the baroque English poets who wrote about their own inflamed hearts as a result of reading Teresa's words, and my own experiences both before and after reading those same texts, four hundred years later. I consider closely the sculptures in the galleries to the right and the left of Teresa and the angel—those figures that are "on stage" forever. To the right, I see four men, and none of them are actually looking at Teresa. But they are talking, talking, and one is looking pointedly away. I think of all the men (and women!) and authorities in general who had a lot to say about Teresa's work and writings but who may not have really seen who she was or what she was truly saying or doing. To the left, I see more of the same: four other men talking, talking, and yet not a single face looking directly at Teresa. I knew she was often the subject of gossip and semi-scandalized criticisms of her writing and the experiences she recounted. And yet she wrote boldly about what God had done in her life and in her prayers—not once but many times.

I return to the back of the church, near the entry doors, and kneel before a painting of Saint Teresa, although the glare of the sun obscures her face. Unexpectedly, into my analytic reflections about perseverance in the face of misunderstanding, a flood of gratitude washes over me. I begin to cry as this deep thanksgiving seeps into my body, heart, and then mind: what goodness this woman has given me through her writings and teachings! She has given me strength as a priest and a pastor; insights that deepened and transformed my faith and my whole perspective on where and how God is present to us; texts that allowed me to trust in Christ's intimate closeness, care, and communication to me, thanks to her author-ity, self-disclosure, wisdom, and humble confidence. I simply would not have the richness of faith and relationship with Christ that I do without her help and guidance. I knew even before I was "grateful" that *The Interior Castle* had been a marvelous map for me as I sought understanding of new terrains in prayer, yet I had never really seen the fullness of the gift or the long-lasting repercussions in my life, five years after opening its pages.

In the cathartic moment when the tears subside, I look again at the painting before me. The saint is holding roses, scattering them. The roses suddenly represent to me the beauty of Teresa's teachings, poured out for others. She had been questioned, mocked, castigated, and censured in her sharing of these teachings; nevertheless, she persisted in sharing them. In seeing this tension between the gift of her teachings and others' misunder-standing of them, I cannot help but think of the book I have just written about my own experiences of God's love in prayer, a love made known not only in my mind but also in my body, and I realize I can expect no less if I am truly being faithful to Christ, in Teresa's footsteps. I should and do expect that many will talk about me or what I have written without truly seeing or understanding, and that there may be moments of misconcep-tion. But now, soaked in gratitude, I hear these words: *Remember the roses.* Remember the beauty and goodness and reality of what Teresa illuminated for you when there is misunderstanding or even mockery. Remember what all of this is about, really, for her and for you: sharing gifts of *God's* good-ness and beauty and passion for us, gifts received in prayer and then scat-tered through writing to others in the world. I have been immeasurably strengthened by Teresa's "sharing," and it has always been my prayer and the only grounds of my writing that others might be similarly strength-ened, healed, or blessed by God, by Teresa's teachings, through my witness.

Only later, I learn that the painting in La Vittoria of Teresa holding the roses, by Giorgio Szoldatics, is actually a representation of Saint Teresa of Lisieux—"Saint Teresa of *the Child* Jesus," not "Saint Teresa of Jesus," as I had mistakenly read it, which would have indeed pointed to Ávila. In other words, the painting is of the nineteenth-century French nun who is often known by her nickname "the little flower," not the sixteenth-century Spanish nun to whom I am so indebted. At first, I think, "How embar-rassing! I had the wrong Teresa! I *thought* her face looked too young!" My

Protestant ignorance on full display. But then I reconsider. Saint Teresa of Lisieux was a discalced Carmelite nun, the order that Saint Teresa of Ávila founded through her reform work. Saint Teresa of Lisieux, like Saint Teresa of Ávila, penned a spiritual autobiography before her death, a text that has been among her greatest gifts of faith to the world. It is not just Teresa of Ávila who shows us this pattern—this has been the way of faith in the world since the most ancient of days: gifts passed from parent to child, from friend to friend, from sister to sister. We do the earthly work given us to do, and we tell our stories of God, full of doubt, darkness, light, surprise, love, and perseverance. And sometimes, in a way that no one can predict or control, the Holy Spirit illuminates the pages, the words scattered for the sake of others, and they become beautiful, fragrant, real: they open a door to the current and close presence of God in our own lives, to a goodness at hand that pierces our illusions of isolation and insignificance, to an insistent love aimed at our very heart.

This is my prayer for this book, now that I have finished writing my story (to this point, anyway). And, after getting to know her better, I can say with confidence that it is Saint Teresa's prayer, too.

INTRODUCTIONS

The Form

As I mentioned in the prologue to this book, in the wake of an unexpected and overwhelming experience of God's nearness and love, I felt God say to me in the quiet of a warm, sunny sacristy, "Turn to Teresa. She will guide you." I knew that "Teresa" was Teresa of Ávila, who had crossed my path only very briefly three other times. I had read nothing of her work in over fifteen years. But after that morning in March, I sought the counsel of my spiritual director, a retired professor of Christian spirituality. She gave me a stack of books on Teresa of Ávila, John of the Cross, and Sarah Coakley (a contemporary theologian). In the meantime, I continued to feel God's nearness and goodness in ways I had no language for, though my spiritual director was an essential and immediate comfort and guide. Finally, in August, I took up God's advice to look to Teresa. I read *The Interior Castle* and found a retrospective guide for so much of what I had experienced and lived, from my earliest childhood memories of being curious about this "God" whom I had continued to seek and doubt and seek.

It was like this:

And in the wilderness
> where you saw how the LORD your God carried you,
> just as a man carries his son,
> in all the way which you have walked
> until you came to this place.[3]

It was marvelous—and I truly marveled—to discover a text that illuminated my spiritual path with such insight, candor, and clarity. I have not yet "arrived," by any definition, and cannot say my experiences resonate with the final dwelling places of spiritual maturity that Saint Teresa describes. But I trust, indeed know, that I am not the only one who might be fed and strengthened by her teachings, half a millennium down the line. This book, then, has two aims: The first is to share Teresa's observations and instructions, from her own experiences, with an audience who knows little about her, as little (or less) than I did. The second is to share, as experienced in my own life and the lives of others, the perpetual truth alive in our day and at the heart of all of Teresa's four-hundred-year-old writings: the love and closeness of a good God, as known through Jesus Christ, seeking to move out into the world, into our very bodies and lives.

I was not, by nature or training, inclined to believe such wild claims. But God is full of surprises, and so here I am, presenting myself as your guide to Teresa of Ávila's *Interior Castle* and the very real "spiritual" dwelling places that she describes, trusting that they may help you navigate or understand the dwelling places inhabited in your own life.

But first, a few introductions are in order.

Of Whom Do You Speak? Naming the Stars and the Star Maker

One day, when she was seven, my older daughter asked me why people stop being married. She didn't even know the word for it. And so I tried to reduce a complex—perhaps unreachable—answer to a simple statement, as parents often do. "People stop being married because they can't find a way to live together in peace," I said.

It is that simple. And, of course, it is not at all that simple.

I have long struggled with this tension between the extremes of simplicity and mystery when it comes to speaking the truth or trying to talk about anything that matters, including—especially—God. There are obvious dangers to both poles: to talk *only* in simple declaratives is to quickly declare yourself a fool, because the created order is simply not that simple. But to stake your claim *only* on the pole of mystery, never venturing toward any clear claim, renders all words superfluous; you might as well declare yourself mute. Such a posture applied to the spiritual life seems to me like pretending our universe is a great blackness of "we don't know," denying the existence of any recognizable light, any familiar stars discovered, named, and pointed to by our ancestors. The stars that do, in ways real and important, illuminate meaning in our lives. So then: How to name the stars, learn to speak of them, and trust at least a few important constellations to help us find our way—without losing sight of the real fact that they are indeed surrounded by so much black?

I can't speak for other cultures, times, or contexts, but I have known in my gut from about the age of fifteen that, as a word—intended for communication, connection—God doesn't work very well in the United States. If *all* conversations about things that matter are exercises in walking on a line strung between the poles of absolute mystery and absolute simplicity (or certainty), then anytime we invoke the name of God, we are walking on that line. *God* is a concept, a word, that should span the whole length of the tightrope between mystery and certainty but instead has begun to be conscripted to one very short fragment on the certainty side. It's as if the ridiculous joke about God being an old man in the sky started to dominate the conversation, and the sad result is that we have millions of people who think that's all the word ever means, ever meant. In the popular understanding of the word *God*, many people imagine that individuals like me who use that word are just happily dancing on the pole of certainty, stubbornly staring into a flashlight and proclaiming that the world is full of stars. This is sad, and frustrating.

Thus, I want to be clear from the beginning that when the word *God* enters this story, the conversation is still on the tightrope between simplicity and mystery. It is a vast expanse. Again, the word *God* ideally signals the biggest sweep of reality, not the smallest space of human closed-mindedness. To speak about God, to think about God, to seek

God, to question God's nature—all of this is for the purpose of engaging "the mystery of faith," an ancient and beautiful phrase that doesn't get much press these days. Yet, for my entire life, as far as I can recall, I have been walking, stumbling, dancing upon the line that this phrase represents, strung across a vast expanse between simple trust and unspeakable mystery. All theology—that is, the study and knowledge of God, and communications about such ideas and experiences—requires stepping off the pole of pure mystery, where nothing can be said, and trusting that there is actually another pole of simplicity, things we limited creatures might indeed know and say with truth, even about God.

The challenges of speaking about God are not new; they are many, and discussing them can quickly grow tiresome for all but the most devout and the most skeptical. So, I would like to include a few simple disclaimers before wandering off into this fraught semantics landscape. First, all language about God is metaphor. We who talk about God are doing our best, as tiny creatures, to describe the Creator and sustainer of the known and unknown universe. God is not male or female, but I will most often refer to God as he/him/his. While I am well aware that this can be problematic in a patriarchal society, I will follow this custom of the Judeo-Christian tradition simply because singular pronouns in English are limited, and this is the pronoun language I was steeped in and naturally think in; to insert female pronouns on principle feels distracting and beside the point for me (because again, obviously, God has no gender). For those who find the male pronouns distracting, you are welcome to replace them as you read. Finally, although God is not a person (I repeat: all language about God is metaphor), I will talk about God in ways that personify him. This, too, is the custom of my faith tradition, but it is also something I have come to trust personally and deeply. Despite being immortal, invisible, and beyond our cognitive grasp, God is interested in knowing us and being known. God is not a person, but God is personal. Maybe, as public theologian Christena Cleveland puts it, "God is *interested* in being personified.... God is relational, and God wants to know and be known. We are so limited by our human cognitive abilities and emotional intelligence. [But] I don't think God wants to let that get in the way of being known."[4]

I don't think God wants words to get in the way of being known, either. We word-users and hearers have a choice to make: Do we want our casual skepticism about misused words to get in the way of actually trying to know something of God? I have nothing against earnest criticism, earnest questioning. Indeed, I have spent a lot of energy wrestling with certain words, phrases, and ideas in the Christian tradition (there are still many terms and phrases, like "God's plan," that instantly raise my hackles). I have nothing against sincere questions about the nature of God's providence and control. But I have also been guilty of using casual skepticism to disengage from certain questions or certain possibilities around experiences of God.

For many years, I was often silently mean and petty and judgmental when people in my life would express confidence about spiritual experiences or insights from God. But there was also a part of me, the more humble and honest part, that was curious, that trusted their sincerity, that wished I might speak with such conviction even as I doubted theirs. I have no need for you to suspend honest, probing doubt, the kind that actually cares about the conversation and the potential for enlightening dialogue to emerge out of differences. I do hope, however, that you will lean into that part of you that is honest and humble, that does not presume to yet know all there is to know about God's activity in our lives or this universe. In other words, I ask you to afford me a generosity of spirit I have often not extended to others. I ask for your grace.

Who Is Teresa of Ávila?

I could be wrong, of course, but I get the feeling that for those who grew up going to Roman Catholic schools or receiving a parish education, Saint Teresa of Ávila is as familiar as the early American presidents—which is to say that her name and stature as an "important person" are well known by almost everyone, but the particulars of her life and teachings are still pretty obscure to those who have little interest in history. Like the early presidents, however, she is wonderfully "knowable" to those who do seek out deeper knowledge of her person, her thoughts, and her time thanks to her prolific writings and all the great thinkers who have reflected on her life and legacy. For my part, growing up as a mainline American Protestant, I remained wholly ignorant of Teresa until the summer between my freshman and sophomore years of college, when I stumbled across an old Penguin edition of *The Interior Castle* and tried to read it because it was lauded as "a classic of Western spirituality," "a masterpiece on the life of prayer." At that time, I found it utterly unintelligible, and I distinctly remember struggling with and abandoning the text after only a couple of days of reading it at the front desk of the Stanford Alumni Center, where I was working as a fill-in receptionist. The contrast between the (to my mind) dark medieval imagery of shadowy rooms with slithering serpents and the sunlit palm trees through the wall of glass doors before me was too great; I could not enter Teresa's world.

My intent now is to at least introduce you to Teresa enough that you might be open to her words and to the ways in which her experiences and writings still shed light on things that happen in *our* world, *so* different from hers in many ways but still filled with human beings struggling to be in relationship with one another and God. To that end, as we embark on the world of ideas she presents in *The Interior Castle*, I'd like to briefly present Teresa to you as a controversial reformer, a writer under obedience, and a "grounded mystic." All of these identities are bound together, of course; but, for the sake of simplicity, I'll address them in turn.

As a means of orienting you to Teresa in relation to these essential aspects of her life, I want to first offer the briefest of biographical sketches—which feels as absurd as writing a few sentences of introduction to the life of George Washington or Queen Elizabeth I. But, assuming you may have little to no knowledge of Teresa, I hope this brief summary provides a basic framework while still allowing us to move quickly into conversation with her teachings on Christian spirituality. It's my hope that you will encounter the essence of Teresa's own distinct voice through the select quotes throughout this book, and that your interest might be sufficiently piqued to seek out her own writings (including her autobiography) or more thorough and insightful academic examinations of her life and legacy (see the "Recommended Reading" section at the back of this book).

In stark terms, then, in a form that might be given at a cocktail party or over coffee, who is Teresa of Ávila?

Teresa (1515–1582) was a sixteenth-century Spanish Carmelite[5] nun, long honored by the Roman Catholic Church as a saint.[6] In 1970, she became the first woman to be called a "doctor of the church," a title through which the Vatican recognizes contributions to theology and teaching. (Since then, three other women have been added to this esteemed list.) Interestingly—by her own admission—her "early" spiritual life was very uneven: she suffered a prolonged illness just a few years into her vocation as a nun, which she began at age twenty; and, in the wake of this illness, she entered an arduous period of struggle with prayer and authenticity that lasted through the rest of her twenties and most of her thirties. In 1554, when she was thirty-nine years old, she had a decisive moment of reconversion and began in earnest the work that would leave such a formidable legacy. For the next twenty-eight years, until her death at the age of sixty-seven, she dedicated herself to prayer, establishing a reformed Carmelite religious order, and writing. *The Interior Castle* is her best-known text.

TERESA THE CONTROVERSIAL REFORMER

What most surprised me when I began to seek out Saint Teresa as a spiritual guide was not her descriptions of rapture (though there is plenty to surprise there) but rather the active, administrative, political, and public nature of much of her work. As Raimundo Panikkar says, "There is…not a little difficulty in classifying Teresa of Avila. If we class her as contemplative because she reached the highest degree of fruition of God and union with Him, we forget that she led an extremely active life. If we rank her among the teachers, we overlook the fact that she was also a reformer…as well as a poet."[7]

I knew nothing of Teresa the reformer. I knew of her only as a contemplative and a teacher. And yet, in reading Teresa the teacher, we find an undeniable emphasis on the balance between what we now might call "the life of contemplation and the life of action." She says that the worth of any prayer is measured by the extent to which it results in more loving action (demonstrable action) in our lives. In her case, this loving action centered on reforming the religious order that she loved, seeking to establish small, simpler communities of eleven sisters in contrast to the large community of 180 she herself had joined as a novice. I will not recount here the political sagas and struggles that accompanied her reform work, but if there is any mythical image of "Teresa of Ávila, set apart from the real world" in your imagination, simply know this: in her determination to establish a new kind of Carmelite house, one that reflected more truly the original simplicity and austerity of the Carmelite rule, she established *fifteen* houses across Spain in the last two decades of her life, often in the face of bitter opposition from civic and religious authorities. Despite all the discomforts of sixteenth-century travel, she spent her last years traversing the country, writing letters, and meeting with opponents and supporters, fighting for the conditions under which future Carmelite sisters might dedicate themselves seriously to the contemplative life.

TERESA THE AUTHOR, UNDER OBEDIENCE

That Teresa wrote is no surprise; *why* she wrote, or under what circumstances, is more intriguing. Apart from her letters, Teresa composed six works. The texts of most interest to a general audience are probably her autobiography, *The Book of Her Life* (sometimes retitled today as *The Autobiography of Teresa of Avila*); *The Way of Perfection* (instructions and observations about prayer for her Carmelite sisters); and *The Interior Castle* (in many ways a synthesis of her autobiography and *The Way of Perfection*). Although a full picture of authorial motives will always elude us, it seems quite clear that Teresa began writing in earnest about her prayer life and the "state of her soul" because she had to.

In an era highly suspicious of claims of spiritual authority (to put it mildly), Teresa needed to share openly with her spiritual directors (male priests) and other church authorities about what was happening in her and how she understood it if she hoped to continue her work on many levels—chief among her endeavors being the establishment of a newly reformed order and the supervision of her Carmelite sisters. Her first proposal for a new Carmelite house "aroused hostile gossip about Teresa's circle," as scholar Rowan Williams puts it,[8] and at least two officials suggested that she defend herself through a description of her spiritual experiences and her methods of prayer. The resulting text, *The Book of Her Life*, mostly satisfied the authorities; early reactions were favorable, and she was allowed to continue with her reforms. However, eventually, in reaction to a negative report by a widowed princess with a personal vendetta against Teresa (really!), the Inquisition offices swept up the original manuscript and all copies of it. Although the manuscript was later deemed acceptable, it was never returned to Teresa.

This background is pertinent to the creation of *The Interior Castle*. About three years after the Inquisition seized all copies of her autobiography, Teresa was in conversation at one of her newly formed houses with a supportive superior, a priest named Father Gratian, who also served as her confessor at the time. According to his own notes, while discussing matters "concerning her spirit" and the continued need for teaching certain insights to the nuns under her supervision, Teresa became a bit frustrated, saying, "Oh, how well this point was described in the book about my life, which is in the Inquisition!" In response, Father Gratian observed that the manuscript wasn't likely to come back any time soon, and he ordered her, in essence, to write it again (about ten years later), this time a bit more cautiously, in order to share the teaching "in a general way without naming the one to whom the things you mentioned there happened."[9]

Thus, once more, Teresa found herself compelled to write, in a way that might be hard for those of us unfamiliar with lives of vowed obedience to understand. While she observed that there were benefits to writing such a reflection anew, particularly because there were things that she had come to better understand through the past decade, it made her task no less of a dreaded chore, and an ill-timed one at that. In 1577, when Gratian ordered her to write this "new" book, she was sixty-two years old and plagued not only by physical maladies but also by serious political assaults on her reform work, exemplified by one series of events that took place in the middle of her writing project. Teresa was elected as prioress of the Monastery of the Incarnation in Ávila, but a church superior who opposed her reforms annulled the valid election. In response, in the reelection, the nuns once more voted for Teresa—and were all promptly excommunicated! In the months before and after this drama, Teresa wrote her book on the sublime mysteries of prayer, the friendship of God, and visions of the Holy Trinity—but, perhaps unsurprisingly, given this context, never in a way that loses sight of the realities and challenges of life on this earth with other humans.[10]

TERESA THE GROUNDED MYSTIC

It is partly Teresa's constant connection with, and concern for, communities in this world that leads me to underscore this third feature of her life and legacy: while it may be evident from even the briefest descriptions of her active reform work, a mindset that wants to segregate "mystical spirituality" from the thorny complexities of real relationships in a dysfunctional world will be constantly challenged by Teresa. She would have found the terms *mystical* and *spirituality* foreign in more ways than one. It was her constant turning from prayer to active love, and the way in which she did this—with so little delusion about what that means—that has caused me to think of her as a "grounded mystic." She was down-to-earth in her prose, her witty and candid teaching, and her lived experience.

It could be argued that every "true" mystic or saint is grounded, or has some element of both the active and contemplative life. That is right, in a sense, but Teresa still strikes me as having been remarkably and robustly balanced in a way that her basic reputation as a mystic sometimes betrays. She was notably resolute in both her defense of the reality of "supernatural" prayer experiences *and* her insistence that this loving movement of God to an individual must then extend *into* the world rather than curve in on itself. What we might call her "grounded" nature even extended into her prayer dialogues with Jesus: once, when complaining honestly to Christ about her many struggles, she heard a response to this effect: "Don't be troubled; so do I treat my friends." Her tart response? "I know, Lord—but that's why you have so few friends!"[11] In many of her waking days, she worried that Christ had so few "good friends" and tried to encourage her contemporaries to become better friends of God. But she was clear-eyed and honest about the things that stand in the way of that friendship, from within and from without.

Who Are You? Where Do You Come From?

Now that I've stumbled through introducing who I'm trying to talk about (that is, God and Teresa of Ávila), it's time to give my best shot at a brief introduction of who I am, this voice that seeks to be in conversation with you, and Saint Teresa, about the love and nearness of God. It is cliché in a postmodern world to say that "context is everything," or almost everything, but I have been sufficiently formed by my postmodern education to nod in agreement. This is basically a spiritual memoir with some much-needed help from the writings of a Spanish saint, so those who continue reading will learn quite a bit as they go along about who I am, where I come from, and how I perceive the world. Nevertheless, some old-fashioned disclaimers might be helpful at the outset, as well as a story or two that might enable you to appreciate more fully the depth of my surprise at certain turns in my spiritual journey.

First disclaimer: the version of Christianity I was raised in, and formed by, is not the normative or most popular version of the religion, at least in the United States. As a mainline-Protestant mutt, spending time in Episcopal, Methodist, and Presbyterian churches on the West Coast, I encountered some variety in perspective, of course; but, overall, it is fair to simply say this: I was raised with an egalitarian, skeptic-friendly approach to the Christian faith. Recently, I was listening to a popular Christian-based podcast, and I found myself becoming annoyed with the hosts' vague posture of self-congratulatory exploration. *Look at us! We're questioning semisacred doctrines of the faith, like calling God "Father"! Isn't this edgy and exciting?* The snide, un-Christian part of me wants to say, "Only if your framework is a relatively new version of Christianity called 'fundamentalism,' and you're unaware of the broad spectrum of Christianity."

This kind of thought is so snobby and ugly that it pains me to confess it. And, of course, it reveals an honest defensiveness that I have struggled to make peace with since I was a freshman in college and first figured out that my admittedly "liberal" version of Christianity was not the norm—that when I say I am Christian, I should expect to be misunderstood. But the truth is, I *do* have to be reminded from time to time that most people in the United States did not grow up with a version of the faith that included male and female pastors (as my churches did), that openly invited and encouraged honest questions about the Bible (or almost any topic, for that matter), and that assumed doubt was a part of any healthy life of faith. And I'm not sure I would still be a Christian if I had landed on any other branch of the family.

Before I learned it was a trademark of my millennial generation and educational culture, I recognized in myself a deep distaste for any expression of unmitigated certainty. I can be, if left to my own instincts, an annoyingly persistent devil's advocate. Nothing sets off alarm bells faster in my psyche than arrogance or overstatement. (My husband learned early in our relationship that *always* or *never* might as well be considered bad words.)

And so, tellingly and not surprisingly, most of the communities that have supported my journey with God generally avoid this kind of (over)confidence with regard to matters of faith. Because I do like scrambling simplistic assumptions about churches, I will add that this description includes the Roman Catholic community that nurtured my faith through my final two years at Stanford.

All of this is to say, I suppose, that if you want to understand where I come from, culturally and religiously, it might be helpful to know that I come from the mainline Protestant tradition, from an educational background, in both college and seminary, that was big on historical-critical method and small on speaking in tongues or other miracles. If those markers mean little or nothing to you, know this: when I was an adolescent, I wanted to be a medical missionary because I could imagine no purer human expression of God's love than curing people's physical pain through the rational insights of modern medicine. The work, I thought, *was* the message. There's a saying popularly attributed to Saint Francis of Assisi that goes like this: "Preach the gospel at all times; use words when necessary." While it's almost historically impossible that Saint Francis said this, I would have gladly carried this saying as the byline of my faith well into my twenties. It was the unspoken mantra of every church I embraced.

Second disclaimer: that's not true of me anymore. I am now a preacher, a pastor, a priest, and an earnest-but-ever-curious teacher of the Christian faith. I am, in the words of one of my slightly befuddled college friends who asked me to officiate at his wedding, a "real-life religious person." I am, in the words of Saint Teresa, a "daughter of the church." If the church is like a grandparent with many gifts and flaws, I think I know her fairly well, and I still love her. She has never hurt me firsthand, though I have witnessed the searing and lasting pain that results when individuals and communities act selfishly or cruelly in her name. She is meant, like Mary, to bear Christ into the world, but we all know that sometimes she is not as faithful or humble as Jesus' mother was. Yet her house is bigger, more sprawling, and more multifaceted than you might imagine, and I live in it still. By the end of this exploration, I hope you will understand why.

One last thing: when I was in my mid-twenties, I traveled to El Salvador over spring break with a small group of college-aged women. The week was primarily a service-learning pilgrimage—learning from the faithful witness and struggle of Christians in El Salvador (including the martyred Archbishop Oscar Romero) over the previous thirty-five years. We also had one day for fun where we could enjoy the country as tourists and go on a river excursion. I had spent a summer in El Salvador before, so, when I packed for the trip, I didn't have a lot of angst about what to wear. On the day of our river adventure, however, I was the only female in a practical, one-piece swimsuit. I didn't think much of it; that's pretty much been the story of my presence in the swimsuit scene since middle school. But the male trip leader, a friend of mine, practically laughed when everyone in the group took off the T-shirts we had worn over our bathing suits. "I just knew you'd be in a one-piece swimsuit," he said. I tried not to be defensive or irritated as I asked, "Why? How? What's that supposed to mean?" He tried to explain: "You just remind me so much of this girl I knew in high school who always wore a one-piece. You're just, I don't know...naturally and obviously *modest*." Honestly, I hadn't realized that I broadcast modesty signals. But, over the years, this uncomfortable encounter has remained with me, a truth about how the world perceives me, and, in fact, a partial truth about who I am, or was. In the years since, this is how I have come to see it: I can let my hair down, but it just isn't very long.

Depending on your stereotypes of Christian ministers, this last story may be superfluous. But because people who know very little about Saint Teresa often still know that she dealt in spiritual "ecstasy" and that there is a Bernini statue of her that might quite accurately be called erotic, it seems worth mentioning. Eventually, alongside Teresa, I will be writing about ecstasy and *eros*, wrestling with both the terms and our multifaceted experiences of them. As you might imagine, this will be at least as uncomfortable for me as it might be for you. But there is a difference between being modest and being prudish, and it is my intent to hold the former while rejecting the latter.

FIRST DWELLINGS:

TURNING IN

"The soul of a person attentive to God's ways is a paradise, a beautiful place; the One who created it delights in it. What do you think a place would be like that delights One so powerful, wise, pure, and full of goodness? There's no adequate image for the beauty of the soul and its vast capacity! No matter how smart we are, we can't understand our depths any more than we can understand God."
—Teresa of Ávila, 1.1.1[12]

Wonder and Terror

I was intermittently attending Sunday school in Methodist and Episcopal church basements in northeastern Oregon since before I have cogent memories, so I cannot give an account of a life that was somehow innocent of religious notions or religious language. Nevertheless, it's a different matter to honestly try to recall my earliest brushes with what I might now call my "soul," or the depth of my being that transcends emotional and social attachments. *Soul* is a word with nearly as much baggage as *God*, so if it is troublesome for you (as it was for me for over a decade), perhaps think of this as an effort to describe early childhood experiences of some spiritual depth or tenor.

In Teresa's metaphor of an interior castle, "turning inward" is the gate of entry to one's soul, where God dwells at the center. I don't remember praying much, apart from repeating prayers at Sunday school and singing table grace. However, I remember certain experiences of "turning in" that stayed with me because they were marked by wonder and awe and occasionally terror at my sense of another reality without material limits in which I was not alone—not by the smug and small satisfaction of pious obedience.

My childhood best friend lived in a double-wide mobile home sur-rounded by enormous fir trees at the base of a large cherry orchard in the foothills of the Eagle Cap mountains. From a very young age, I felt com-fortable staying the night at her house; it seemed like a second home to me. Our mothers both worked full time, and we had been cared for by the same woman in our small town of about five hundred residents since we were born. One morning, when I was about four years old, I had stayed the night with my friend, and I found myself in the bathroom, sitting on the toilet and looking up at the window to my right. The morning light was streaming down to the faded brown linoleum floor, but my eyes were fixed on the ever-expanding beam suffused with golden particles: dust, shimmering, surrounding me. I had this notion, no doubt articulated by my Sunday school teacher, that God is everywhere, and suddenly I was struck by the thought—perhaps awareness—that God was indeed right there, right in the bathroom, right in the beauty of the light and the dust, right with me even *here* in this mundane place of humble necessity. I was in awe and a bit overwhelmed, but I reveled in this moment, in this wonder, long enough to seal its place in my memory as my first thought about God.

There were other such "spiritual" moments that punctuated my more typical childhood memories of having fun with my friends, squabbling with my siblings, experiencing the delight of speeding on a sled onto a frozen pond, and wandering the halls of our home in the wretched fever-dreams of strep throat. Yes, I recall, as a little girl, praying to Jesus to protect me when I was scared, imagining that someone was following me up the dark stairs when I journeyed from the garage to the main level of our house. But I also recognize, in retrospect, engaging in a different kind of prayer. Sometimes, when I was alone, I became aware of what felt like another dimension of my being. I didn't have words for it, really, and when I tried to talk to the adults in my life about it, the words I did find failed to express the depth of my feelings.

One day, when I was nine or ten, as I was sitting near the piano and looking at the wood floors under the dining room table across the room, I began to enter a space of self-reflection about what it meant to "be," about the very fact of my existence that somehow seemed unchanging in God's eyes even as I knew the years were passing. This idea felt both heavy and wonderful, scary and exciting. There was even more to it, an intensity of awareness that I can't describe to this day. I also remember trying to talk to my mother about it, and her obvious lack of comprehension. Yet how *could* she know what I was saying? I learned that there was a certain solitary nature to these explorations and encounters with a presence or reality beyond myself and what I could see; these experiences were most likely to happen, though not exclusively so, when I was alone, and I couldn't explain them fully, then or now. In time, however, I would also gratefully learn that there *were* teachers—most notably Teresa of Ávila—who could help me understand and see this vast interior world just a bit more clearly. Teresa's writings in *The Interior Castle* helped me to place these early childhood experiences of "turning in" as one example of prayer, as depicted in the "first dwellings."

Concerned with and for "Souls"

Teresa kicks off *The Interior Castle* with a prologue in which she understandably complains about having been ordered to write a new book about prayer. She is occupied with what any typical leader would consider administrative nightmares, is physically unwell, and wonders if she will end up repeating things she's said before, "like parrots [do]."[13] At the same time, she wishes she *could* have access to the memories and words of teachings she has previously penned, "that [she] was told were well said"[14] (presumably so that she might repeat these "well said" words), just as any good teacher wants to repeat past successes. She dryly and darkly notes that "if the Lord *doesn't* help me in this way," at least there might be some personal benefits to the self-sacrificial task of writing, "even…if what I write is of no use to anyone."

It seems the Lord did help her to remember, to reconstruct, insights from the past and gave her images anew, too. In the end, the manuscript that was written for her colleagues—nuns in the monasteries of our Lady of Mount Carmel—has offered benefits of spirit and truth to untold numbers of others, despite Teresa's deflective protests. "It seems ridiculous to think that I can be of use to anyone else!" she writes, focusing her gaze on those who might at least listen to her because they know and love her: her sisters in the Carmelite order. She never completely loses sight of those of us outside the monasteries, though. It's as if she can't help herself. The book she ends up writing reveals that she is concerned with and for *souls*,[15] with and for all the people in the world, and wants Christ to have more devoted friends wherever they might be found. She will settle for the nuns "prais[ing] Him even a little better" as a result of her efforts, but it seems God is not entirely indisposed to the "ridiculous."

A Tour of the Ways We Relate to God

The Interior Castle is a book about the ways and places within ourselves where we come to know more and more of God, intentionally and specifically through prayer. It is a tour, of sorts, of the different ways that we relate to God within ourselves, with varying intensity, awareness, and intimacy. In Spanish, the book is simply titled *Moradas*, or "Dwellings," a title that I find more appealing and helpful than the standard English title of *The Interior Castle*, mostly because "dwellings" sounds approachable, universal, and less precious. In our day, castles do not represent unmitigated goodness and beauty and strength, if they ever did, but it is important to remember that the English title comes directly from an image that Teresa *hopes* will convey such truly admirable traits:

> While I was praying today that God might speak through me (since I was severely struggling to even begin this task of writing), a thought came to me. It's a foundational image on which I might build. I started to think of the soul as being like a castle made of diamond or crystal, with many dwelling places—as there are in heaven.
>
> Considered in this way, sisters, the soul of a person attentive to God's ways is a paradise, a beautiful place; the One who created it delights in it. What do you think a place would be like that delights One so powerful, wise, pure, and full of goodness? There's no adequate image for the beauty of the soul and its vast capacity! No matter how smart we are, we can't understand our depths any more than we can understand God: for we are created in God's image and likeness, as He himself says.[16]

Subversively, there is nothing elitist about this "interior castle"; it is simply part of Teresa's Christian anthropology on how we are made. She later clarifies that even if we are not "a person attentive to God's ways" (or do not believe ourselves to be), we cannot eliminate the essential presence of God's light in us, the glorious "center" of our soul: "Take note: it's not the spring, or the brilliant sun in the center, that loses splendor and beauty. Nothing can remove or diminish this central loveliness."[17] We can, however, "cover" the source of light within and live in darkness; that's our human prerogative born of free will. Teresa cannot and does not maintain a strict boundary on her metaphors for the soul and its center; and, in her exuberance, we are given many images: "this pearl, this tree of life planted in the living waters of life"; "the Sun..., as the giver of all this splendor and beauty"; "a crystal...inherently capable of reflecting the sun"; "a clear spring"; "a tree [sustained by a spring that brings fruitfulness]."[18]

For those of us accustomed to thinking of ourselves in strictly material terms, as marvelously complex animals, the surprising point of this array of ideas evoking clarity, brilliance, and life is that we all have been given a gift more marvelous than the mere existence of our human brains and bodies. We have been given *a capacity in and through* these created elements that is not on any anatomical chart and that is not obvious at first glance but is just as universal. For Teresa, the beauty, dignity, and grandeur of our soul—a place where we might know something of God—is simply an aspect of who we are and what we are given, by virtue of our creation and existence. And it is not like one small hidden room with a light in it that we must feverishly search for. It is a magnificent wealth of places—a castle!—with light radiating throughout, where we all might explore, live, rest, refresh, learn, cry, play, and work in response to the very One who is the source of it all and who ever invites us closer to the center, into deeper relationship. It is not just that we have the "capacity" to encounter the light of God; we have *capacities*—many ways and places where this might be so.

Teresa has no illusions that this concept is easy to grasp. In fact, she says quite plainly that we will never comprehend it. Don't wear yourself out trying to clearly see the beauty of these spaces in your interior life, in your soul, because that would be like trying to outline God: "the fact that His Majesty *says* the human soul is made in His image means we can hardly conceive of its dignity and beauty."[19] Still, in typical Teresan (and Christian) paradox, we are urged to strive toward an awareness of this mysterious reality. It is the first instance of what quickly strikes the reader as a theme in the text and in her teaching: don't expect to understand or to receive gifts from God that help you see. Be humble! But, then again, don't rest there in complacent unknowing; in humility, seek to know more and more of who you really are and who God really is. Strive on!

If Teresa were content with the incomprehensibility of the castle, the book would end after five hundred words. But she wants the reader to "try to discover what we really are" and not "live our lives thinking only of ourselves as our bodies."[20] *Moradas* is an attempt to draw people's attention away from "the rough setting of the diamond, or the outer wall of the castle—in other words, our bodies" and toward our souls' "qualities, their precious value, [and] who dwells there."[21] Let us consider this castle (these dwellings), she says, even if we can never really understand its beauty or dignity. Let's work with the feeble insights we do have.

The notion that there are different dwellings within this interior castle is the outline Teresa presents for aiding exploration of our soul's capacities. Now, metaphors of all sorts get tricky when we try to be too exacting. They have their limits, and Teresa is quickly faced with the difficulties of even a seemingly spacious metaphor like a castle with many *moradas*: she is clear from the beginning that these *moradas* are not "neatly lined up in a row" for our orderly progression. One way she honors the complexity and diversity of our spiritual explorations is spatially: "This castle contains many dwelling places all around: above, below, and to each side; in the center of them all is the central dwelling place where the most secret, hidden exchanges take place between God and the soul."[22] Some artists have rendered Teresa's castle as a spiral-shaped edifice, for good reason. At another point, she herself uses the shape and layering of a palmetto as a point of reference:

> Don't imagine these dwelling places as neatly lined up in a row, but focus instead on the center. This is the room or grand dwelling place—a palace—occupied by the King. Imagine a palmetto, with layers of leaves surrounding and enclosing the central kernel within (which have to be removed to see and eat the kernel). In the same way, around this central room are *many* more rooms, and

many more above it, too. The soul must always be thought of as spacious, vast, lofty. There is no danger of exaggeration, because the soul's capacity is greater than we can imagine. And the Sun, from within the central palace, reaches every part of it.[23]

So, although for purposes of teaching, Teresa divides her text into seven sets of dwellings, it is important to note that the units are always in the plural: "First Dwellings," "Second Dwellings," "Third Dwellings," and so on. Also, she addresses as directly as possible the potential contradiction of needing to "enter" our beautiful castle: "How can we enter it? This seems a silly question, because if this castle is the soul, and we are the castle, we are, in a sense, already in it! But," she continues, "there are many ways of 'being' in a place. Many remain in the outer court of the castle.... They are not interested in going inside, have no notion of the wonders it holds, how many rooms it has, or who lives in it."[24] It is clear that Teresa is wrestling with her own metaphor and working it out as she goes. This isn't problematic for the reader because it's always clear that the point is not a detailed map of the castle but simply the provision of a *frame* for her teachings and observations about a life of faith, and specifically about prayer. The dwellings are merely a "comparative image" that Teresa hopes "maybe God will use" to explain some of the gifts God gives through prayer, and the differences between these gifts.[25]

It's worth pausing here to face a few of the obvious obstacles to entering with Teresa into her comparative castle, even in our imaginations. Obvious barriers are the very notions of a soul and of the language of the soul, which even Teresa notes are inherently difficult concepts but which have become only more so in the centuries since she wrote. She says, "Because we've heard it said, and because faith tells us so, we know that we have souls. But," as noted before, "we rarely consider their qualities, their precious value, or who dwells there, and so we don't bother to care for them."[26]

The first part of this statement might feel very far from us: "because we've heard it said, and because faith tells us so...." Hmm. Maybe not. Growing up, I did not really hear, anywhere, that I had a soul. Even my communities of faith, my churches, did not tell me so, presumably because they wanted to avoid—and were reacting against—the false dualism of "soul" and "body." My teachers and pastors and parents (who didn't use language of faith) talked about the whole self, a personhood of depth and with the capacity for wholeness or brokenness, vitality or deficiency. I was given the image of a holistic personhood assessed in terms of health and wellness and ethics. Through my education, the books I read, and the movies I saw, to this basic perspective was added an intensified emphasis on the physical and biological aspects of the self: I was in high school when the implications of brain-scanning became popular fodder for discussion. These biologically driven concepts of what it means to be human continue to dominate our current culture. The assumed ability to trace and analyze all human experience within the confines of our neural pathways or other bodily systems remains present in most conversations about behavior, knowledge, experience, and spirituality that are being held in the fields of science, medicine, psychology, and sociology—and even around the family dinner table or between friends. Add to this the fascination with genetic mapping and gene therapies that has defined the last twenty years of popular biological discourse, and a recent flurry of easily accessible DNA tests to clarify ancestry, and we twenty-first-century Americans mostly find ourselves in a landscape of human anthropology where there is no room for a soul.

Who are we? We are human beings, infinitely interesting creatures defined by genetics, body, brain functioning, social dynamics, and community. To say we have souls, if this is said at all in this cultural space, usually means one of two things: One, that we are, in a very vague way, more than these biological markers—there is an essence or depth to us that is greater than the sum of these parts, or not fully defined by them. Something is "soulful" if it touches these transcendent depths of our humanity. Or, two, talk of "souls" can stand in defiance of the dominant assumptions of stark materialism, often, but not always, within the context of conversations about eternal life. In this framework, the soul is usually presented as a reality distinct from the body, a reality of personhood that can still be quite self-contained. The phrases "save your soul," "soothe your soul," and "lose your soul" all indicate this kind of "alternate dimension" perspective.

Although it is related to both of these views, Teresa is saying something different through her metaphor of the soul as a castle. She often uses the term "soul" as a substitute for "person" (e.g., "Many souls remain in the outer court of the castle,"[27] which also might be called…the soul!). The way she does this again and again, over time, began to work an inversion on my modern mind: what if "a soul" is the more capacious definition of who we are, not a subset entity that we must somehow "get in touch with"?

For Teresa, it seems obvious that the soul is not a little interior part of us that makes phone calls to God-in-heaven through prayer. But, more to the point: it is important to note that, in her explorations of the castle as the soul, and the dwellings as rooms *in* the soul, this is a dimension that exists only because of God's presence in and to us, just as we are— as human creatures. In other words, it is an "alternate dimension" of ourselves, but not one that we can explore or develop on our own, in isolation. It radiates into our lives and bodies through God's close presence. In sci-fi terms, it's like a portal. It is ours, *and* it does not belong to us. Yes, only we can come to know this meeting place, to plumb its depths, and it is the vessel in which we might come to know more of who we really are—but the light by which we search and find is not of our own making. (The same could be said of our bodies, of course.)

If the soul is a castle, then it is always a shared dwelling; it is the place or places where we connect with, seek out, and learn something of the One who created us—the One who, as Teresa always reminds us, is always present at the center. The soul is a relational place, not a solitary place. Likewise, the life we are given as people, or "souls," as Teresa would use the word, is essentially relational, not solitary.

As an American who carries the temptation to look at the soul, if I consider it at all, as one more interior landscape for my self-improvement projects, this idea has been very hard—but essential—for me to grasp. My soul is mine! What can I do here? How can I make it better? Stronger? Healthier? More beautiful? These are not Teresa's concerns or temptations when thinking about the castle of the soul (fasting in her sandals through the unheated winters of Castilla, she's more attuned to our dependence on God for life than I am, eating cookies by my space heater in San Diego), but they are mine, and might be shared by others.

Here we return to Teresa's first teaching: the *moradas*, the interior castle, our very soul, is a beautiful dimension of ourselves because it is the place where we might explore and connect with the divine mystery. It is the space where we can draw close to the goodness of God and become more aware of God's constant closeness to us and presence in us. We do not earn this capacity or make it; it is a gift of creation. And as we choose to enter in, God might indeed give us other gifts we didn't believe could be possible or real, no matter the century of our birth.

Writing to a World of Many Skeptics

I turned to Teresa's book on the *moradas* of the soul because Christ had come close to me, in prayer, in a way that even churchy people like me don't usually talk about. When I picked up the book, I assumed that I would be entering a world, historically, where such experiences and language were commonplace. I thought, in a subliminal (and simplistic) sense, that because even I vaguely knew of Teresa of Avila as a writer with wild, intense, incredible prayer experiences, she must talk about them with a candor and confidence that would have the power to blast through five centuries. And I assumed that such confidence could *only* come from a cultural and religious context that constantly affirmed the potential for God's close presence to people.

Yes, I turned to Teresa, specifically, because God pointed me in her direction: "Turn to Teresa. She will guide you." But I also naively assumed that she was just one articulate voice in a sixteenth-century world where the gift of God's undeniable presence in prayer was the usual experience and culturally unremarkable, as if I had been given an obscure antique utensil and wanted to read some historical commentaries to better understand it, since back in the day every household had one. To my great surprise and immediate encouragement, it's obvious from the beginning that Teresa is writing to a world of many skeptics, even in the church. In chapter 1 of "First Dwellings," even as she is laying the foundational metaphor of the interior castle, she rhetorically detours to a preemptive defense of why she is writing about "the various gifts [God] gives to souls,"[28] since quite evidently they are not shared by all or accepted as possible by all.

From the first chapter, Teresa presents us with the central term and idea of "gifts from God," as known particularly in prayer. Most English translations of *The Interior Castle* frequently use the word *favors* for these divine actions or experiences. Yet what is implied by this term? In Spanish, as Teresa wrote it, we find the word *mercedes*, a word directly related, through a shared origin (the Latin *mercedum*), to the English word *mercy* (*merced* in Spanish). Today, we primarily hear the word *mercy* used in abstract terms, as an unmerited kindness or pardon. But *merced* also has uses and connotations that are less emotionally situational and more concrete: the term can be used as a synonym at times for *obsequio* or *regalo*, words rendered clearly and consistently in English as *gift* or *present*.

The example in one dictionary hints at the unequal power and unexpectedness of a gift understood to be a *merced*, a mercy, a concrete kindness: "*Este caballo es uno merced de tu rey*" ("This horse is a favor [gift] from your king").[29] It is a favor from the king, unable to be repaid. It is a kindness of unexpected proportions. This rudimentary word study makes richer our understanding of Teresa's use of *merced* (singular) and *mercedes* (plural): she wants to talk about mercies, gifts, favors, kindnesses that God sometimes offers souls in prayer. She knows the whole idea can be difficult for people in her world to fathom or accept, and the same is true in our world.

To extend the metaphor in a way that's rather silly but also rather reasonable, kings don't just go around giving out horses. For many people, the whole idea would be preposterous. ("I don't believe you! It just doesn't happen. Where'd you *really* get that horse?") For others, their incredulity would be laced with understandable envy and desire. ("Even if the story *were* true, and the king did give you—or someone else—a horse, what's the good of telling me about it? It's never going to happen to me, so why share your fantastic fortune?")

Teresa lived in a world, like ours, where the idea of God's love and goodness being known, *received* in some fashion, by mere mortals was suspect. From the beginning, Teresa can hear the objections of some readers because she has heard them in the flesh, from men and women she has encountered throughout her life who doubted what she said and mocked her piety. But by the time she writes this particular text, she offers the sage solidity of a woman in her early sixties who is not deeply bothered by detractors. She steadily stands on her story about God's manifold *mercedes* being given to her over the years, but she takes seriously the questions raised by what she shares. She has given them thought, and she wants to address them at the outset, long before she describes the rooms in castles where such "questionable" gifts are sometimes given.

Directly after introducing the metaphor of the castle with many dwellings, which she hopes God will let her use to "show you something of the various gifts [mercedes] He gives to souls,"[30] she situates herself with humility and hints at what (potentially unbelievable) gifts are coming. "I'll do my best to explain them," she says. "There are so many different gifts that no one can possibly understand them all, especially someone as simple and deplorable as I."[31] In other words, this is not a definitive list of the mercies of prayer. But then she sharply turns to the background questions: Why talk about these things at all? What's the point of drawing any attention, ever, to the gifts the King has given? Here's why, by her lights:

> If the Lord gives you these gifts, you'll have the consolation of knowing that such things really are possible. If not, you'll have the consolation of praising God's goodness in giving them at all.
>
> It doesn't hurt us, spiritually, to think of those blessed to be enjoying God's presence in heaven—it can actually bring us joy, too, and inspire our perseverance. In the same way, there's no harm in seeing that it is possible even here on earth for our glorious God to commune with the foul-smelling worms we humans are and for us to love God all the more for this goodness and mercy. Anyone who is offended by even the thought of God giving such gifts to others must be lacking in both humility and love. How could we not rejoice that God offers such grace to one of our family members? Especially when these gifts to others do not hinder the possibility that they will be given to us! His Majesty grants an understanding of His greatness to whomever He wants.[32]

It's a practical argument: for those who find themselves, quite unexpectedly, to be the recipients of such good gifts in prayer, it will be helpful and encouraging to have heard about these types of experiences beforehand, or to have another voice affirm the gifts as "possible" afterward. (This was my own great consolation in reading *The Interior Castle*.) For those who are never granted these kinds of gifts in prayer, what's the harm? Isn't it helpful for everyone to be reminded that God is not "above" communing with human beings, in all of our obvious absurdities and limitations? Might it increase in us all a trust in God's goodness and mercy, which can admittedly be hard for humans to see? And if you feel pained by this knowledge of gifts you have not personally received, it might be worth evaluating the depth of your humility and love: it's not a zero-sum game, she notes, so we shouldn't begrudge our brother or sister for a kind of goodness we have not yet experienced. After all, they didn't take it from us!

Teresa takes a calculated risk in writing about favors of communion with God that "seem impossible."[33] She knows that some people will not believe what she says and will be scandalized by it. In this passage, she categorizes such people as "the weak," *los flacos*, the ones with skinny faith. It's a designation that seems a bit lacking in charity, but it's possible she meant it compassionately, referring to those whose faith was not steady and strong enough to carry such ideas without stumbling into false concepts or expectations of prayer. Nevertheless, she makes her wager and presses on: "But less is lost by such disbelief than by the missed opportunity to strengthen those who have known such gifts. Such readers will rejoice and will awaken others to a renewed love for the God who so generously gives such mercies...."[34]

And "anyway," she supposes, most of the sisters I'm writing this for won't have this problem of deep skepticism; "they know that God gives even greater evidence of His love than what is described here."[35] Nevertheless, it's worth reminding them of a few basic truths about how she thinks this works: if you firmly don't believe such favors are possible, you won't experience them. "So don't set such limitations on God's actions or gifts to others, sisters, if the Lord does not lead *you* by this road."[36] Once more, you get the sense, even without reading her biographies—which testify to the same—that, in the past, people had often doubted God's generosity to her.

Finally, before we even move into the first dwellings, we are given a few basic thoughts on *who* receives these favors, or gifts, and why. Why some and not others? Between the lines: why her? Teresa will have more to say about this later, but it's interesting to me that she can't resist correcting some false assumptions at the outset, before the reader even knows what she's talking about. "He gives these gifts...so that *His* greatness may be made known," she explains. It's emphatically not a meritocracy, the kind of "favor" or "gift" that is really a reward or payment: God doesn't give gifts "because the *recipients* are holier than those who do not receive them." Why, then? Again, "so that *His* greatness may be made known. We see this dynamic in the lives of Saint Paul and Mary Magdalene."[37] The horse given by the king to his subject does not stay hidden in the stable but somehow or other helps the surprised recipient to bear witness to the unfathomable goodness of the giver.

Entering the Castle

> As far as I can tell, the way into this castle is through prayer and meditation. I'm not saying mental prayer *rather* than spoken prayers, because all prayer must include internal meditation. If someone is not mindful of whom they are addressing, what they are asking, and who *they are* in asking, that's not prayer at all, no matter how much the lips move. True, sometimes we can pray without paying direct attention to all these things, but that's only because we have considered these matters before.[38]

As in our day, there were discussions during Teresa's age about what "real" prayer is. Some people espoused a division in prayer that Teresa found consistently annoying and false: a sharp distinction between "mental" and "spoken" prayer. A whole school of thought (and then resistance to it) described an interior advancement in the techniques of prayer without spoken words—"mental prayer"—in contrast to the most common understanding of prayer, then and now, which is "said" prayers or verbal prayers. From the beginning, Teresa wants to insist that *all* prayer includes a "mental" or interior dimension, an *intentionality* in trying to communicate with God, whether your lips are moving with this communication or not. She will have more to say later about the helpfulness of sometimes speaking the words aloud; but, for now, she simply wants to kick aside this popularly held dichotomy.

Finally, this is the way we enter the castle: reflecting in earnest about who we are, as small and limited creatures, and somehow—even implicitly—taking a leap of faith that we are nevertheless "naturally endowed with the power to converse with God himself,"[39] even if there is nothing to prove that idea. Thus: pray. Try to converse with God.

Teresa knows that this "simple" beginning is not a given; she observes that "there are souls so weak, so used to keeping busy with outside affairs, that nothing can be done. It seems they are incapable of entering within themselves."[40] A modern reader with modern prejudices about religion as unthinkingly oriented toward traditional (external) dogma may be surprised to find this consistent emphasis on self-reflection and critical self-examination—what Teresa calls "self-knowledge"—as characteristic of most beginning prayer. She fears that these weak souls "will be transformed into lifeless pillars of salt for not looking within themselves, just as Lot's wife was because she looked back"[41]—imagining they might get stuck in this inflexibly outward orientation.

Perhaps in a way that is more in alignment with our impressions of traditional spirituality, Teresa seems to take for granted that the first "rooms" we enter in prayer and self-knowledge will quite often be those that bring us face-to-face with the shadow parts of ourselves and the honest cry of our hearts to acknowledge our failings and less-than-noble patterns of thought and behavior. This is what the English writer Francis Spufford calls "the human propensity to f[***] things up."[42] "Why did I do that? Why do I *always* do that?" we ask ourselves. In fact, Teresa makes the surprising claim that we come to know ourselves best and most truly as we strive to know and relate to God, an idea that turns an image of fruitless navel-gazing on its head. That's not how it works, she implies. In even stepping into the dwellings of prayer, however briefly, we are more likely to be faced with holy mirrors that show us things we struggle to see—perhaps cannot see—without intentionally placing our thoughts in the presence of God.

Here is one poignant example from a woman I know who had reached a point of deep cynicism about the church and all of Christianity: she decided to give God one final shot, practicing a form called "centering prayer" in which the pray-er strives to simply rest in God's presence without words (save one word to help "recenter" when the mind wanders). She describes how, after she had practiced this form of prayer for many months, God placed a truth in her lap, unexpectedly but undeniably presented: *You have been a yeller.* "I knew, but I didn't know," she said. "I had never faced it, never wrestled with the family roots of the yelling, or the way it affected my relationships with my children." The idea came to her with a forceful spirit of both truth and love, which is how many such painful convictions are given to us: on a plate of mercy. She began to change in a way that she could not have without this inward knowing.

Such honest and clear-eyed self-knowledge of both our strengths and weaknesses (i.e., true humility) is both a beginning of prayer and a consistently evolving fruit of our efforts to explore the castle, no matter how old we are or how much we think we already know ourselves (and how "advanced" we think we are in matters of the spirit). As Teresa writes,

> A soul must not be forced to stay for a long time in a certain room… well, unless perhaps it is in the room of self-knowledge.
>
> Listen closely: this room is essential, even for those whom God keeps close in His very dwelling place![43]

> Self-knowledge is so important that even if you were drawn directly into heaven in prayer, I wouldn't want you to relax your practices of humble and honest self-reflection. As long as we live on earth, nothing is more important than humility. So, I say again that it is an *excellent* thing to start off in the space where one learns humility, instead of flying off to other rooms. That's the path to progress.…
>
> …From my perspective, we'll never truly know ourselves unless we seek to know God. Thinking of His greatness returns us more clearly to our own small and limited nature; looking at His purity, we see more clearly our marked flaws; meditating on His humility, we see how far we are from being humble.[44]

Compared to the One behind the mysteries of all creation, who are we, really? Can we inhabit the room of who we are enough to find out, as Teresa wants us to, that, even in our "small and limited nature" and "marked flaws," we are still also bearers of God's presence and light? To this end, she takes a moment to talk about sin, and what it does (and doesn't) do. For Teresa, sin is any action or thought that obscures to us the light of God's constant presence. In "sin," we cannot see that light, and others cannot see it—but it doesn't mean we are cut off from God, that the soul's capacity to know more of God's love is closed off forever. As Teresa explained earlier:

> Take note: it's not the spring, or the brilliant sun in the center, that loses splendor and beauty. Nothing can remove or diminish

them. But if you place a black cloth over a crystal in the sunshine, it obviously will not reflect the sun's light.[45]

She continues,

O Jesus, it's so sad to see a soul without abundant light![46]

At first glance, this idea is not so different from the Sunday school teachings I received on "what sin is" (i.e., those things that separate us from God), but there are some subtle and consequential differences. For Teresa, a soul is "without" God's light in *effect* but not separated from it in *essence* or reality; the light is still there, close at hand. Removing a veil (the "black cloth") seems less formidable than crossing a chasm of separation from God. Her image of our potential for relationship with the divine is an intrinsically hopeful one because the divine light of God is always near, always within, giving us our very lives. We just have to trust this enough to pray. We are invited, but never compelled, to explore our interior lives and seek to draw closer and closer to the One at the center.

From the get-go, Teresa encourages the reader toward this exploration, urging them to expand their imaginative vision of this place where we come to know God and ourselves more truly. We are not meant to just hang out in the prayer room of self-flagellation and penitence ("God, I'm so sorry for all the ways I mess up"), praise and thanksgiving ("I'm so grateful for my life"), or supplication ("Help me; help us"). It may be true what Anne Lamott says, that most prayers can be categorized as "help," "thanks," or "wow."[47] But Teresa wants us to take time to explore, not just hustle in and out with a summary, prefab interaction. As she says:

> The soul must always be thought of as spacious, vast, lofty. There is no danger of exaggeration, because the soul's capacity is greater than we can imagine. And the Sun, from within the central palace, reaches every part of it. Whether one prays a little or a lot, it's very important that there is no false sense of constraint or limitation. Because God has given each soul such dignity and value, each must be allowed to roam freely among these dwelling places—above, below, from side to side. A soul must not be forced to stay for a long time in a certain room.[48]

Now, even Teresa might admit she's getting ahead of herself in this encouragement, because the first dwellings are metaphorically the habitations of those who don't pray very often, who gather themselves to pray in earnest on occasion but aren't very comfortable doing so and thus rush their prayers. After pondering the sad state of those who *never* turn inward in prayer or self-reflection (those who "remain in the outer court of the castle"[49]), she cheers herself by refocusing on the topic at hand: what it's like for those who first enter the castle, and what their typical state of mind is about the whole thing. What she writes is wonderfully down-to-earth and specific:

> Let's consider those souls who *do* eventually enter the castle. These, too, are absorbed in worldly and exterior affairs, but their desires are good. Sometimes—though infrequently—they turn to our Lord. They think about the health and state of their souls, but not very carefully. Filled with a thousand preoccupations, they pray only a few times a month. Generally speaking, they are mentally consumed by the affairs of their life to which they are most attached: where their treasure is, there is their heart also. From time to time, though, they shake off these mental shackles. It's significant progress when they know themselves well enough to realize they aren't heading toward the castle door at all. Eventually, they enter the first rooms on the ground floor, but so many reptiles slip in alongside them that they can't appreciate the beauty of the place or find any peace there. Still, they have achieved a fair amount just by entering.[50]

I love the matter-of-fact description of those of us whose "desires are good" and who "sometimes…think about the health and state of [our] souls." Who "pray only a few times a month" with minds "filled with a thousand preoccupations." Who sometimes manage to "shake off these mental shackles" but then don't find the space of prayer to be a very calm or beautiful room. We can't calm down; so many reptiles[51] and distractions from our active lives are with us there that it doesn't seem a particularly peaceful place. To this harried crowd, Teresa offers a little pat on the hand: "Good for you! You have 'achieved a fair amount just by entering.'" From my own experience, I would add, "Don't despair. This is normal."

Imagining one of these first dwellings of prayer in material terms, I see a sunlit but dim bohemian lounge, filled to the brim with knickknacks and pillows and stuff from our everyday lives—calendars and keys and laundry lying about—along with cats and dogs roaming around and canaries singing in cages. It is a beautiful place, yes, but it is also full of distractions. The cats and dogs won't leave us alone. The calendar beckons, or the laundry leads us into meditations about the state of our wardrobe or figure. We sometimes like to go in, although it's not a place where we can really relax, where we can connect with deep meaning. But it's interesting and somewhat alluring, so we go back occasionally. We know there's something good there—or somewhere in the house.

"Having some good desires" and "praying only a few times a month" would define the first twelve years of my life very well (and other seasons intermittently, too). It is a description of those times when God is just one interesting thing in an endlessly interesting and stimulating world, where I am too busy defining myself by what I do and the relationships around me to give any real space to anything else. Self-reflection sometimes occurs, but in a hurried fashion, and it is quickly forgotten in the press and drama of life.

I was a well-loved child growing up in a sunny and beautiful small town, trying to make my way in a world that included, but was not defined by, religious notions. Like many people, and with a pattern that would repeat often as I grew through adolescence and young adulthood, I didn't try to really explore the interior castle, the *moradas*, where I might know something of God, until it began to rain, until deep sadness came to life outside the castle walls.

SECOND DWELLINGS:

SEEKING

"In some ways, these souls have it harder than those in the first dwellings. But in reality, they are in less danger, because they now seem to understand their position. There is great hope they'll be able to go farther into the heart of the castle.

I say it's harder for them because those in the first dwellings are like those who are unable to speak but also unable to hear, so their lack of speaking ability is not particularly frustrating. Those in the second dwellings are like those who can hear others speaking but cannot talk themselves. This is much more difficult, more frustrating. But that's no reason to envy those who can't hear. After all, it is a wonderful thing to be able to hear and understand what is being said to us."[52]

Beckoned (by World and Word)

When I was twelve years old and in the seventh grade, I would come home in the evening to find my house with all the lights turned off and my mother on the couch, crying. I could hear her before I saw her. I would make my way over to her in the dark, then sit next to where she lay on the plaid, mission-style sofa. My father had left her, moved across town in the wake of an extramarital affair he didn't want to give up, and my mom's grief would not be contained. Not that night; never, fully.

In my adolescent rage, I wrote accusatory letters to my dad and gave him the silent treatment on the weekends when he would pick up my siblings and me in his truck and drive us to the farm where he lived—the farm my mom had thought we'd *all* be moving to as a family. My brain and body were shifting into adult gear just as my domestic space and deepest relationships suffered an earthquake, and so it was no wonder I found myself often pondering the ragged precipices of existence that emerged from the rubble:

What did it mean to be a good person? What was love, really? When was forgiveness merited? And who could be trusted, leaned on, when your dad had gone elsewhere and your mom was sobbing in the dark?

One evening, after Wednesday-night youth group at the First Presbyterian Church, a Filipina college student named Rhonda listened in the stairwell as I told her that my parents had separated. Her sweet round face instantly shifted in compassion, her eyes mirroring my pain and disappointment. "I'm so sorry," she said as she gave me a hug. With my blonde best friend by my side, she talked to me for a while there in the dim passageway before saying goodbye. By the time I finally stepped out of the church basement into the clear winter night, I had at least part of my answer as to who could be trusted—an answer that would continue to evolve in the coming decade, but the course of which was largely set in that "divorce year": the church.

I didn't have much to say about God then (although I had plenty of questions); but warm, solid, loving faces like Rhonda's would lead my adolescent heart to wonder more deeply about the divine figure who was at the center of this stable community, all these kindhearted people. I can tell this story now with casual simplicity—the church was a rock when everything else came crashing down; the church was my safe harbor in the storm of that year and the sadness beyond—but the truth is, when I slow down and take time to remember and honor that season, I recognize the depth of vulnerability I experienced during that period, and it still brings me to tears. And there is a deep mystery about the goodness that I encountered in it, that I tasted, that defies my attempts at accounting.[53] What—or who— did I find in those months? What do I remember?

I remember trying to pay attention to the sermon in the peach-colored sanctuary as the bearded minister went on and on about God's love. I remember closing my eyes as we made a circle in the basement at the end of the youth group meeting, standing on the industrial brown carpet, and were all invited to pray, people saying words into the dark as if God heard. There was a strange light behind my eyelids, and I didn't know if God heard us, but I liked those words of care for other people; I liked the way I felt afterward.

I can read my experience sociologically, a-theistically: at a tender developmental time, young girl finds companionship and stability in religious community. Attaches self to religious community. Forms nascent identity around religious community. At times, this is basically how I understood it, and how I would account for my religiosity when my immediate family members had little of it themselves. But a utilitarian accounting of faith communities has never actually stood up under scrutiny in my own life. As I am a West Coast millennial in the mainline tradition, my primary church communities have *never* been cool and have always been full of people whom popular culture would quickly dismiss as weird. (I say that as the terrible kind of person who has often wanted to believe she is one of the few non-weird ones, full of hubris and empty of logic.) If it were social assets I was seeking and finding, there would have been (and were) lots of other places to have those needs met: The volleyball team. The tennis team. Our warm and wonderful and funny neighbor's house, a second home offering comfort two doors down from my mom, my siblings, and me as we struggled through the post-divorce years in our new home across the state.

By the time I was in eighth grade and we had made this 370-mile move, it was definitely not the social relationships that kept me coming back to the strange institution we call church; sadly, but tellingly, I cannot remember the name of anyone in my youth group from high school except for the youth minister, a smart woman with grey hair and sad eyes. Was the short, friendly runner named Gus—or Ben? They were not my *friends* like that. But I kept going back, because in the midst of the busy mayhem, I felt better after I left that place where God was at the center, the raison d'être. We always prayed, somehow. We talked about what it meant to be a good person in a way that went beyond my good grades and my anxieties to get into a good college. I wanted to be a Christian because it seemed, somewhere deep within me, a truly good thing to be, even though my faith was earnest and fervently seeking when I was in the church building and largely forgotten when I left it.

When I was a sophomore in high school, I did begin to make an effort to seek God outside the church walls, too, sometimes trying to pray in my bedroom. I scanned the clearance racks at Borders Books and came home with hardcovers by Mother Teresa (a Catholic nun devoted to the poor in India) and Charles Swindoll (an American evangelical living in Orange

County), not knowing then that they represented wildly different visions of Christianity. I read these books in fits and starts, beginning programs of devotion and prayer that quickly got buried in the shuffle. But I would *try*, buying a special leather book in which to record "spiritual thoughts and questions" that remained mostly empty, pondering if I would ever know God, because Mother Teresa said God's language was silence, and that seemed patently absurd (and devastating). I didn't hear anything in silence. One night, though, I sat on my blue-and-white-plaid Ralph Lauren bedspread and somehow found myself reading John 21, somehow felt time stop when I read that Jesus said, "Feed my sheep," because, although in the words on the page, he was talking to Peter, for the first and only time during those years that I remember, it seemed the words on the page were talking to me. That's what I'm supposed to do, I knew. I was arrested for a moment by the conviction, caught in a reality that seemed to engulf me like a transcendent bubble and then slowly faded away, releasing me but not the memory of the moment. *Feed my sheep*. What did it mean? I couldn't say, but I also couldn't forget it.

In retrospect, the years from age twelve to twenty could well be described as my season primarily spent in the "second dwellings," as Teresa understands them. They are the spaces where a person can hear the Lord calling,[54] sometimes, in various ways (mostly indirectly, through other people, books, and sermons), but they can't really answer directly or consistently; they haven't found their inmost voice. These are the spaces of fitful spiritual striving and seeking, where a person has a desire to move deeper than the occasional prayer and self-reflection of the first dwellings; but Teresa diagnoses both a lack of consistent determination and an honest struggle over ultimate values. As she describes it:

> This chapter concerns those who have begun to practice prayer and who see the importance of not staying in the first dwellings but who can't quite yet bring themselves to leave for good…and don't avoid occasions of sin that keep drawing them back…. It's a great mercy when they manage to escape from the destructive, distracting elements, even if it's only long enough to see that it's good to get away from them.[55]

For here, the forces against spiritual progress show you the things of the world, and pretend that earthly pleasures are practically eternal. They remind you of your reputation, your friends and relatives, the way in which your health and strength will be endangered by any generous act of self-sacrifice (which one always wants to do upon entering this dwelling place), among thousands of other kinds of stumbling blocks.[56]

In Teresa's Spanish text, "the forces against spiritual progress" are called "devils" and are metaphorically represented as snakes, reptiles, and occasionally beasts. They are noisy and poisonous and always sneaky, with aims of deception. This was the language I found so off-putting when I first picked up *The Interior Castle* at age nineteen, language and ideas that effectively created roadblocks to the landscape of her worldview for my postmodern mind. The truth, however, is that Teresa is not particularly interested in demonology; she is not obsessed with what we might call "spiritual warfare." But she is *aware of* and attentive to the reality of our resistance to moving into a more conscious connection with God, resistance from within and without. She is realistic about the real tensions and competition between alternate claims of value, purpose, meaning, and success in our human experience.

Whether or not we relate easily to the notion of devils or can even assent to the more abstract idea of "forces against spiritual progress," can we listen long enough to her words to relate to the still-relevant reality of fleeting distractions, the constantly cloying sources of self-satisfaction that never bring lasting satisfaction, the evident tensions within ourselves over what really matters? Who cannot relate on some level to the desire to succeed brilliantly according to the terms of current culture or familial values, whatever they may be, in tension with a different desire to align oneself with a purpose that transcends those most obvious metrics of "success"?

There are those who can stand over a grave and say, "Better get the good stuff of life while you can" instead of reflecting on the temporality of material comforts, but most of us have a different response. At such times, we ask ourselves, "What really matters? What is worth aiming for in life?" Teresa tries to describe the very real and often extended struggle over these questions, with different aspects of ourselves offering different "arguments," especially in this second dwellings territory of our spiritual journey. Teresa laments:

> Oh, Jesus! These forces bring such confusion. The poor soul is greatly troubled and doesn't know if it should continue on farther or go back to the room it just left. But then, on the other hand, there are forces that help: Reason tells you that earthly things are of little value compared to what you are truly seeking (and it's a mistake to think otherwise); faith teaches what you must do to actually find satisfaction; memory reminds you how all these earthly goods come to an end, drawing to mind the death of those who enjoyed such things greatly.[57]

It's all there: One part of us says, "Don't be a zealous fool! The world has plenty of wonderful satisfactions to offer." Another part listens to what all the major religious traditions of the world, including Christianity, say about lasting fulfillment and how it's not found by winning the terms of the current economic or cultural game. Yet another part considers—however fleetingly—our own death, or, Teresa implies, at least reflects on the death and legacies of the status winners. If they were not people of greater substance than their joy in riches, who remembers them long? "How quickly their lives can be forgotten by all," she reminds us.[58]

More compelling than postmortem reflections, however, is the goodness of the One who keeps beckoning us closer. As we seek deeper meaning for our lives and begin to devote some time to prayer and reflection, God, as described by Teresa, is like a good and steady neighbor who is patient with our confused, fraught, and uneven behavior:

> They are getting closer to the central place where His Majesty dwells, and He is a very good Neighbor as they approach. His mercy and goodness are so great that even when we are engaged with our worldly activities, business, pleasures, and struggles, as we are falling into sins and getting back up again—because the deceptive and destructive elements are so active, it would actually be a miracle *not* to stumble and fall while in their midst—still this Lord of ours deeply wants us to love Him and seek His companionship. And so He calls us ceaselessly, again and again, to come

closer. And His voice is so sweet and obviously good that the poor soul is grief-stricken because such obedience, such progress feels impossible.[59]

When I was sixteen, I was invited to be a chaperone for middle schoolers on a trip to northern France as a reward for my diligence in French class. My two primary memory streams of that trip are like a comic parody of the second dwellings. One: I spent much of the time feeling sophisticated and self-important for being in *France*, speaking *French*, and trying to decide if I had a crush on the rosy-cheeked sophomore who was another chaperone. Overlooking Paris from the steps of Montmartre, I boldly asked him to give me my first kiss, because what could be better than a first kiss in view of the Eiffel Tower? But, immediately, I knew it was all wrong; I had used him for my romantic fantasy and didn't really care for him. I went to bed feeling sick to my stomach and trapped in the quasi-relationship my grasping had created. Two: we visited the stunning cathedral in Chartres, and after the historical tour, I pulled away from the group to sit in a pew and stare at the rose window. I knelt, tried to pray. I would not have said then that I heard God's voice, but I was suddenly attuned to the intended recipient of all this labor, sacrifice, and beauty. I dissolved into tears at the "impossibility" of what I perceived was commanded of us all, which was to somehow, vaguely, in a way I did not understand, live in a way that was much more oriented to the glorious reality reflected in the soaring gothic space and much less oriented to the "perfection" of my clothes, grades, body, social life.

I wanted to devote my life to God, like the craftsmen who made each shard of the stained-glass windows. But I also wanted to wrest a kissing-story into existence that I knew would impress my friends *forever*. It's funny, now, but there was nothing funny or false about my tears of anguish then. I *did* want to do better by the goodness I intuited to be at the heart of this whole Christian thing, but I was also not able to let the world's goalposts out of my sight. I can see that, in some ways, my teen years would have been easier if I hadn't been trying to seek God at all; I can see why Teresa says that those who hear God's voice find it "more difficult, more frustrating" than those who can't hear it.[60]

In his summary and analysis of the *Interior Castle*, Rowan Williams offers a sensitive and encouraging perspective on this trial, because it reorients the struggle to the love of God:

> We suffer more in this second stage than in the first simply because we have fewer defences against God. God has taken us at our word: if we have turned Godward, God will be eagerly desirous of bringing us closer still (II, 1.2), and we shall find ourselves less able to deceive ourselves about our need and weakness. We *know* more clearly what we are meant for (*wanted* for, as in L 9), how far we are from this, and how deep-rooted are our evasions and self-delusions. Thus, although we shall feel some kind of affective warmth here, the primary *emotional* coloring of this stage is a sense of fear or despondency at the conflicts which seem to be intensifying all the time. In a way, it would be quite easy to slip back (II, 1.4); but we only do so at enormous moral cost, because that would involve something like a denial of the truth about God and ourselves that is in front of our noses.[61]

At peaks of devotion, at moments when I took time to reflect on the central teachings of faith via book or pamphlet or Bible or mixtape given to me by a now nameless youth group friend, I would connect with the impulses and thoughts and "will" toward God that Teresa describes burgeoning in these dwelling places:

> The will moves us to love One in whom it has seen so many acts and signs of love—desiring to return some of the same. In particular, the will shows you that this true Lover never leaves but is always present, giving life and being. Then the understanding comes along and helps you realize that you could never in your lifetime hope to have a better friend: the world is full of deceptions, and the alluring "goods" coming to mind bring difficulties, burdens, and annoyances. Understanding also tells you that security or peace will surely never be found outside this castle, and says to stop wandering from one house to another, searching for satisfaction, when your own home is full of good things—if you would only sit down to enjoy them.[62]

It is not *irrational*, Teresa thus points out, to conquer the allurements of distraction. Our own intellect is capable of seeing the inadequacies of a life lived by the simple yet ruthless rules of social status and success. "But oh, my Lord and my God," she bemoans, this never seems to be enough for us: "How the whole world's habits of getting involved in worthless vanities ruins everything! Our faith is so lifeless that we want what we can see with our eyes more than the things faith tells us about."[63]

Alas, Teresa, it is true. Still true. We are beckoned by a voice unseen and even unheard in words we could repeat, but we are also beckoned by the visions of goodness and joy we can see in the images of human happiness all around us, the ones that call us to self-fulfillment through ambition and pleasure and human perfection. Only individuals who are asleep to their own multilayered desires can mock the seekers—those who find themselves in that landscape of their soul where they are actively caught between these beckoning sources of proclaimed goodness, where all is fraught.

Words Heard from Good People

One of my favorite discoveries in Teresa's work was the understated affirmation that throughout our life, but perhaps especially in the early stages and seasons of our faith, God "calls" to us through other voices. Our creator "invites" us "through words heard from good people, or through sermons, or as we read good books, or through sicknesses and trials, or through truths God teaches us when we are praying. (However weak our prayers may be, God values them highly.)"[64] She even adds a general category, as if to cover the manifold means by which this happens that we are already familiar with: "There are many other ways God calls us, as you know."[65] There are so many things I love about this small passage—including her familiarity with lukewarm, half-hearted prayer—but the primary treasure here is implicit. Teresa *assumes* the quotidian work of learning and the very ordinary, familiar ways we tend to approach God—by listening and talking to people who seem to have surer footing than we do when they speak about the divine, reading books, reaching out in crisis, and even mediocre prayer times, all of these—are a real and important part of the journey through the dwelling places. They are mediums through which we might be drawn closer to God, if we are willing to listen and follow with discernment. In my case, this passage immediately brought to mind those books and sermons and friendships that seemed to have a disproportionate effect on my life, the ideas or "words heard from good people" that I remember to this day because it somehow felt like I was receiving them under the very eye of God. Teresa reassures me, without fuss: that's because you were.

It might be considered a cliché maxim of faith to say that "God speaks to us in many ways," but I was not taught this idea explicitly (or the message didn't sink in). To my mind, it was unlikely that God would speak to us, appeal to us, lovingly *beckon* us at all (because we are so small, so insignificant), but *if* you were going to put a divine claim on communication or prompting in your life, it would likely come via prayer or Scripture. The other stuff, like books, sermons, articles, memorable experiences of insight, conversations with teachers and friends—these were like the human how-to manuals for living "a Christian life," or, in contemporary terms, "a wise, wholehearted life." They were secondary, albeit helpful, commentary on the ultimate. That God would *employ* these "secondary" mediums to speak to us, guide us, care for us...well, that perspective matched up brilliantly with what I had lived, but I had never heard it stated so plainly. It reshaped how I understood those memorable times of insight, transforming them from intellectual "breakthroughs" to moments of caring communication, as if God were saying, "This is the key for the current cage you're in, love. Why don't we move on?"

It is not just in your head, Teresa reassured me; God was there all along, calling you into greater wholeness and maturity, into new dwelling places, through the voices of other good and wise people. These kinds of words don't come every day, but they are also not once-in-a-lifetime experiences. A friend of mine says it happens for her, with a book, every couple of years. We know these moments of encounter, often recognized in the moment but only confirmed by the sifting of time. They are the words with more weight than average words, the books, the conversations that strike and tend to our hearts, ones we remember receiving long after the details of the message have faded.

"Associating with others who are walking in the right way is very helpful," Teresa writes; "don't just mingle with those in the same rooms where you find yourself but with those whom you know have progressed to rooms nearing the center."[66] Of course, Teresa was creating just such a "conversation" by writing down her own observations about prayer and the spiritual life, and I have found it "very helpful" to hear her speak across the centuries. But many other voices have spoken to me about walking through this interior castle using different terms, and there have been other times when, in retrospect, I have recognized God's appeal to me to take a step into the next room.

The most memorable instance from my late teens came through my struggle to achieve a healthy relationship with food—and my own body. Through my senior year of high school and the first two quarters of college, I had been waging and mostly losing a mighty internal battle in which I very much wanted to stop thinking about food, calories, and the state of my body (because it seemed so obviously wrong, so obviously a waste of my energy), yet I also believed that to be the perfect eater and exerciser in optimal health was to be "good" (not to mention admirable, lovable, worthy). I was living by the sadly common theology of popular magazines: "Be ye perfect, and then"—only then—"will you know abundant life." This is a terribly false and unbiblical amalgam, but it is so easily mistaken for God's truth, whether or not one is religious.

I was caught up in it in a bad way, and, almost twenty years later, I can see the unnamed shadows pressing in on my eighteen-year-old psyche, which sought self-disciple and tighter control: my mother's mental health struggles and then breakdown during the fall I went away to college, which caused her to take a leave of absence from work while I determined to hold it together in every way, helplessly separated from her, five hundred miles down I-5. At the time, I didn't see this sadness as part of my battle. All I saw was unwanted obsession, unwanted binge eating, a new escalation to purging when I returned to campus after Christmas. I went to the university's psychiatric clinic to see if I qualified for research counseling for eating disorders. Sorry, they said. I didn't meet the criteria for having bulimia—I had only purged two times. On my way out the door, I ran into the girl who lived across the hall from me. We smiled at each other politely. *Funny meeting you here!* Later that night, we began to talk.

At first, I doubted whether two confused people sharing with each other could possibly make either one of us better. But exposing our secret thoughts and behaviors robbed them of their power. By offering forgiveness and compassion—and always, laughter—to each other, we learned to be gentler with ourselves. One time, she asked me to keep a box of chocolates in my room that she didn't trust herself not to eat. "Sure," I said, "I'll keep them safe." Then, on a binge, I pulled them out from underneath my bed and ate them all up myself. When I confessed to her, ashamed, she had only sympathy: because the chocolates were out of reach, locked away in my room, she had gone down to the communal freezer and eaten a bag of frozen garlic bread. Soon we were crying with laughter. And grace crept in, unnamed but almighty. We began to offer each other the love and compassion that we had not yet learned to offer ourselves.

But there were still depths of healing unattended to. In mid-March, I was caught facing the toilet when a stranger walked in on me in a bakery bathroom. He probably thought nothing of it, but I felt incriminated: Through a stranger's eyes, the sick nature of binging and purging was magnified. That was the last time I self-induced vomiting. I knew enough by then not to promise instant reform. Yet I still needed to construct new ways of thinking about God, food, and how the two were related.

Less than two weeks later, during spring break, I finally moved to a new, brighter dwelling in my interior castle. It happened not because I finally got enough willpower to move my stuff but because, unexpectedly, a door opened, and I was invited to walk through it unencumbered. I was sitting on my uncle's brown couch in his little Los Angeles bungalow, reading C. S. Lewis' *The Screwtape Letters*. Then, and for years afterward, I would have said I had a "spiritual breakthrough" on that sunny afternoon. Now I ponder with some wonder Teresa's hermeneutic: What if it wasn't me "making a breakthrough" but rather God breaking in to my consciousness through Lewis' words? In *The Screwtape Letters*, I finally received an idea—a word—that illuminated my misdirection: my greatest offense against God wasn't eating forty-eight cookies; it was my excessive, inordinate attention to food, body, and self-perfection. My new favorite word became *inordinate*. In that reading, I saw and heard with great clarity that I had made an idol of my diet. When I had prayed all those months for God to help me not be so "out of control," I was, in effect, asking God to help me do a better job of serving my other god. In those hours, I heard old concepts in a new way. Certainly, I had read before, and often, that our love for God and neighbor is primary—everything else is secondary. It was not a new idea. But, suddenly, as I read, I was swimming in that truth. It was another instance of time outside of time, of the memory lens collapsing around this moment when I was somehow receiving the good words I'd needed all along but hadn't been ready or able to hear.

I asked the kindred-spirit friend who accompanied me through freshman year how she would describe those moments when a book or speech seems to speak into our very heart, opening up a new way or new understanding. She mentioned something I had never thought of: it's not just where these revelatory and incisive moments lead you that's notable, but the ways in which they suture up our past experiences, too. There is a coming together of the past in a way that allows movement into the future to proceed differently.

This is part of what happened to me that afternoon with *The Screwtape Letters*. Suddenly, the terribly foggy mess of my spirit and psyche seemed so clearly outlined. I was looking in the wrong direction for peace, love, satisfaction. My dieting and exercise tracking were an obscure form of gluttony, a fixation on that which is unworthy of so much attention. *Oh! That's what was happening.* Suddenly, I could see this with greater clarity, though, of course, I would have intellectually assented to the same throughout my disordered eating days. But at the right moment, as I continued to seek healing, I heard this truth through Lewis' words in a way that also gave me power to actually live into it, to move toward it with greater and greater steadiness in the coming months and years. Food became an amiable friend, not the viciously volatile lover she had been for years. I think now that C. S. Lewis would be the first to say such a transformative moment is not the work of his words, exactly, but rather his words put to work by a much greater healer: the One with power to suture our pasts and draw us into a new way of life.

Peace in Our Own Home

So, if you sometimes fall, don't lose heart or stop trying to progress. Even from your fall, God will bring good.... Can any evil be greater than that which we discover in our own house? How can we hope to find rest in other people's homes if we can't rest in our own? No friend or family member is as close as our own thoughts. We always have to live with them, whether we like it or not. Yet our own minds seem to create inner conflicts, as if they resent the conflicts created by our bad choices. But sisters: the Lord said "Peace, peace," to his apostles, again and again. Trust me, unless we have peace and strive for peace in our own home, we won't find it elsewhere. Let this inner war cease…. I beg you—those who haven't even started this inward journey and those who have just begun—don't let such inner conflicts and confusion turn you away from prayer or cause you to retreat.[67]

The internal battles of competing priorities may be an inevitable part of "start[ing] this inward journey," but Teresa wants to make clear that the journey is still more than worth this cost of admission. Toward the end of "Second Dwellings"—which is her shortest section, containing only one chapter—she moves once more to a voice of encouragement and coaching: "So, if you sometimes fall, don't lose heart or stop trying to progress." This acknowledgment of falling, failure, backsliding, and a later reference in the chapter to "the temptation to give up on prayer" (for which she says there is "no solution…except to start again at the beginning")[68] are reflections born of her own experience. At one point, when she was in her twenties, she became so discouraged by her own losses in "this inner war"[69] that she felt it was better to give up trying to pray. In her autobiography, she writes candidly about nearly eighteen years of disconnect between her actual prayer life and her holy reputation, which includes this particular misstep. It seemed that no prayer at all was better than feeling like an imposter before God, keenly aware of all the ways she knew she was still not really loyal to the central claims of faith. This was a decision she deeply regretted and frequently warned other sisters against. *Do not let the war make you turn back. Keep walking, keep moving, until you come to a place of greater peace.*

Shortly after this message of encouragement, Teresa writes something that points to the paradoxical key of both striving and humility in the spiritual life, a message with many refrains in her work:

Remember: recollection can't begin through hard work or mental fighting. It must come *gently*, and eventually you'll be able to experience this quiet prayerfulness for longer stretches of time.[70]

Here it seems she is speaking specifically about prayer and the ways in which we try to forcefully clear our minds of all thoughts in a combative way that only creates more disturbance. This is an important tenet of her teachings on prayer, expanded upon more fully in other texts. But the basic idea is now established wisdom in teachings on contemplative Christian prayer and other forms of meditation: when you find yourself engaged with other thoughts, gently return your attention to the intended focus. Don't beat yourself up or get caught up in the distraction. It's like saying, "Let those unwelcome and distracting thoughts walk by. Turn away, again, without fanfare. Set your eyes upon the horizon once more. Don't go and try to push the interlopers off the sidewalk of your brain. It never works for long, and then we just end up in a brawl and leave our inner landscape, feeling defeated."

I hear her words as illuminating an important truth behind my own journey to greater peace outside the arena of prayer, too, in the general "war" within. *"Recollection can't begin through hard work or mental fighting. It must come gently, and eventually you'll be able to experience this quiet prayerfulness for longer stretches of time."* Although the peaceful resolution of internal battles requires intentionality, persistent attention, curiosity, and patience ("trying to progress"), that quiet space of open possibility ("recollection") usually arrives with a spirit of gentleness, not force. The inflection point in my battle with food is but one example, but the more I think about this notion, the more it shines through most of my transitions from war to peace. I see the light of this gentleness—perhaps God's persistent gentleness with us—in the season when I began to experience greater "peace in my own home," the summer I spent in rural El Salvador, staying in a convent, after I turned twenty.

I was at an age and in a circumstance that make for common stories of personal growth and transformation; there is nothing extraordinary about the journey toward greater self-assurance and maturity that took place within me in the village of Arcatao. What does strike me as extraordinary, all these years later, is the way that the inner shifting I experienced lines up so strikingly with Teresa's schematic for the dwelling places. Looking out at the mountains on a cooling summer night, I knew I had been following other voices in my quest to be "the first honest politician," as one Vietnam veteran wryly put it when I told him my then-intended major. What I actually wanted was to study literature and history and culture, and seek the possibilities for hope and change within those disciplines, those areas of the human experience. Journaling and crying and indirectly praying in my *convento* bedroom, I wrote heartfelt adolescent poetry in which I finally found my way to accepting that I might not be "the best" at anything (i.e., loving God, being a friend, being a student, being a human...), ever; but, nevertheless, I was "good enough."[71] *Enough, enough, enough.* I remember that poem, that tear-filled night, and I see gentleness raining down. The healing of my forceful perfectionism in learning to approach the things I wanted to "battle against" with gentleness allowed for a new kind of peace in all areas of my life, not just in my body or my faith. It was, in retrospect, the end of an era. Not that there wouldn't be other conflicts or disturbances or even battles down the line, but they would take place on a different level or plane of commitment.

After living among the nuns and priests, traveling in the back of a white pickup truck to celebrate *misas* on mountainsides, it is perhaps not surprising that I felt more at home in my Christian identity, with a greater longing to understand—and share—the deep trust in God exhibited by those around me, and which illogically and powerfully ran through the horrendous stories of the civil war. In the land of Oscar Romero, I no longer felt ashamed of my faith; I learned to be comfortable in it, and, at the same time, I began to yearn for some sign, some consolation, some experience of God in prayer that would anchor my faith, that might initiate me to the province of the solidly faithful. Teresa speaks back to me with a humorous chiding:

> There's one thing so important to say that I will knowingly repeat myself here. At the beginning, one must not think of such things as spiritual gifts or favors, for that's a very shabby way of starting to construct such a large and beautiful building.... Because it is not in these dwelling places that it rains manna, but in the ones farther on. Once there, the soul has everything it wants, because

it only wants God's will. It's an odd and funny thing: here we are, coming across barriers, stumbling, and suffering from imperfections by the thousand, with newborn virtues so undeveloped they can't even walk (God granting they have even come to life at all)— and yet we are shameless about wanting consolations in prayer, and complain about periods of dryness. Sisters, don't let this be true of you.[72]

How else can we come to love this Lord? May it please God to give us this understanding: how much we cost Him, that the servant is not greater than his Lord, and that to enjoy His glory we must work....[73]

I was willing to work—at least, in my imagination, I was willing. As Teresa incisively describes this brand-new sense of allegiance and devotion:

You might think that you *would* be full of determination and able to better handle the challenges of your life...if only God would give you inward gifts in prayer. But His Majesty knows best what is right and good for us; it's not for us to boss Him around about what to give us, for He can rightly respond that we don't really know what we're asking for.[74]

I was in the land of modern saints and martyrs. I thought that if only I were to be given a vision of Jesus, one that would alleviate all my misgivings about him, I could be like them. I could do great things for God (!). I just needed a little extra divine fuel and the opportunity. Thankfully, I didn't pursue this line of "boss[ing] Him around about what to give [me]" and begging for chances to prove myself, largely because I was surrounded by wise people who would never have encouraged such a path of thinking or prayer. Thanks to these wise mentors and the central teachings of the church community, I learned a simpler, wiser path: Try to walk in God's ways. Try to love God and love your neighbor, with sincerity and justice. As Teresa puts it:

All the beginner in prayer needs to do is to work, to try; resolutely preparing oneself as much as possible to bring one's will into alignment and conformity with the will of God. As I'll say later, you can be assured that the greatest perfection attainable on the spiritual road lies in this conformity..... We don't need sophisticated terms or efforts in spiritual practices we don't understand. All our well-being is found through seeking conformity to God's will.[75]

Teresa will say it again and again on this journey into some of the greatest mysteries of faith and prayer: there is no mystery, really, in how we approach God on the spiritual path. It is a matter of the mature reshaping (perfect conformity) of our lives to be in alignment with "God's will"—that is, for her, always and ultimately, practical and down-to-earth self-giving love in community. Other features of "God's will" in the Christian tradition more broadly include honesty, obedience, compassion, unfathomable forgiveness, and justice. Not easy, but not mysterious. A journey we are willing to pursue, with all of its uncertainties, once we are more settled in the fact that we actually want to; and that, in that desire, we are better served by gentleness and humility and the practice of receiving grace than by forceful achievement of "doing well" and "being good." Once we accept this paradox of life with God, we might begin to have a grounding of peace in our own house.

THIRD DWELLINGS:

COMMITMENT

"Through God's goodness, I believe there are many such souls in the world, people earnestly desiring not to offend God. They avoid committing even small, unconscious sins; love to give of themselves generously and sacrificially, and to make up for it when they do wrong; spend hours in prayer and meditation; use their time well; practice works of charity toward their neighbors; and act very thoughtfully and intentionally in their speech and dress and in the management of their households, if they have one. This is certainly a desirable state. There seems no reason why they should be denied access to the final dwelling places. And the Lord will not deny this movement, if they *truly* desire it."[76]

Devout Life, Stable Life

When I returned to Stanford for the fall quarter of my junior year after spending the summer in El Salvador, I entered a sunny San Francisco season with clear autumnal skies that radiated joy throughout my life. I had come to that "peace in my own home" that Teresa talks about toward the end of the second dwellings and was bathing in the "great good" of having so much inner turmoil behind me. Settling into a major that matched my deepest interests and gifts, I felt academically at home and affirmed. At peace with my Christian identity and less stressed about external labels and assumptions regarding what that meant about me, personally and politically, I signed up for a weekly Roman Catholic small group gathering of women. I was their "closet Protestant," but after a summer steeped in Catholicism, I felt comfortable there and enlivened by what I was learning through this new community of faith. I attended the 10:00 p.m. candlelit Mass on Sunday nights and continued my somewhat typical undergraduate balance of studying and completing class work, doing paid work, talking on the phone to my boyfriend (still in El Salvador), and spending time with friends.

Beneath those ordinary rhythms was the satisfaction of the third dwellings—the peacefully devout life, the stable life. At that time, I would have simply said I'd "found my place" and "hit my stride," which was true, too. But such phrases might be seen as colloquial equivalents of "finding peace in our own home" and then walking through our days with the basic integrity that flows from such peace. Either way, it was a really good autumn, providing a foundation of stability I would need in the years to come.

In the third dwelling places, we are in the land of fairly steady commitment to God, or at least to the values and communities of God. The deep angst resulting from a troubled search to discover where ultimate allegiance, meaning, and satisfaction in one's life are found is mostly left behind. (Careful, though! There is always, always, the possibility of backsliding, Teresa hastens to add each time she describes such progress.) The soul in this third stage has come to greater clarity around the *telos*, or end, of life's strivings: learning to walk in God's ways of love, healing, and self-sacrifice for the good of the world—as exemplified by Jesus—using the gifts and circumstances given. This goal now takes hold, deeply, as a peaceable priority.

As we know based on observations from both within and outside of the religious life, to have a clear and consistently held intention or priority does *not* make for complete consistency or perfection, but it is a very powerful force in keeping us headed toward our goal. If we are actually clear about what we seek, day in and day out, our lives will be structured and built up around this desire. (Maintaining such clarity is difficult. This difficulty is one of the main reasons for honest self-reflection and prayer.) And if our desire is for greater alignment with God's ways—remembering that God's ways are primarily about learning to love God and other humans—then this deep desire is no different. Our lives begin to reflect this aim, slowly and imperfectly, even as we seek it with full knowledge of our continued shortcomings.

Herein lie the tensions and temptations of the third dwellings, which Teresa jumps into immediately: on the one hand, such a person is "blessed," "on the path to salvation."[77] She boldly says, "I'm convinced that the Lord always gives a person who has overcome inner strife a certain security, a peace of conscience, which is no small blessing." But then she quickly pulls back, revealing the possibilities for other insidiously false paths to be followed yet: "I say 'security,' but that's probably the wrong word because nothing is completely 'secure' in this life. Whenever I say it, please know I mean and imply 'unless they stray from the path they've begun.'"[78]

Perhaps reminding her readers to stay grounded in the awe (or fear) of the Lord (*Beatus vir qui timet Dominum*)[79] is at the front of her mind as she begins this chapter because she knows that the temptations toward, and possibilities for, smug self-satisfaction and self-righteousness begin in earnest here, too. Or worse—delusion of oneself and others about what's *really* going on inside us. Indeed, as she meditates on the blessedness of remembering our smallness and vulnerability before God, her mind wanders to the ways in which she, too, has been at fault, the ways in which her life has been "misspent," and her own reliance on the mercies of God.[80] Between the lines, she reveals that the desire for hero worship was as strong in communities then as it is now. She acknowledges that often the sisters become "sad" when she reminds them of her own falls and weaknesses (they "want to think that [she has] always been holy"), and yet she will not complain, as if "God stopped giving [her] all the help [she] needed" to carry out her commitment to him and actually live a more holy life. But based on her own experience of fooling others and herself while living as an esteemed Carmelite nun, she urges against a posture of settled security, ever, even in the most rigorous communities of devotion.[81]

After giving this extensive warning and caveat, Teresa moves to a clearer depiction of the third dwellings and some of their good and desirable aspects, too. This is, as one Teresan writer puts it, "the normal state of most good people."[82] They long not to offend God and are intentional about self-sacrifice, prayer, and self-reflection; they "use their time well; practice works of charity toward their neighbors; and act very thoughtfully...."[83] It is "no small favor" for them to have moved through "their initial challenges," and, in a sense, Teresa wants to celebrate this movement and such people's ubiquitous presence: "Through God's goodness, I believe there are many such souls in the world."[84] These people are, in many ways, "the ideal" or at least "the good" Christians of our world, or as close to it as we think we'll see in our lifetime if we don't make a pilgrimage to meet a saint. They are those whom local churches refer to as "saints" in a truly loving and fond way (drop the cynical twist, for a moment): "She's a saint." Or, "Why don't you ask so-and-so for advice? He's amazing." We can think of people we admire who seem to have this evident thoughtfulness most of the time, made known to us through their intentionality, wisdom, and hospitality, their true and practical love for their neighbors. I have known many such individuals, couples, and sometimes whole families. What's not to like? Here Teresa waffles.

She wants to acknowledge the good parts of this state (or stage) of faithfulness, but she also does not want us to mistake it for the highest good, as the world and church often do. Right on the heels of a very brief description of the third dwellings and the assurance that "this is certainly a desirable state," she presses onward: "There seems no reason why they should be denied access to the final dwelling. And the Lord will not deny this movement if they truly desire it—such a desire is excellent preparation for the granting of every kind of favor."[85] Do you hear what is happening between the lines? Do not think *this* third dwelling of stability, obedience, and measured good works is the final destination. You can move on fur-ther—*if* you actually want to. Will you desire to know the Lord more fully and not remain satisfied by your carefully crafted life of love and obedi-ence? Such a deep desire will prepare you for something more fulfilling but also riskier, she says.

Here she finds an image and story from Scripture to illustrate the threshold she's describing—the story of the wealthy and pious young man who approaches Jesus, asking how he might have eternal life.[86] "Ever since I started to talk about these third dwellings, I've had that young man in mind," she tells us.[87] Here's his cameo, as seen in the gospel of Mark:

> As [Jesus] was setting out on a journey, a man ran up and knelt before him and asked him, "Good Teacher, what must I do to inherit eternal life?" Jesus said to him, "Why do you call me good? No one is good but God alone. You know the commandments: 'You shall not murder. You shall not commit adultery. You shall not steal. You shall not bear false witness. You shall not defraud. Honor your father and mother.'" He said to him, "Teacher, I have kept all these since my youth." Jesus, looking at him, loved him

and said, "You lack one thing; go, sell what you own, and give the money to the poor, and you will have treasure in heaven; then come, follow me." When [the man] heard this, he was shocked and went away grieving, for he had many possessions.[88]

This passage usually raises questions and prompts conversations about the place of wealth in the Christian life, but that is not what interests Teresa, who has already committed to a life of personal poverty, as have her Carmelite sisters. Instead, she wants to draw our attention to this common spiritual posture: although we may *say* we want to know God more fully, more closely, even in this earthly life (alluding to the "final dwelling" of full union with God), the depth of our desire is suspect. Teresa writes:

Oh, Jesus! How could anyone ever say they have no desire for such a wonderful thing? Especially when they've gotten through the troubled stages leading up to this? Surely no one could, or would. We all *say* we want to live fully with and in God—but…. Words are not enough, just as they were not enough for the young man at the moment when Jesus told him what he needed to *do* if he wanted to be perfect.[89]

Teresa knows that many of her devout sisters—like many of us—are "exactly like him,"[90] and she wants those in the third dwellings to acknowledge this potentially unwelcome truth. We can get stuck here due to a lack of willingness and a lack of true humility, a state in which we are actually "doing **good** and being good"[91] in order to "receive good" from God. Here is the crestfallen face of the wealthy young man: the limits of his will are exposed, and his system of rewards-for-service seems to have cracked with Jesus' hard invitation. We are invited to look on him with love, like Jesus does, as we ask, "What does he really want? What do *we* really want?"

Teresa addresses this often-hidden fissure line, this "obscure unease"[92] in the lives of "good people," through a topic that may seem strange to us at first because we don't talk or think about it nearly as much as she and her colleagues did: How patient are we with "dryness" in prayer? Can we accept the fact that God doesn't feel or seem as close as we think he ought? In the Christian circles I grew up in, people didn't expect much "richness" in prayer; "dryness" was the expected norm. But for Teresa and her compatriots, what happened (and didn't happen) in prayer was a hot topic.

Many books about prayer and prayer methods, including some of Teresa's favorites, were banned under the Inquisition. (Teresa gave them up reluctantly but obediently.) There were assumptions and instructions about how these kinds of "desirable" prayer experiences were achieved. Although it's not a perfect metaphor, it brings to my mind the culturally common conversations around variations of the "prosperity gospel" in the United States. Ironically—especially given the story of the rich young man—we are such a materially wealthy nation, and so oriented to material well-being, that our conversations about what it means to be "blessed" by God often imply material rewards. In this twenty-first-century American version of the "the good Christian life," if you do right, you will be rewarded (financially, tangibly, circumstantially). In the sixteenth-century Carmelite convent version of "the good Christian life," if you do right, you will be rewarded (spiritually, richly, in prayer). So what do you do when you are "doing everything right"—or are trying to—and yet are not receiving your rewards? Worse still, when you hear and see that other people in your community *are* being "rewarded"! How do you respond? With indignant impatience? Or patient acceptance, including gratitude?

In his book on Teresa, Rowan Williams beautifully describes this common shadow side of the well-ordered third dwellings life and summarizes Teresa's analysis and response:

> The great danger is in supposing that our regular and controlled lives give us some sort of claim upon God, so that we become bitterly resentful if God is apparently not at home to us in the way we should like (III, 1.6). If we continue steadily believing ourselves not to deserve anything at God's hands, we shall never lose sight of the truth that God is consistently giving to us and "serving" us (III, 1.8); and if our inner unsettlement is not buried by religious self-congratulation we shall be able to keep this in view.[93]

Teresa raises her signature antidote to such frustration born of "religious self-congratulation": a combination of humility ("believing ourselves not to deserve anything at God's hands") and striving. We will see this paradoxical combination of humility and striving throughout *The Interior Castle*—though, in this place, the tension between the two postures is more evident than usual. It's as if the rich young man who has kept all the commandments since his youth is *about* to approach Jesus, and she wants to encourage him to approach (and then do what is required of him!), but she also doesn't want him to feel entitled to the invitation into the inner circle. She vacillates, rhetorically, between warning against a posture of entitlement (the appeal to humility) and encouraging continued effort and the exercise of his will in seeking God (the appeal to sustained striving). The tension is close and unadorned, except by the mystery of God's freedom, and the careful reader finds that Teresa goes back and forth between the two admonitions, sentence by sentence:

> Souls in the third dwelling places know that nothing would persuade them to seriously defy God in sin—many of them would not even commit small sins intentionally or knowingly—and they make good use of their lives and their possessions. But then they can't be patient when the door [to the inner rooms of the castle] is closed to them, and they can't move to the King's presence. They consider themselves to be God's dedicated servants, and, in fact, they are. But even an earthly king might have many devoted servants, and not all of them get to enter into his personal room. Enter within yourselves, daughters, as far as you are able. Stop circling around your petty good works. These—and more!—are your basic duties as a Christian. It's enough to serve God; don't try to get so much that you achieve nothing.[94]

Be content. Go on, enter! Wait, don't be greedy, she says.

Such dynamism might be frustrating if we are looking for a simple how-to manual, but I find it reassuring because this mix has evident depth and wisdom, born of Teresa's long journey with God. I trust both her encouragement to a bold pursuit of God and her discouragement of a posture of entitlement that is prone to bitterness. Why wouldn't both be essential? It has the natural balance of evident wisdom. Besides, as the fullness of the manuscript reveals, there is so much that is outside our control, so much that is up to God, not us, both within and outside of prayer. Teresa is really urging us toward a disposition that is well-suited to a long life of faith on this unpredictable earth, with many trials, both within and without. You must *want* to receive God's grace as directly as possible, always. But that grace may come to you in many different ways, and often not in the ways or places you'd like, or expect. Thus, a question comes to us alongside the graces, again and again: "Will you accept the food that God gives in rooms that you never wanted to visit?"

Unexpected Trials

Although Teresa writes directly about trials that test our trust and detachment, she also says quite plainly in her writings on the third dwellings that she is not going to discuss what we might consider the most significant difficulties: "I'm not talking at all here about interior trials, which disturb many good souls to an intolerable level, and through no fault of their own, nor am I referring to those who suffer from depression and other illnesses."[95] It seems to be simply outside the purview of the *Moradas* text, these "intolerable" trials that are "no fault of their own." Eventually, we will return to the "symptom" that Teresa does want to talk about (dryness in prayer), but first I must depart from Teresa's structure for a bit. Because I simply cannot tell or make sense of the story of God's presence in my life without talking about the trial that nearly led to my abandonment of the quest for a "good life in the ways of a good (?) God," among other worthy commitments.

In late December of my junior year, my mom called my siblings and me into the living room of her apartment to tell us that she had breast cancer. In late November of my senior year, my mother called me at my dorm room and asked me to find my best friend or my boyfriend so they could sit with me while she told me something: the cancer was back, and it was terminal. She then said she had "maybe six months" to live, but I learned later that the doctor had said two. It would turn out to be one. In between these milestone calls, I watched my mother, sometimes from afar and sometimes up close, as she went through surgeries, chemotherapy, radiation—all the grueling clichés of cancer's horrors, writ large and nuanced when we witness their affliction on a beloved body.

And yet that was not all for her: she financially collapsed, too. After her surgeries but before the chemotherapy, she had to give up her apartment and go live with a friend in a nearby city. Just shy of her sixteenth birthday, my sister went to live with our dad across the state. When I received the news that my mother had to move, that she was broke, I was studying abroad in Oxford, sitting on a lilac-colored duvet and looking out on High Street. She had insisted I go—I would be home for the summer, after all—and yet I'd never allowed myself to imagine the story could get worse than *single mom faces cancer*, at least not within a few months. Yet things were darkening in the spring, and quickly.

Over the summer, living with my mom and her friend, I watched the chemo transform my brave and vivacious pioneer woman of a mother into an emotionally paralyzed, anxious wreck. She was afraid to be alone, so I would watch the clock at my summer job, skip lunch, and slip out at four on the dot so I could return to her for the evening hours. At the end of the summer, we thought the worst was behind us: she was given a cancer-free scan in August, and radiation would be a breeze after all this, wouldn't it? We threw a pink-themed "I Beat Breast Cancer" party at Crescent Lake, where our extended family gathers each year, to celebrate and mark the milestone. My mom was still bald, but we thought a different future was just around the corner. Instead, after braving radiation by herself through September and October, she began to notice back pain in mid-November. It would turn out to be the terminal metastasis to her liver, which became clear on November 22. She died on December 21, the winter solstice.

The night my mother died, my brother and I lay next to her warm body in her hospital bed after she took her final breaths and tried to absorb the last vestiges of comfort and memory we might draw from the woman who had given us life so joyfully and so selflessly. Then, weeping silently, we stood outside the hospital on the cold concrete in our socks and watched the black van take her body into the night.

What this rushed account of my mother's final year leaves out is the real story of her death, at least as experienced by my siblings and me. The death of a beloved mother at age fifty—when her three children are twenty-four, twenty-one, and sixteen—is very sad under any circumstances, and likely to cause deep questions about the goodness or reality of God; but my mother's death felt particularly hope-less, a death at the bottom of a dark V curve that seemed to cut off all possibilities of redemption and eclipse any claims of love's victory. Here's the story of the last decade of her life that I saw on the coldest days of that winter:

At age forty, she is rejected and dumped by her husband in one of the most humiliating and searing ways. Despite his affair, she's willing to make it work. Just choose her or us, she says. We'll get counseling. He chooses the other woman. So, she moves back to her hometown with her three children and tries to make a life for herself, and us, giving us everything that she thought we should have, prodigally loving and spending. My mother struggles with anxiety and depression, the teenage rebellion of one of her children, and the painful, stereotypical contrast between her increasingly spent life and the life of her ex-husband, who is now remarried and thriving in a big house on a hill.

Nine years in, broke and still brittle-hearted despite all she has managed to tenaciously forge for herself and her children through the pain, she gets cancer. In the midst of her treatment, my dad files to reduce his child support payments. More possessions and vestiges of the old life are shed; her younger daughter moves out, and she moves into a spare bedroom in the suburbs. When her cancer treatment is finished, she is all alone, facing the prospect of spending her days teaching two hundred middle school students once she is well enough. A little over a month later, the cancer returns, and she dies, after offering parting words of love and wisdom to her sixteen-year-old daughter and welcoming her twenty-four-year-old son home from Spain just in time to witness her final days. On her deathbed, as my mother lies unresponsive, her closest friends tell me that she was just so tired, she really didn't have the will to live anymore. I can hardly bear the words, but they are not inconceivable. They have the sting of truth. They close a decade of rejection, selfless suffering, and loneliness with a fittingly tragic end. The imaginary gentle man that I'd nicknamed Larry—the man who would love horses as much as my mother did and appreciate my mother for all her worth, with whom she'd ride into the second act of her life—never came. A new hope never dawned for her on this side of the veil.

So it wasn't "just" that my mother's life was cut short. It was *where* it was cut short that seemed to undercut any claims of redemptive victory. I thought the Christian story was all about joy coming in the morning after a night of weeping. I had kept faith through the weeping, trusting that joy would come. I was resolute in this—probably annoyingly so—until the plug seemed to be pulled on the light that might bring a new day.

For many people, Christians and the vaguely spiritual alike, there is an "easy" answer to this sort of short-circuiting: the afterlife; the continued existence of the soul. But this had never been a primary focus of my faith, and what I might previously have said theoretically about it quickly condensed to vapor in the vacuum of grief. People all around me would look at me with hungry and eager eyes, wanting the comfort of my comfort: "You feel her still with you, don't you?" "You know she's still watching you, don't you?" The truthful answer was, "No, I don't. I wish I did. But I don't." The truth was closer to the first half of the lovely Ysaye Barnwell song I cried through at the Stanford baccalaureate: "I am sitting here wanting memories to teach me / To see the beauty of the world through my own eyes."[96] I didn't know if humans had souls, if there was life for anyone beyond the grave. At that moment, it seemed not only possible but probable that we simply return to dust, leaving love and memories in our wake as we disintegrate.

Strangely enough, I never moved to a place where I thought there was no God; I could never ignore that question every atheist must: of why there is something instead of nothing. But I did shift to a place where God was much more the rational, removed force of the Enlightenment. One night, I got on my knees, with my pajamas draped on a frame too thin from grief, and cast my searching glance heavenward. "Are you even there? Do you even exist?" *I am* was all I got, a dark and interstellar feeling more than the warmth and power of the burning bush. *I do.* "What about my mom?" Silence, nothingness. I had a God but no assurance of love.

It was eighteen months before I saw a sign that indicated to me that my mom continued to exist in God's love in some way. That doesn't sound like a long time now, but in a loss so searing, the doubt felt cavernous. I can still connect to its memory when I sit with people in their spaces of utter disbelief.

It's possible that during my mother's illness, however, I was more firmly established within Teresa's third dwellings than I knew. I sang the hymn "Be Thou My Vision" to her in the hospice bed and offered the prayers for the departed over her body from the blue prayer book she'd received at her confirmation. My paradigm for life was a frame of faith and service, and, apart from these private moments, I was even building a public identity around that. I won the Stanford Spirituality and Service Fellowship in my junior year but gave it up to go home to be with my mother through her chemotherapy treatment—a different kind of fellowship, less prestigious but still approached with the same lens. I served. I sought to be a vessel of God's love, even in the toughest places. "I am a modern-day martyr, a modern day MLK or Dorothy Day in training," I believed.

I never would have expressed this idea so clearly then, of course, and I'm not trying to be cynical or mocking about my sincere intentions. I did want to love. I did want to serve. I was willing to sacrifice. But my faith in a good God fractured quite quickly when my mother's story took a seemingly dark and irredeemable turn. I cannot help but see elements of the frustration Teresa describes with those in the third dwellings who *say* they want to suffer for God but then quickly grow outraged, indignant, or despairing when suffering comes. To be fair, I do think Teresa is talking about smaller sufferings than the death of a loved one (the examples she gives are much less painful). But I still feel convicted by Williams' keen observation about this aspect of the third dwellings:

> Basic to much of what she says here is the gulf between the suffering we can choose and control ("penance") and that which takes us by surprise. We may believe we have great qualities of endurance because of what we *choose* to give up or put up with: we never really put ourselves at risk, however. Calculating reason is still very much in control.... But God calls us to cope with what has not been planned, what we are not confident of having strength or resource to meet, and it is our response to this that shows whether or not we have been deluding ourselves.[97]

If, indeed, our response to "what has not been planned…shows whether or not we have been deluding ourselves," it's fair to say that I had been deluding myself and others—not entirely, but quite a bit. How deep was my desire to reflect God's goodness, really? I look on my younger self with compassion, but still I see the thoughts and impulses no one else would have known at that time. In the shock of grief, I felt untethered from all moral structures and patterns, and I thought about breaking up with my boyfriend (now husband) for no reason apart from seeing if my childhood crush would finally affirm my worth and beauty after all. I toyed with this idea, this impulse to abandon a loving and supportive and wise partner, for nearly eleven months. One could honestly make the assessment that the only reason it didn't happen was a lack of external encouragement; but, in retrospect, I see other agents of grace, moments and people that guarded me from abandoning not just Colin but the gritty pursuit of a lived faith that we shared. The habits of going to church and of being in relationship with other people who wanted to live good lives in pursuit of a good God remained like trails and fence posts in this strange landscape, guiding me even as I wandered within.

One summer night, when I was restlessly intent on taking the latest excuse as a chance to end my relationship, I called a friend from college who was the only married person my age I knew. After I told her what was happening, what I was thinking, she spoke through the phone in a way that had the same effect that reading C. S. Lewis had had on me years before: time stilled and expanded as I recognized the presence of an invitation to truth and freedom. *It's normal, what you're going through. But don't end a good thing because you're confused.* I joked then that she was like an angel. Later, I learned the definition of angel—"messenger" (of God)—and saw the whole thing with a little less levity. As I considered fleeing the castle, eyeing the way out, Christ kept calling me in different ways. I nearly left the building for the outer grounds to sow my (not-so-wild) oats and have a "typical" experience of twenty-something life, post college. But different things slowed my exit, including a brief witness of the pain I'd cause with my feckless rebellion. In time, I decided I didn't want to leave after all. Teresa says this: "I'm not referring to the great interior trials I mentioned earlier, because of course this kind of 'dryness' is about much more than a lack of devotion. Let us prove ourselves, sisters, or allow the Lord to prove us. He knows how to test [our depths of faith], although we often refuse to understand Him."

To prove has many meanings, but among the concepts that seem to apply here are to set in place, to firm and strengthen, and to make a lasting mark. I did not prove myself in the wake of my mother's death, but, thank God, the Lord proved me. I was set, held, stilled until I was capable of recalling what I really wanted. It turns out, in the end, my deepest desire wasn't the cheap thrill of being unpredictable. I did want to stay close to the people of Jesus, watching and learning and questioning, even if I did not yet trust the One at the center of it all.

Learning to Fly While Thirsty

I didn't know it then, but my grief-induced doubt and unease, which produced genuine humility about my faith (because it was clear I was no trust-filled saint) were actually vessels of grace. Because the great danger of the third dwellings is to get stuck there forever, intent on our well-ordered and valiant efforts; the "obscure unease" of the rich young ruler who *knows he lacks something* is important. Rowan Williams goes so far as to say, "This obscure unease is what matters most in the deceptively smooth waters of this stage (III, 1.6–7)." Dryness and frustration in our prayers can "keep alive a proper uneasiness here," as can "harder things" like depression, illness, misunderstanding, and—in my case—grief.[98] Although I had not been raised in a way that made me worried about God's seeming distance or the dryness I felt in prayer, in retrospect, the grief created a greater *longing* for personal assurance of God's goodness and closeness (and, potentially as an added bonus, confirmation of comforting ideas like the afterlife). And it was this longing that kept me close to the church, to other people striving to live lives of integrity and faith. And it was these many wise people, in turn, who taught me the truth that Teresa restates around every hinge point of spiritual hunger:

> Perfection
> as well as its reward
> does not consist in spiritual delights
> but in greater love
> and in deeds done
> with greater justice and truth.[99]

For five years after my mother's death, I slowly learned from others how to lean in to the inherent rewards of simply seeking to grow in love and engage in actions that contribute in some way to justice and truth. Not as a solo endeavor, either, but in relationship, where virtues are almost always born, raised, and realized.

I was following Teresa's advice, not directly but instinctively. She advises those who are in this third state to find a wise teacher, a mentor, who can teach them to fly:

> What I think is most helpful to those who are in this state, by God's goodness, is that they seriously seek to practice obedience. (It's no small mercy to be here, on the brink of rising higher.) Even if they are not in a religious order, it would be extremely beneficial for them to have someone they can go to for advice and direction. This can prevent them from following their own will [rather than God's].... They shouldn't look for someone with the same overly cautious approach to the spiritual journey—they should pick a person completely lacking in illusions about the things of the world. In learning to know ourselves, it's very helpful to have a conversation partner who sees the world [and human nature] for what it is.
>
> It's also very encouraging to see that things that we thought were impossible *are* possible for others, and even come easily. It makes us feel that we might eventually fly ourselves, like they do. Like young birds, we may not be ready for great flights, but we can gradually learn by imitating our "parents." This is a huge benefit, I know.[100]

I was fortunate to have many people I could consult, wise men and women whom I could tell were more free than I was from the illusions of the world. There were the three gracious and strong women who stepped in from the sidelines to mother me as I navigated my emergence into adulthood without my mom: my aunt, my former neighbor, and my mother-in-law. There was the down-to-earth, strikingly smart, and caring couple who befriended Colin and me in the small-town Methodist church of my childhood. There was an abundance of riches, mentor-wise, when we left

Oregon for a yearlong internship at a Christian peace and justice organization called Sojourners in Washington, DC.

I share just one story of learning from that time because it echoes what Teresa says about the value of learning from others, with others, as we seek to grow—not only in our times of acute joy and sorrow but perhaps especially then. After the first stormy months of grief, I fell prey to what Karl Rahner calls "the rubbled-over heart."[101] As Kathleen Norris writes, evoking this term by Rahner, "When one's life is dusty with ruin, it can seem reasonable to bury oneself in the wreckage rather than expose oneself to more suffering."[102] The normal numbness of my grief transitioned to perpetually subdued expectations. I was not depressed, but I couldn't decide what to do with myself (fairly normal in one's early twenties), and I could no longer identify any passion (not normal). Dante's hell haunted me; I remembered that it held those whose passions were lukewarm. While living in Washington and approaching the second anniversary of my mom's death, I felt vaguely muted, but I couldn't articulate the root problem. This passage in Ivan Goncharov's *Oblomov*, highlighted by Norris, well-defines my state then:

> He was painfully aware that something good and fine lay buried in him as in a grave, that it was perhaps already dead or lay hidden like gold in the heart of a mountain, and that it was high time that gold was put into circulation. But the treasure was deeply buried under a heap of rubbish and silt…something prevented him from launching out into the ocean of life.[103]

My mysterious sense of spiritual lethargy was exposed to the harsh light of day by Vincent Harding, the civil-rights leader who wrote Martin Luther King Jr.'s Riverside Church speech. Sitting with the Sojourners staff in a big circle in the organization's conference room, the seventy-five-year-old Harding answered people's questions over the lunch break. It was exactly two years since the day I'd left college to be with my mom as she died, but I didn't notice the date then. I sat and listened to the first few questions, awed by his apparent wisdom—he emanated *sage*—and satisfied when a fellow intern asked the question that I would have said was closest to my own: "I think some of us are wrestling with questions of what to do with ourselves after this year. I wonder if you would talk to your vocation, and sort of how that unfolded for you." Yes, I thought. This is my problem. I don't know what to do with myself, how to find my passion. I listened closely to Harding's answer.

> If you allow yourself to really hunger and thirst for what is right and just in this world, you will be filled. And I have felt more and more and more that that is meant to be taken very seriously. That kind of powerful invitation is really meant to be an antidote to our anxieties about whether we can do it or not, an invitation for us not to resist that sense of hunger and thirst, which can drive us crazy but which may also drive us sane. But the context is not simply, "Can I really do this in this crazy world?" but "Am I willing to allow that hunger and thirst to take me over, and to move me?"[104]

As he spoke, a heated wave of protest rose in me—that rare, hotheaded sense of turmoil that tells me I either must give voice to whatever is rising up or leave the room. I raised my hand. "My name is Laurel Mathewson. I'm from Oregon. I guess I want to press you further on that sense of 'allowing yourself to hunger and thirst' for an authentic life." And then, unexpectedly, my voice caught and tears fell. I told him my mom had died under tragic circumstances, her life at a low point. Underneath the tears was my hopelessness, rising in protest to meet his advice. *No*, it said, *if you hunger and thirst for what is right and just, you will not be filled. God and life and people will come up short. You can't let that hunger and thirst move you; that's just setting yourself up for more bitter ends.* I hated to admit it, but, at that moment, I saw my buried hope for what it was. I had stopped believing change was possible, even in the long game.

"I used to have a lot of optimism," I said, "and I want it again. But I struggle to feel it. And so I was wondering," I said, slowly and meekly, "if you have any suggestions of ways of opening yourself up to that sort of hope?"

Gently, he asked for my mother's name. "Elizabeth," I squeaked, and "Elizabeth," he echoed back, beautiful and smooth and sure. He held her name in silence for some time, and then he gave a response that drew up and watered my newly uncovered hope, still shriveled and squinting. "Laurel," he said, "I am very proud of you, and very grateful to you to open up such a personal kind of question in our midst."

I didn't have a choice, I thought. Harding continued:

I think that one of the ways I would just begin to respond to the cry that you are expressing is [to say] that I have lived my life... among just such a magnificent set of witnesses to love and compassion that I know that in spite of what I run into in certain dry periods, I know that the universe is full of that kind of love and compassion; everywhere I go there are people who manifest that. And so I know that that is not in short supply.

And part of what's involved is simply being willing to let my hunger and thirst be known...and out of that comes a response, almost automatically, in ways that would have to be called miraculous sometimes. But crazy folks who are involved with things like quantum physics tell us that that's the way the universe works. When we let certain energies flow out of us, they attract certain energies that are almost waiting for that call and response. And all I'm trying to say, Laurel, is that the encouragement towards hope that you are crying out for is already present, and is going to be surprising you around one corner or another, or even around this circle. And the great challenge is not to be afraid to expect it.

In response to a follow-up question, he explained:

As I understand it, one of our major purposes for being human is to engage the grief and the joy of other humans. And, indeed, it seems to me that we can't even be fully human without exercising that gift that human beings share with one another. I have this dear father of my faith, named Howard Thurman, who used to say, "The things that appear in the Bible are not true because they're in the Bible; they're in the Bible because they're true." And what I find all through the accounts of the biblical experience is testimony to this whole idea that we exist to help mediate the loving presence of God—to each other, through each other, with each other, in each other—and that, in a deep sense, we're not meant to grieve alone, nor are we meant to rejoice alone, that the connecting web is one that, in a sense, it's like a cord that needs to be plucked for us to really know both the depth of the grieving and the possibilities of the healing.

We were created to be with and for each other. When we miss that, we miss the point of our creation—and that's why we feel so miserable sometimes.

I relied on the spirit of this outpouring until the green shoots of my hope stood firm, if not tall. I looked around at my own cloud of witnesses—the people in that room, that circle at Sojourners; my husband; his family; my family; my friends; the three wise women who'd mothered me—and I began to watch for "the encouragement *toward* hope" in their presence and in those relationships. He was right. It was already there. I was surrounded by people, both there and in the coming three years in San Diego, who would not just lead me into the possibility of hope and joy again, but also lead me in learning more about what it meant to live as a Christian in the real (post-college) world, what it meant to pray in community, what it meant to be part of a church for reasons beyond my own edification or solace. These friends and mentors listened to my angst-filled questions and gave honest and care-filled answers; taught me anew about the heart of the resurrection story and mysteries of redemption, both born in senseless suffering; and gave me the language I needed to express the meager faith I did have ("death is not the end of the story"). They laughed and cried with me, and, little by little, I recognized myself, and God, in these hopeful words of the psalmist:

> You who have made me see many troubles and calamities
>   will revive me again;
> from the depths of the earth
>   you will bring me up again.[105]

In my manner of life and even in my critical thinking, I tried to imitate the "parents" of this steadfast faith—both those present in the flesh and those encountered on paper: people who knew *something* about flying with God because of the way they walked the earth with a purposeful intent toward truth-filled justice and yet a humble insistence on perpetual grace and service.

One of the implicit "tasks" of the third dwellings is continued detachment from desires and impulses that detract from our ability to love God and others well, including our attachment to being "rewarded for good behavior." It's for this reason that our responses to suffering or loss of status or unfulfilled expectations are so revealing: What do we really think we're doing in this life of faith? After giving many examples of indignation or flailing from those whose steadfastness is tested, Teresa offers this advice, even to nuns who think they have been stripped of every worldly preoccupation: "From such situations you find out if you are really detached from the worldly things you've left behind. Small challenges and troubles do come up that give you the opportunity to test yourself and discover if you have mastery over your passions." Immediately afterward, she offers advice that seems applicable to *all* third dwelling place residents, whether they are cloistered or not:

> What matters most is…whether we strive to practice the virtues of our faith, surrender our will to God in all things, and bring our lives into alignment with what God wants for them. We need to desire in all things that not our will, but His, be done…. Humility is healing ointment for our wounds. If we are truly humble, then (even if there is a delay) God, the physician, will eventually come to heal us.[106]

Perhaps because it is bread-and-butter Christian teaching, not just the wisdom of Teresa, this is thankfully the essential message I received and lived by in those five years after my mother's death as I continued to try to inhabit the stable, generous third dwellings life of faith: *strive to practice the virtues.* This is solid advice for every age, but we also know how quickly this kind of striving can sour our hearts and diminish others when carried out in self-righteousness rather than in humility. Rowan Williams nails what contemporary expressions of this look like:

> To be "good" without humility is to be condemned to a really wretched life, "weighed down with this mud of our human misery".… We are committed to the strenuous job of constant

repression, projecting our own fears and uncertainties on to others and showing aggressive zeal for their improvement. Teresa would have had no difficulty in understanding the shrill censoriousness of modern Christian zealots for the moral reclamation of society; she might have had equally sharp words for the self-consciously consistent radical Christian, obsessed with the creation of an uncompromised lifestyle. As she herself patiently repeats, it is good to know where you stand and to have a measure of control over your life; not to feel at the mercy of intolerable inner tensions all the time. But we need to see the sensation of stability as a *gift* that is given to help us forward, not a possession or acquisition.[107]

I laughed aloud when I first read this passage because I easily saw (and still sometimes see) the arrow landing on my brand of striving as "the self-consciously consistent radical Christian." It's probably enough to say that my husband and I moved into a Christian commune (as a school of discipleship in simple living and just peacemaking, of course) seven weeks after we got married, where we (sometimes) argued over whether it was more righteous to buy organic milk or give that extra money to the hungry, or whether we were the "kind of people" who bought juice. Thankfully, there were many shrewd and mellowed mentors around us who could point out the dangers of a life obsessed with "keeping down with the Joneses," competing for righteousness points through conspicuous sacrifice or simplicity or social justice showboating. ("How many times have you been arrested in anti-war and anti-poverty protests?")

And so, though there are things from the early part of our marriage that I look back on with a wry smile, mostly I see a sincere day-to-day striving, guided by people wiser than we were. We gathered with other Christians regularly—on Sunday mornings in classes and worship at an Episcopal cathedral where we were confirmed in the Anglican tradition, and on Sunday evenings with a small house church, Hawthorn House, in our neighborhood. We also shared meals twice during the week with a few other couples and singles in our neighborhood, rotating the hosting. With the house church community, we wrestled with living our faith with some evident Christlike distinction from "typical American life," even as we cared for one another in mostly quotidian ways, like cooking, doing dishes, and sharing the ups and downs of real life. From classes at the church, we learned how to pray at home in a sustainable way, saying short, set devotions from the prayer book. We led cross-border trips to an orphanage in Tijuana on the weekends and helped to raise money for the same organization in small ways.

When I became a campus minister, I took the students to El Salvador for the fortieth anniversary of Oscar Romero's martyrdom, approaching the whole trip as a pilgrimage of faith. Upon the advice of an Episcopal priest, I also began seeing a spiritual director, someone skilled in accompanying Christians on their journeys with God—like a wise friend who is particularly and persistently attentive to your soul and how you seek and respond to God's presence in your life. There were moments of joy and warmth and insight, and assurances of holy grace, woven through these years, mostly in the voices and faces in our circles of community.

In all of this activity, in all of this *striving to practice the virtues*, I was, in essence, learning to fly, but it was also a time characterized by what Teresa notes is a common challenge of these dwellings: spiritual dryness. Here I had one "advantage" over Teresa's Carmelite sisters. As I have mentioned, unlike them, I didn't expect God to be richly present to me in prayer, especially after my mother's death. The faith that had taken shape for me over many years, before and after that personal sadness, was marked by obedience to moral principles and a trust that, in the long run, God's justice would prevail. It was the faith of "The arc of the moral universe is long, but it bends toward justice."[108] It was the faith of "If you've come to help me, you're wasting your time, but if you think your liberation is tied up in mine, let us work together."[109] It was faith in God's slow but steady behind-the-scenes redemption of the tangled messes we weave. It was a faith that invited our striving to "be good and do good," to steadfastly do justice, love kindness, and walk humbly.[110] It was not a faith that expected or required personal encounter with, or attention from, God. Teresa advises her sisters, who are prone to feeling a bit entitled to some spiritual gifts in prayer, in this way:

> We [must] see ourselves as servants to whom nothing is owed... and realize that our Lord is in no way *obligated* to give us such gifts. On the contrary, the more we've been given by God, the more

deeply we are indebted to Him. What can we do for such a generous God—who died for us, created us, gives us being—without considering ourselves simply fortunate to be able to repay *something* of what we owe Him for the way He has served us?... All the time He lived in the world, He did nothing but serve. So, can we serve without asking for *more* gifts and favors?[111]

Teresa's voice was not yet in my ear; nevertheless, this was my point of view, but with an added layer of undeservedness. The Lord owed me *less* than nothing. I was, in fact, in debt in ways that extended beyond the classic gospel of sin. You see, I was rich in all the categories of the world: white, American, upper middle class, my belly full after every meal. The eyes of the Lord and the love of the Lord were upon the poor, for good reason. The preferential option for the poor appeared to me not only biblical but also ethically preferable to any other theology. I had received my rewards. For those to whom much has been given, much is expected. As Teresa says, "What can we do for such a generous God...without considering ourselves simply fortunate to be able to repay *something* of what we owe...?"

Teresa follows this idea by affirming, "You can be assured that when true humility is present, even if God never gives gifts in prayer, He *will* give peace, and resignation to His will. With this peace, a soul may be more content than others are with such gifts."[112] In many respects, God did give me "peace, and resignation to His will," without dramatic gifts, which allowed me to walk for quite some time in relative contentment, or at least steadiness. I thought I could do the will of God—again, love justice, love kindness, walk humbly—without an assurance that this God of justice loved me. That was irrelevant in my intellectual and moral framework, like a greedy child demanding lollipops when you've asked her to set the table for dinner guests. I could do what was right; I could set the table; I could even teach other people to set the table.

Other people in my life, though, noticed a hunger and thirst I was not willing to admit, maybe for fear it would never be satisfied. My spiritual director listened to my monthly delivery of questions and observations and reports on obedience, and she tried to talk to me about God's love. I took down the notes, wrote the quotes with diligence. Another priest, noting my detachment, asked me what I felt about Jesus. *Felt?* "What do you mean?"

I asked. Finally, as I was entering a crucial stage in my discernment about entering ordained ministry, my spiritual director, a steady Midwestern RSCJ (Society of the Sacred Heart) nun with blonde hair, looked over her thin-rimmed glasses and said, "I think you need a silent retreat." Maybe she saw, in all my striving, that though there were touches of something deeper, I was still on the "near side of the great chasm that crosses the Christian path, the disjunction between effort and grace."[113] Maybe she saw that I would not be able to walk much longer, or for many years of seminary and ordained ministry, while thirsty—yet I was convinced that I could not expect water from God. "Buck up, buttercup," my ego said. "You've been given everything you need to do the job you should do."

But, below the surface, another part of me cried out for more, aware of the weakness of my faith, the real potential for it to become brittle, crack, and blow away. Teresa reminds her sisters that "often...it's to the *weakest* that His Divine Majesty gives extra gifts in prayer,"[114] and I think that's probably true. I know they're in the world, in spades, these stronger steadfast servants who need so little extraordinary assurance to trust in the goodness and presence of God. I admire them so. In the end, however, I wasn't cut out to be among them. I have to be honest, though, as Teresa is in her follow-up acknowledgement: "I don't think we would ever trade these gifts for all the natural strength given to those who continue to make progress without them, journeying through spiritual dryness."[115] We are greedy children that way, but it would turn out to be true what the preachers always said: God loves us nevertheless.

FOURTH DWELLINGS:

AWE

"I must once again commend myself to the Holy Spirit. I beg the Holy Spirit from now on to speak for me so you might understand what I'm going to say about the dwelling places not yet addressed. Because supernatural experiences begin here, and this is extremely difficult to explain....[116]"

For me, one of the most wonderful and frustrating things about reading *The Interior Castle* was discovering terms that might have helped me make sense of different kinds of prayer experiences I'd had over the years. Even in the Protestant tradition, Saint Teresa is acknowledged as a wise teacher of the faith. Why had no one ever shared with me some of her wisdom, her framework for our spiritual journey (even as one among many)? Teresa has many things to say about prayer that *had*, in some form or other, made their way into the teaching I received in seminary, though they were not directly attributed to her. This is because much of what she has to say about the basics of prayer is not unique. For example, I was instructed on prayer essentials, such as practical tips on praying with and through distracting thoughts. Teresa addresses these essentials in the first three dwelling places. Yet it seems obvious that, in writing *The Interior Castle*, she is eager to move beyond these dwellings—not because they are unimportant or insignificant, but because she recognizes that much has already been written about them, and there are many other resources available that address "how to pray" from the perspective of what *we* can do to try to draw near to God.

Teresa has something else to add to the tradition: under the obedience of her spiritual director, she wants to explore more fully a kind of prayer that is related to, and in continuity with, these "typical" prayers and yet also distinct from them. She wants to talk about how we faithfully and carefully proceed in prayer in which God gives us a *different* sort of grace, where we find ourselves infused by God's presence, when it is clear that he is acting in us. Her favorite metaphor for the difference between these two kinds of prayer is one involving water: in the first sort of prayer, we are busy carrying buckets and tending irrigation systems, working hard to bring water to the garden of our souls, our hearts, with God's help. And this is not a waste of time: we can, and do, experience God's grace and receive the gift of God's holy water in this "acquired" way. But in what Teresa calls "the prayer of quiet," God makes the one praying aware of a spring welling up, bubbling, providing water from within, without a sense of striving.[117] The water is instilled, not acquired. Teresan scholars Kieran Kavanaugh and Otilio Rodriguez refer to this dynamic as "passive prayer" or "infused prayer." Both forms of "watering," or prayer, are a partnership, and both begin and end with God, but our human experience of them is different (only God knows why, Teresa says).

To this end, Teresa distinguishes between these different experiences of God's grace, life, peace, and presence with the help of two words. She uses the Spanish word *contentos* to denote experiences of joy, peace, satisfaction, and comfort that are not infused but are acquired. The most commonly used translations of Teresa's work render this word *contentos* as "consolations." To denote infused experiences, on the other hand, Teresa uses the Spanish word *gustos*. This is often rendered as "spiritual delights." This translation may sometimes make these experiences sound a bit precious, a bit frivolous, like an ice cream sundae. However, while *gustos* does mean pleasures, delights, gifts, or favors, I don't believe there is anything frivolous about them.

I say this now, as if I know what I'm talking about, but I can only speak from the ways my own experiences align with what Teresa describes. I didn't know these words, these terms, this framework when God first gave me *gustos* and for the seven years that followed—until I read *The Interior Castle*. And so, while I would have said these experiences were wondrous and wonderful, I would not have used the term *delightful*. As I entered what Teresa calls the fourth dwellings, where the natural and supernatural are intermingled, where acquired prayer intermingles with infused prayer, I felt something that paradoxically held more freedom *and* more weight: I was a beloved child, living in awe.

The Problem of Implausible Love

> These dwelling places are getting close to the place where the King dwells. As a result, they are tremendously beautiful and contain such exquisite treasures that the intellect simply cannot describe them accurately.[118]

Even as I filled out applications for seminaries and divinity schools, understanding in my mind how the work of ordained ministry aligned with my gifts and values, I continued to wrestle with the vexing question of God's love and personal care for humanity. I could pray with integrity, trusting that in some mysterious way this was good and right and helpful, even if it was simply a matter of reorientation toward humility and justice. I could talk about following the way of Jesus with integrity—the way of forgiveness, reconciliation, truth telling, healing, humble service, compassion—trusting it as a holy path of justice and healing. It seemed to me a path that was simple but not easy, full of hope for the world's transformation if we paid heed. But I recognized, even if obscurely, something I felt I could not do with integrity: proclaim God's love for the world, or for any particular person. This notion seemed to keep coming up in church, seemed to be a big part of the minister's work each Sunday. I could fight its importance to the tradition, and I did, but I could not deny the reality of its centrality.

One night, I lingered after a Theology on Tap gathering, where a theology professor from the University of San Diego was talking about how we draw theology from Scripture, to press this point about God's love. "It seems like a big stretch of interpretation," I said, "to conclude from these complicated texts that God loves the world, that God is love, or that Jesus loves us. From a literary perspective, it doesn't seem clear that this is the main theme." She responded in an open, evenhanded, intelligent way, suggesting that I consider the two thousand years of interpretation from various men and women who had come to this conclusion, and offering that the witness of these texts is held in balance and augmented by experiences that testify to a God of love. I pushed back again, explaining that I was hesitant to trust these more personal, experiential accounts of God's love and questioning if they were simply projections of the same generous and wishful reading of the Bible that led people to think that God's primary trait is gracious love. She paused. Then, she looked me in the eye and said, quite deliberately, "I think if you reject the conclusion of the broad and ancient tradition, and aren't willing to trust more personal expressions of the same idea, you might want to ask yourself if this is something you don't *want* to believe."

But who doesn't want to believe that God loves them? That God *is* love? Well, someone who doesn't trust the claim to be credible, believable, but who still wants to hold on to the truth of a good and just God (if not a loving one). My spiritual director at the time had sat with me every few weeks for nearly a year, watching me take notes on what she said, observing me as I scribbled my life around this question, not even realizing it was the question at the center. After hearing about the Theology on Tap gathering, my spiritual director told me, "I really think you need a silent retreat." *"How long?"* I asked. "Oh," she said, "it takes at least three nights." And so, ever obedient, I made plans to stay at a small Roman Catholic retreat center on the other side of San Diego, a house near Sunset Cliffs. That New Year's Eve, a week and a half before the retreat, I was writing in my journal, reflecting on what I wanted to do in the next decade. Some of it was specific, but I ended with this generality: "I want to live out the love and service that I know we are each called to… (or at least I cling to the hope that we are called and created to love and to love again)." I hoped that love was at the center, that we were created for and with some purpose, but I was aware of the effort it took to hold that concept in my mind.

When I arrived at the retreat center the first morning, I met with the white-haired RCSJ sister, previously unknown to me, who would be my spiritual director throughout my retreat. I would meet with her once each day to check in; otherwise, my time would be spent in silence and solitude. She provided some basic suggestions for my times of prayer, affirming that "seeking understanding" is my form of faith but also noticing that I yearned for something more. "This is what you will be trying to do: come to know the heart of God through the word of God," she said. *"Listen!* As you pray these verses, just be noticing, not analyzing." She spoke in direct terms about the kind of prayer that is honest and personal. "What is the grace that you seek? Be very clear about this. What are you looking for? What grace are you asking of God?"

She suggested that I follow a basic form: First, meditate on the verses "Be still, and know that I am God!" from Psalm 46:10[119] and "Behold, I will do something new" from Isaiah 43:19.[120] Second, ask God for the grace I know is my heart's honest desire. Then, continue by praying various suggested Scripture excerpts throughout the day—listening, paying attention. At the end of the day, reflect on how the grace has been given.

"In the midst of it all," she said, "trust that God is at work!" It seemed she saw right through my big talk about God as she spoke about trust in a personal way—as if there might be some point to "paying attention" beyond obedience and discipline, and that's the kind of trust I didn't have. I realized this in my first period of prayer and reflection, right after I met with her, as I considered her question about what I was looking for, what I sought. I recognized that my honest fear was not that God didn't exist but that it was impossible to *know* God, that he was absolutely inaccessible. That God was at work, but not in any way that we could ever know. The grace that I sought was to know that the God of the universe was *somehow* accessible, that I might somehow hear or know of God's work in my life and the lives of others, even in small part.

I had lots of time and no one to talk to, and so I journaled after each prayer session. What happened over the course of the next four days transformed my understanding of God. The experiences were sufficiently indelible that I had not looked back at the pages that contained my time-stamped descriptions of them until I began this book project. There was no need. (It took me a full day's search to even find the journal that contained them.) Now, however, I want to look at the details of these experiences, the sequence of prayers, the weird shifts in perception and understanding, with the hope that such nuance is instructive and might provide insights as I attempt to convey what even Teresa admits is the "messiness" of the fourth dwelling places, where acquisitive seeking and passive receiving comingle. Here, then, are some of the details of the experiences of this time as they progressively occurred, along with my current reflections on them:

Monday, January 11, 2010

On the first day of the retreat, I spent my initial prayer session trying to get to the heart of the grace I sought, and sleepiness led me to take a break for lunch and a walk by the beach. I returned to my retreat room in the early afternoon and tried to follow instructions in both the small and the big sense, attempting to trust that God was working within me in some way that I might notice or comprehend.

I sat down with a selection from Isaiah 55 and asked to know that the God of the universe was somehow accessible, and, more specifically "that I might HEAR."[121] Looking back, I find this detail fascinating because it points to a limitation that I didn't even know I had: "hearing" was the only way I thought we could know God (apart from genuine experiences of love, I might have added in an academic manner). People in the Bible "heard" the voice of God, the word of God. Not surprisingly, I was focused on this physical sense. So, that was my prayer as I settled into a comfortable place with the single-page Scripture list, dwelling on my retreat leader's assigned prayer, including these verses from Isaiah 55:3 and 43:19: "I will make with you an everlasting covenant"[122] and "Behold, I will do something new."[123]

Isaiah 55 was not new to me; my husband and I had selected it as a reading for our wedding, and it is one of my favorite passages. The idea of *lectio divina* was not new to me either—the practice of reading a relatively short text and meditating on whatever phrase or word strikes a chord in you, for whatever reason. But on this afternoon, I was trying to engage God, trust God's closeness, in a new way. What I experienced, and what I recorded, was not exactly the stuff prayer manuals are made of. Looking back, I'd say it's a mess, the kind of journal entry about voices that would make the most generous-hearted agnostic run straight for the arms of atheism. But it was an honest struggle.

Here's what happened: I ended up focusing on verses 3–5 of Isaiah 55, probably because the question of whether I should pursue ordained leadership in the church was at the forefront of my life:

> Pay attention and come to me;
>   listen, that you may have life.
> I will make with you an everlasting covenant,
>   the steadfast loyalty promised to David.
> As I made him a witness to peoples,
>   a leader and commander of peoples,
> So shall you summon a nation you knew not,

and a nation that knew you not shall run to you,
Because of the LORD, your God,
   the Holy One of Israel, who has glorified you.[124]

The phrase that struck me as an invitation to meditation and prayer was "As I made him...a leader." I began to reflect on this phrase, asking questions about its implications for my own life. In time, I sensed that another voice was answering my questions, and I engaged it with great skepticism, asking, "How do I know this isn't just a part of my own inner voice?" In response, the voice said, "You know." (As an aside, I had no trouble referring to this voice as "it" in my journal, because I had wisdom and caution not to assume a holy *he* or *she*. Anyway, I felt half-crazy, but I was willing to engage, willing to challenge and dig in to this experience. "What else is a prayer retreat for?" I thought.) When I focused my energy on the part about summoning a nation, which had inexplicably caught my attention, I asked other things, like, "What does this mean for me?" In response, the voice said, "It's too early"—to show me or tell me, I guess, which seemed like a pretty convenient response from the probably-not-voice-of-God. Nevertheless, I kept engaging this voice, even if it was just my own inner voice, just to see what would happen—or perhaps seeking to "prove" that it wasn't (or was) my own.

At the time, what I found most annoying, or interesting, was how the phrase "I know" kept coming up. For instance, I'd say, "I want to be a mother," and even before I'd finish the thought, the voice would almost interrupt me with an "I know." And, surely, I can't be the only person in the world who, when having such an inner dialogue with a voice of unknown origin, wants to see if there might be information available about the future, a sort of prophetic clarity about any number of things. Alas, the voice didn't play that game. If I'd try to ask a specific question like *"Will* I be a mother?" there would be no answer, or perhaps something vague like "In some way," which only revived my suspicions that this was my own inner voice masquerading as something more interesting and wise. But encountering this voice in the quiet and intentionality of the prayer space, coupled with the surprising element of interruption, intrigued me. As did the emerging theme of this inner "conversation"—it was unquestionably *patience*. I don't even remember what I was pressing for, but apparently I kept hearing "Wait and see." I think I must have been pretty explicit in my (admittedly greedy but seemingly relevant) desire to understand the voice of God, to hear God, in response to which I heard, "You will." Then silence. "Apparently," I wrote, "not at this moment." My concluding thought at that time sounds like a frustrated teenager self-consciously parroting her parent: "I guess I'll have to wait and see." It is cringeworthy, but I know that I actually didn't mean it that way. I meant it in earnest. I was willing to wait and see. I didn't have any cherished faith in a personally close and loving God to lose.

In general, my journals are far from meticulous—they are sprawling, scrawled entries made sporadically and with much hand-wringing about their inconsistency. Yet, for some reason, I recorded the time of my prayer sessions with meticulous detail. Perhaps the retreat's spiritual director suggested this approach. Whatever the reason, they are funny, these time stamps of random intervals attached to deep interior struggles: "Prayer = 5:55–6:18; Prayer = 9:30–9:45." I notice how many of the first sessions were twenty minutes in length and feel convicted once again of how little time it takes to at least *try* to engage with the Source of all life—and how unwilling I often am to give that time.

But on a prayer retreat, it's different because such time has specifically been set apart for this purpose. And so, after a solitary dinner of soup from a can, toast, and cheese, I sat back down to pray, choosing Psalm 63 this time as my focus. Once again, I asked for the grace to "HEAR," noting that I had earlier decided to "ASSUME that God was/is with me and willing to speak to me" (without evidence, the all caps implies). Over the years since the retreat, I've absorbed biblical language that helps me broaden my understanding a bit: I recognize that the mercy I was asking for is that I might have "ears to hear." I understand it is more likely that *I* need transformative help than that God needs to respond more clearly to me (as in "Speak up, Holy One! I can't hear you!"). I have consciously realized that, in my case, there's nothing to lose from this approach, this almost Kierkegaardian leap of faith. As I wrote that day, "It seems better than endlessly milling about on my own, wondering about whether or not the Almighty God of the Universe cares for a lowly worm like me [smiley face]." Smiley face? I am covering for, trying to round the edges of, the anxieties of existence that Kierkegaard describes so well but would *never* adorn with a smiley face. This is so much the product of our age, so American: I think I may be a "superfluous pawn"[125] in a potentially superfluous species, but I don't want anyone to think I'm really bummed out about it.

In the late afternoon, before dinner and prayer, I had gone down to the beach to watch the sunset and felt that I saw the word "wait" written in the clouds. I was aware, as I entered into my time of prayer on Psalm 63, that this was a central theme of the day: wait and see; be patient. I had previously heard this phrase, a biblical one, to "wait upon the Lord," but if I had ever thought about it at all, it was probably in service terms, not patience terms. On this day, I remembered the phrase and tried to apply the other obvious meaning, but, not surprisingly, I was not very good at something I had so little practice with. "I was feeling ready to be patient," I wrote, "and it was still hard."

My attention and my prayers were drawn to verses 2 through 6 of Psalm 63:

> O God, you are my God—
>   it is you I seek!
> For you my body yearns;
>   for you my soul thirsts,
> In a land parched, lifeless,
>   and without water.
> I look to you in the sanctuary
>   to see your power and glory.
> For your love is better than life;
>   my lips shall ever praise you!
> I will bless you as long as I live;
>   I will lift up my hands, calling on your name.
> My soul shall be sated as with choice food,
>   with joyous lips my mouth shall praise you![126]

Initially, the verses that struck a chord, drew me in, compelled my focus were those that described a life of praise. I experienced them as an unexpected affirmation of priestly ministry, with the clear caveat that I didn't even really understand what I was getting into. "I will lift up my hands, calling on your name. My soul shall be sated as with choice food, with joyous lips my mouth shall praise you...." I heard this as a word upon my life, as in: "You will be fed by singing my praise, even if you don't yet understand how." Looking back, I notice how little attention I seem to give this moment—a moment that now seems fairly significant. I record it like a curious but detached observer, still longing for something more than a vocational vision, unsatisfied and impatient.

As I turned my attention to the line about looking to God in the sanctuary "to see your power and glory," my impatience began to burst through with an honesty, intensity, and weakness that is older than the crowds who demanded signs from Jesus to prove his authority. I thought, "*Yes*, this is what I want. This is what I need. Show me your power and glory so that I can *really* believe." I was demanding, and, unsurprisingly, nothing happened. I'm not sure what allowed for a self-conscious correction of this pushy posture toward God. There is an intriguing quote scribbled on the side of this journal entry: "I'd love to, but there's no space." Did I sense this response?

Regardless, somehow, I recognized that my clamorous desire was akin to trying to boss God around, and I remembered a powerful image given to me from another nun: "Prayer is not just standing on a pile of rocks from our lives, instructing God about how and where and when to move them. Prayer must also involve time for clearing away the rocks, pushing them out away from us, creating an open space so that God might then enter and speak." And so I tried to do this. I actively imagined clearing a space for God to come into, as if I were creating a large firepit, and I expressed a more humble (but still honest) statement of yearning: "My soul thirsts for you, O Lord." As I repeated this prayer, "a fairly remarkable thing" (as I referred to it that day) happened: I began to feel "filled up," like I was a balloon being filled with warm air, especially in my chest, even though I continued breathing regularly. I found my head and chin lifting up gently without my conscious intention, and again had a sense of warm inflation and fullness. The light behind my eyelids appeared brighter, and this experience seemed, most simply, to be a tiny moment of elation. By reminding myself to remain open to God and not critically analyze what was happening too much, I allowed this moment to last long enough that I actually could sort of pay attention to what was happening. It felt like some kind of response to the words I kept repeating: "My souls thirsts for you, O Lord." I was grateful and earnestly intent to remember "the lesson": don't boss God around. Instead, try to make space for a more perfect wisdom, that famous "peace that passes understanding."

Later, I prayed according to Jeremiah 17:7:

Blessed is the man who trusts in the LORD, whose hope is the LORD.[127]

Trust is such a basic concept of any brand of faith, and yet I could see in a difficult moment of reflection that I still carried so much accumulated skepticism and intellectual judgment toward this kind of person (the poor simpleton!) "who trusts in the LORD, whose hope is the LORD." At the same time, I also obviously yearned to trust, to hope, to be more like such a person. I realized that the movement of the day's prayers had been toward a different sort of trust than I had ever held: trusting in God in a given moment rather than resting on an abstract sort of trust in the big-vague-universal-providential picture, the sort I might have proclaimed. The day felt like an invitation to trust that God was already with me and that encountering even a hint of this presence, a whiff of the Holy One, was, as I put it that night, "worth this sometimes crazy-seeming effort."

Now I marvel at the staggering implication that encountering a trace of God's presence within might not be worth the effort of sitting in silence for a few days, but I try to remember how uncharted this territory and this movement felt at the time. After all, what "seemed crazy"? The idea that I might know something of God, and that God would care enough to help me know that same something. Many voices in my education, culture, and even churches considered this illogical, fantastical, or make-believe in the most darkly literal sense. I used language like "crazy" because I had no other category for this endeavor of personally engaging with the divine.

The Prayer of Recollection

First, in this work of the spirit, the person who thinks less, and desires to do less, actually does more. Here's what we have to do: beg like a needy and poor person before a powerful and rich emperor, and then lower our eyes to the ground and wait with humility. When we seem to realize (through the secret signs He gives us) that He *is* hearing us, it's good for us to remain silent, since He's allowed us to be near Him. It wouldn't be wrong to try *not* to work with our intellect—that is, if we even can work with it. But if we aren't sure that the King has heard us, or sees us, then we must not hang around like fools. The soul remains really foolish when it tries to grasp this kind of quiet prayer; it experiences more dryness, and the imagination is perhaps even more restless due to the forceful effort to "think nothing!" The Lord just wants us to ask things of Him and to remember that we are in His presence; He knows what is most fitting for us. I can't persuade myself to use human effort in matters where it seems His Majesty has set a limit and wants to leave the action in such places for Himself. There are lots of other things not reserved in this way that we *can* do (with His help), like sacrificial generosity, good works, and prayer—as much as our weak human nature is able to do.[128]

In "Fourth Dwellings," Teresa is trying to chart the rocky and often uneven territory between the benefits of concerted effort in prayer and the kind of spiritual gifts we cannot work for or toward at all. It is as if she is navigating the complexities of a border region, and her description is understandably meandering in both image and explanation. First, she tries to mark this border relatively cleanly between *consolations* and *gustos* (spiritual delights), but, later on, she turns her attention to part of the prayer landscape that she recognizes as a sort of borderland, a space that one enters in the transition between *contentos* and *gustos*. She refers to this space (or "work of the spirit") between striving and effortlessly receiving as "the prayer of recollection."

Teresa says the prayer of recollection "almost always" begins before "the prayer of quiet," where one first experiences spiritual delights—those gifts from God that well up from within. Teresa uses diverse metaphors to try to describe what is happening in the prayer of recollection, but admittedly it is one of the hardest terms to grasp because she is not consistent in her terminology. As translators Kavanaugh and Rodriguez note: "Sometimes she speaks of a recollection that is not infused…; at other times of a recollection that is infused; in the *Life*, [she uses] the term indiscriminately with 'quiet' to designate the first degree of infused prayer, and in [another book] to designate the first faint experience of mystical prayer that prepares the way for the prayer of quiet."[129] It makes sense on some level that this "borderland" term would have all the messiness of borders themselves. As with other good "border" writing, we get a sense of the place only through images, which are accurate and helpful even if they are incongruous or seemingly haphazard. So, what images does Teresa give us for the prayer of recollection in *The Interior Castle*?

1. *"A building…being constructed."* In a way that is "supernatural" or beyond our abilities ("without any human effort," as Teresa puts it), recollection creates space, makes a structure, within which one can then receive the spiritual delights of infused prayer. "The senses and all external things seem to gradually lose their hold," she writes.[130] But why? How? We don't know, of course, but she explores this process more fully with the next image.

2. *The beckoning whistle of God.* This is the most elaborate metaphor, and my favorite, because it demonstrates the dance of God's invitation (often in ways that are imperceptible to us) and our response(s), both voluntary and seemingly involuntary. Imagining a person who remains outside the castle of their soul, the castle of prayer, Teresa graciously acknowledges that many such people are of good intention: "They aren't traitors, or *against* the castle anymore," she says, "and they're wandering around the castle." It is as if we can circle the dwelling places of prayer, not sure whether we want to or can go inside. But such seekers still haunt the grounds, drawn to the environs. Then comes the unexpected invitation and the possibility of response. As Teresa writes:

> In His great mercy, [the King] desires to bring them back to Him. So, like a good shepherd, with a whistle so gentle it is *almost* imperceptible, He teaches them to recognize His voice; He stops

them from going off and getting lost and brings them back to their dwelling place. This Shepherd's call is so powerful that they abandon the exterior things that were causing such alienation and enter the castle.[131]

3. *A gentle drawing inward: a hedgehog curling up or a tortoise drawing into its shell.* This image is a simple one, but I love its illustration of entering into a deeper interiority during prayer. Although there are many forms of prayer, many ways of talking with God (including visual and physical means that involve the senses), this ability to withdraw a bit from the world and the physical environment, slowly, tenderly, awkwardly—like a hedgehog or tortoise!—is a bread-and-butter element of most traditions of prayer and meditation.[132]

4. *Deeply listening to God.* Teresa's description of "recollection" is quintessentially complicated: "Giving thanks also helps prepare the soul for greater gifts. And this state, or disposition, enables us to *listen* as certain books advise," Teresa writes. "Instead of running after God through reason and words, the soul is intent on discovering what the Lord is doing. But if His Majesty hasn't yet begun to absorb us, I can't understand how *we* can stop our thoughts in a way that doesn't bring more harm than good."[133] It seems Teresa is saying that there must be a depth of quiet attentiveness before God ("the soul is intent on discovering"), but that we are not capable of achieving this kind of quiet, really, without God's help. Thus, recollection might also be thought of as God "beginning to absorb us," or as stopping, slowing, or focusing our mind in some way so that we can respond with real focus and attention.

Invoking the image of adjoining rooms, or perhaps even a doorway, Teresa writes this: "The prayer of recollection is much less intense than the spiritual delights of God I've been talking about, but it's often the beginning, the first step toward them. In the prayer of recollection, meditation and the work of the intellect do not need to be set aside."[134] In other words, our minds are still active in this prayer, even as God is "absorbing" us or present to us in new ways. To my mind, these images are diverse but also still coherent, and each resonates with what I might now call experiences of "recollection." A space is created for dialogue and an encounter with a living and surprisingly close God, and to enter that space requires listening, movement, attentiveness, and trust on our part—but also gracious assistance and beckoning and guidance on God's part. Remember, as Teresa said, "Supernatural experiences begin here, and this is extremely difficult to explain."

To Be Known

Tuesday, January 12, 2010

I met with my silent retreat's spiritual director again on Tuesday morning, and my notes from that time are a collection of diverse prayer advice that makes me wonder about our conversation: How long did we meet that we were able to cover such varied ideas? Was she rambling, or was I? Nevertheless, I notice a few lines that I didn't expect. Honestly, the only concept my memory (without looking at the journal) attributed to her teaching was of naming what we need in prayer so that we recognize how God responds. I also remembered her giving me specific Scripture passages. In revisiting my notes, however, I discover she had much more to say—direction and insight that later opened up dramatically and profoundly, in a three-dimensional way. I had forgotten she planted those seeds, those two-dimensional treasure-map clues I scribbled down but later overlooked in the wake of a windfall beyond hope or expectation.

"God reveals Godself to people differently!" she told me. "Look for the ways that God comes to you in your marriage! This is your first vocation," she said a bit later. "This is the image of God's love for us." Assigning Psalm 139 and Isaiah 43, she said, "Be utterly yourself; it is utterly safe." Finally, she exhorted me to acknowledge my longing to know God's love more and more deeply. "Tell God that you long to know God's love for you in some new way," she said. The words sound good, like most words about God's love do. I have no doubt I took them to heart, as I had with many wise and caring words from spiritual mentors. But I really can't overstate the unexpectedness of God taking those words and making them more than words.

At around eleven thirty in the morning, I sat in the recliner in my retreat room to pray, holding a single sheet of paper with an excerpt from Psalm 139 printed on it:

> LORD, you have searched me out and known me;
>   you know my sitting down and my rising up;
>   you discern my thoughts from afar.
>
> You trace my journeys and my resting places
>   and are acquainted with all my ways.
>
> Indeed, there is not a word on my lips,
>   but you, O LORD, know it altogether.
>
> You press upon me behind and before
>   and lay your hand upon me.
>
> Such knowledge is too wonderful for me;
>   it is so high that I cannot attain to it.[135]

The excerpt from the psalm continued from there, twelve more verses, and at first I read it all the way through, staying in my head (intellect). But I thought back to the advice to ask for the particular grace to know God's love, and to the invitation to *wait*, trusting that God would somehow come into the space I managed to clear. I asked for God's Spirit to help me pray, too, ever more aware of my need. Then, I started to meditate prayerfully upon the first verse, "You have searched me out and known me," repeating it slowly over and over. This repetition soon morphed into the real and deepest question of my heart: *Have* you searched me? *Have* you known me?

As I asked—almost accusingly, but also very truthfully—trusting that God would answer in some way, my body began to again feel warm, a bit like the night before but with new features, too: my legs were shaking, and a trembling seized me, drawing my attention to warmth and internal movement through my feet. It felt like God was saying, "All the way through the blood in your feet to the tips of your toes, I've known you; every part." I was shocked, and I moved into a new prayer in response: "You have searched me; you have known me," but even yet this didn't seem right, and I kept trembling when I said "known." I realized, through a sense of pressure, correction, that I needed to express this in the present tense; it needed to be "know": "You have searched me, and you *know* me." I kept praying in this way, caught up in both fear and awe at what was happening.

I am loathe to describe the particular physical elements of my experience because such descriptions invite skeptical analysis, as they certainly have for Teresa. It is obvious that she tries to minimize these aspects, too—though, in the end, they are present; they are part of her work. And, tellingly, they are the parts of her work that many people who have never read her know something about: "Didn't she levitate? Didn't she feel pierced by fiery arrows?" This is the "crazy-mystical" stuff that both attracts and repels attention, in a way that sometimes has very little to do with genuine interest in the movement of God. I will write more for the sake of those who do genuinely care to know more about such movement.

What I have written thus far doesn't do justice to the sense of power and otherness that moved my body with fear and trembling. It was frightening in its newness and unexpectedness, the way it ruptured my understanding of how God would or would not be present on this earth, in these times, to insignificant individual humans, and more particularly a cold-blooded white girl like me, formed by the staid spiritual expectations of the frozen chosen. My full journal entry after the fact includes the words "fear," "scared," "scary," "frightening," and "freaked-out," along with the admittedly "silly" observation that "I'm not Pentecostal, but this is still happening to me."

This. The overall physical effect might be compared to a mild seizure that just kept shaking me again and again as I prayed, drawing tears and yet leaving me with full presence of mind, the capacity for observation and bewildered engagement in this foreign conversation, but also the (real and terrifying) awareness of another power affecting my physical being. As I moved further and further into this prayer of "You know me," the fear and awe eventually overtook me and transformed my words to "Holy God." As the experience intensified, even this gave way to a simpler prayer: "I'm scared."

In my fear, I turned to Jesus: the name of Jesus, the idea of Jesus, the Jesus to whom I had never prayed for help more urgently or earnestly. I don't know why I thought Jesus might help me, except that I figured if anyone knew what it was like to be seized by the Spirit of God, it was he. My prayer was like that of Jesus' friends who thought they might die in the storm, and so I begged him for relief. Suddenly, I grasped—and pinned my hope to—the notion of Jesus as the Christ, the priestly mediator, the one who can stand between small creatures and their Creator, the one who cannot just bridge this cosmic divide but also provide a sheltering wing for the frail human psyche. This thought came later, of course; in the moment, I just cried out to Jesus because he was a human and divine figure I trusted, despite all my intellectual qualms. There seemed to be no other place to turn when I wanted out of the boat. Slowly, gently, there was relief. Calm settled over my limbs and my heart. I lay there in stillness for a moment, then uttered an exhausted prayer of thanks. In spite of the fear and the confusion, I was awake enough to say thank you to God for this gift, this sign that I am known, every particle of me. I opened my eyes and looked across the room to the alarm clock next to the bed; about thirty standard minutes had passed in this time when I felt out of time.

I stood up, bewildered. As I wandered toward the bathroom, I wondered, "Did I just conjure that whole thing? Did I somehow *make* that happen?" I washed my hands with the light off, and I began to doubt that it was God after all. Suddenly, I was seized by the Spirit again, and my knees buckled beneath me. I made my way back to the chair, where I prayed and put my head down in my lap, again asking for Jesus to be with me. I cried, overwhelmed by God's insistence that I not toss aside this great gift. I cried, seeing clearly that I had always thought I wanted a mystical experience of God, but I should have been smart enough to fear it a little more. It felt like I had been given the very slap in the face that I had been praying for, and I was embarrassingly surprised.

You dare to ask if I know you? If I have searched you? I am in every part of you! Moving in you, even as you don't understand what is happening, knowing your very thoughts before they are on your lips.

I didn't know where to go from there, other than to the place that the line from the psalm led me, where I could rest in wonder, at least for a bit: I am known. It is what I could say with every part of me, even as my mind continued its habits of protest: "I am known."

To Be Loved

The spiritual delights begin in God, but our human nature feels and enjoys them as much as it does consolations, and indeed much more. Oh, Jesus! I wish I could be clear about this! I can see a very marked difference between these two things, but I'm not clever enough to describe it very well; may the Lord explain it for me.[136]

Later that day—I assume after lunch and a walk outside—I returned to my retreat room for another time of prayer. I sat at the top of the bed, legs crossed, with my back to the wall, and again tried to quiet myself, attune my thoughts to the realities of my heart. In the words of the week's spiritual director: What mercy do I need? What grace do I seek? I can still feel the meekness of my honest answer. "Okay, God, I get it. You know me. But…do you love me?" It is a different question, an embarrassing question, one I did not assume the answer to, and one that is not inherently answered by knowing that one is known. We all know, quite painfully, that there can be knowledge without love. And so I named this question, this yearning, with meekness, with a quiet fear, with the vulnerability of a creature who has just caught whiff of the fact that there is nowhere to hide but is still unsure of the character, the demeanor, of the One whose gaze is upon her. I began to read Psalm 139 again:

Where can I go then from your Spirit?
    where can I flee from your presence?

If I climb up to heaven, you are there;
    if I make the grave my bed, you are there also.

…

If I say, "Surely the darkness will cover me,
    and the light around me turn to night,"

Darkness is not dark to you;
the night is as bright as the day;
    darkness and light to you are both alike.

For you yourself created my inmost parts;
    you knit me together in my mother's womb.

> I will thank you because I am marvelously made;
>   your works are wonderful, and I know it well.[137]

As I came to and through verse 12 of the psalm, I was again seized by Spirit in a way that arrested my reading on this line, inviting me to repeat it again and again: *"For you yourself created my inmost parts; you knit me together in my mother's womb."* This time, however, it was not my legs that were trembling. Instead—unexpectedly, inexplicably—I felt trembling in my "inward parts," the organs inside my chest and gut shaking while the rest of my frame remained still. It was as if God were employing my very body to confirm the truth of these words, which I repeated as I looked upon what was happening with awe: "For it was you who formed my inward parts; you knit me together in my mother's womb."[138]

And then, seamlessly and yet still surprisingly, the conversation point shifted. I was holding on to the verse like a lifeline as the energy and movement changed from the strangeness of trembling organs to the relative familiarity of sexual encounter, of being loved in and through my body. I was once again alarmed, caught off guard, but I felt safe enough to continue to sit still in wonder and awe and joy, paying attention to what was happening as the experience expanded and intensified, marveling at the beautiful bluntness of this communication, which was completely contiguous in my experience with what came before: "I *made* you. Of *course* I love you, more deeply than you could ask or imagine."

It seemed to me then, almost instantaneously, that I was receiving a truth spoken previously only in the language of my marriage. I could hear, understand, and even receive this expression of love because I had been strengthened by a nearly ten-year relationship with my husband that made the metaphor a clear one, and a welcome one. To be loved as I was loved in my marriage—completely, wonderfully, even in our missteps and imperfections—was without a doubt a good thing. There were also a few phrases from the Christian tradition that helped me receive this experience initially, even though I also felt and acknowledged in my journal that the whole thing "sounds REALLY weird." One such image was God as the "lover of our souls," and the other was the teaching that marriage, as an "outward sign of an inward and spiritual grace" (or sacrament), pointed in some way to the mystery of God's love and steadfast faithfulness toward humanity. I had never been drawn to either of the images (to put it mildly), but suddenly they were helpful and relevant.

I both wrote and remember that I was so bewildered by this unexpected experience of God's love that I didn't even know how to say thanks, how to *be* adequately thankful afterward. "I tried to say thank you appropriately, but I fear I haven't *fully* learned the lesson and my thanks didn't seem complete. I'll keep practicing the thanks." I now look upon this young woman with such tenderness, and I want to say the following in a way that won't be heard as teasing, as dismissive: "You're right, sweetheart. You haven't fully learned 'the lesson' of God's love. You may find in time that your thanks will never seem complete, will never be complete. But don't worry. God's love doesn't end over such trifles."

Sarah Coakley, the systematic theologian who writes brilliantly (and at length) about how divine desire and human desire are perhaps our most foundational elements, claims that "the very act of contemplation—repeated, lived, embodied, suffered—is an act that, by grace, and over time...instigates an acute awareness of the messy entanglement of sexual desires and the desire for God."[139] Indeed, perhaps such experiences of *eros* mingling with what we previously thought of as pure, disembodied *agape* are practically commonplace, if one finds the stamina to live the day in, day out Christian contemplative journey. As a pastor and priest, I now hear of this dynamic in prayer from some people in my congregation, directly and indirectly. And anyone listening carefully to Christian music picks up on these themes in lyrics written in nearly every age (including by contemporary artists). Yet, before this day, *no one* had alerted me to the idea that this "very act" of contemplative prayer might lead to such overlays. Little in my roughly twenty-five years of Christian formation had prepared me for the possibility of this "messy entanglement," with the vague and inadequate exception of songs I used to make fun of for having "Jesus-is-my-boyfriend" lyrics, like "Jesus, Lover of My Soul."

I feel the power of the silence (and the implied shame) around such experiences even as I write, for I can still hear the derisive laughter of some of my most wise and thoughtful seminary classmates when we briefly covered the prayer life of Teresa of Ávila and pondered Bernini's evocative statue of Teresa being pierced with fiery darts. "That's messed up," they sneered. "God is not your lover—not like that." It seems that such reactions are based on fear that such allusions are more than a "messy entanglement," that they are somehow a perversion of the nature of God's love or that they distort our own responses to God. These are questions that I will address more fully at a later point, but my interest now is to look at my immediate response to such "entanglement." Where did this taste of divine *eros* lead me at the time?

My "general reflections" at the close of January 12 give some clues:

> No matter what happens from here, I can't imagine that this won't be a red-letter day in my life of faith. I have the sense of not wanting to celebrate or rejoice *too* much, because I know this is just the beginning of a long journey; the first lesson. It's almost as if I'm already turning to the teaching and asking, "Now what?" And I am heartened by [my priest's] interpretation of Saul's conversion—that it takes *time* to figure out what experiences like this mean. And I need to be careful with my words and diligently truthful to my experience, even as I know I will be tempted to qualify or equivocate. But here is the short of what happened in one day: I felt God's Spirit in me; I was seized by the Spirit with the very convicted and "in my face" truth that "you know me": I was shaken with the realization, quite literally once again, with the words that God formed my inward parts and loves me like a husband, with intensity, and that if I continue to seek Christ in the Eucharist, I will meet him there.... My Word! My God! Holy Lord—God of Power & Might. I asked. You answered. Thank you. Guide me on...I pray.

It almost makes you cringe to read this—at least, it makes me cringe, even as I trust the sincerity and truth of the words. It is enthusiastic and passionate, but it is also full of Christian truisms that have become dull and off-putting through sometimes trite overuse and also patterns of dismissive misunderstanding. The truth is, I was not walking on new ground that day. I did not learn anything that faithful people have not known and taught with much greater eloquence for thousands of years. But this is where I landed, with a new depth of conviction and sufficient trust to carry my study into seminary: the One who created us knows us and loves us—knows us better than we know ourselves, and loves us more than we could ask or imagine. The same is true for your neighbors, made by the same God with the same love. It is not the answer to every question. But it does seem to me like solid, old-fashioned footing for a life of faith, a life that tries to trust God and God's ways. In human hands, perversion of good gifts is always a possibility. Yet it does not mean we deny the reality of the gifts or the invitation—always—to in some way share their goodness.

Why Me? Or Why Not Me?

I've just remembered a Scripture verse that we say at the end of the last psalm at Prime. The last words are *cum dilatasti cor meum*—"when You enlarged my heart." For those with a lot of experience, this [line] is sufficient for explaining the difference between the two [consolations and spiritual delights]. To those who have not, more explanation is needed.[140]

In the weeks following my retreat, I related the basic outline of what I had experienced in prayer with select friends and companions whom I knew would receive this vulnerable and wondrous witness with care: three priests in the Episcopal Church who were my mentors, my husband, my spiritual director, and my best friend from college. I remember them sharing in my joy and wonder as I told them, and I never once questioned or pondered why I had been given such an indelible experience of God's knowledge and love. If anything, I assumed that this was the only way God could get through to me—by bypassing my overactive and hypercritical mind to imprint the knowledge of God's omniscience and love, cutting through my tangled but honest mess of yearning and doubt. In other words, I saw it as God's kind response to a deficiency in my faith, an indulgent willingness to reach me across the boundary of physical experience when so many people don't *need* such a holy shaking. One mentor interpreted it as an anointing, a blessing, before my journey into seminary. I did experience it as a grounding in the basic tenets of the Christian faith, a grounding that would allow me to walk toward theological education with (still) an endless supply of questions but also the trust that they were worth wrestling with. I assumed that this experience would be once-in-a-lifetime, and, actually, one priest told me to expect as much: "It tends to be the case that these sorts of things happen less and less as we journey on in the life of faith. It doesn't mean this isn't important. I just don't want you to be alarmed." I took him at his word; I didn't expect to experience the presence of the Holy Spirit in such startling and wonderful ways ever again. Largely due to my religious context, I was not intentionally seeking *gustos* from God, did not feel I was entitled to them, and did not think that they might continue to be a part of my life in any significant way.

The cultural and religious assumptions that shaped my attitude differed greatly from those of Teresa, who primarily addressed *The Interior Castle* to Carmelite nuns eager for rich prayer lives—of the sort they'd heard much about from Teresa and others. Teresa walks a fine line, encouraging her sisters to be bold and seek the King in prayer, to *strive* to align their wills with that of Christ, and to *assume* Christ is near, but also frequently reminding them that they cannot *expect* anything; these are God's gifts to give, when and if and how God sees fit. (I sometimes imagine that if Teresa were born an American millennial, she would have at least two tattoos: on one wrist, we might find "Strive onward, needed friend of Christ!" and on the other "Expect nothing, wretched lowly worm!") I did not feel the questions then, but I see them and understand them now: Why does God move into some people's lives in this way but not others? Can we make any sense of how, and why, and the best way to approach our natural desire for such intimacy with God once we have heard about its occurrence in the lives of others, past and present?

These remain important questions, present questions, and Teresa's insights on them are characteristically thoughtful and paradoxical. First, she acknowledges the natural desire we have for such experiences in prayer as an extension of our desire to be closer to God. And she forthrightly admits that some of this simply cannot be understood by proxy; more than Keats' notion that such matters must be "proved upon our pulses,"[141] Teresa implies that some things might only be *known* upon our pulses:

> I know you'll now want to try to attain this way of prayer, my daughters, and this is right and good. As I've said, the soul can't fully understand the gifts that the Lord gives there or the love with which He draws the soul nearer to Himself. Clearly, it's desirable

to try to understand how to reach, or attain, this gift. I'll tell you what I've learned about it.[142]

Teresa foresees (and has likely heard) cries of "That's not fair!" from faithful sisters who feel such favors have been squandered on souls who have not paid their dues, in the convent or chapel or simply through years of living. The same accusation was thrown at Teresa herself. She responds with a measured tone:

> It does seem that a person must have lived in the other dwelling places for a long time in order to reach these spaces. As a rule, you need to have been in the third dwellings, but there is no *infallible* rule: as you've probably heard before, the Lord gives when He wills and as He wills and to whom He wills. Because the gifts are His own to give, there's no injustice in this to anyone.[143]

Then she gives the common-sense disclaimer that sometimes these things will happen to people who are not on any spiritual path at all, not even seeking to pray: there will be outliers. God can do what God wants to do. She writes, "We'll leave aside the times when the Lord wants to give these gifts because He wants to and for no other reason. He knows why He does this, and it's not for us to interfere."[144] But we are rational creatures, and so she knows her sisters want something more applicable, something that follows some sense of logic. (God's freedom is wonderful until we want God to respond predictably, right?)

It is obvious that Teresa has thought a great deal about this matter, and she tries to be both careful and kind. First, she says, we must do "what should be done by those in the previous dwelling places [the first, second, and third dwellings]."[145] She often summarizes those things that we can do—apart from any *gustos*—as prayer, penance, good works. It is basic Christian teaching: pray to God, trusting in God's closeness without feeling it. Love others, forgive others, serve others with the humility of Jesus. Then, Teresa says, after this is done, and as this is done: "Humility! Humility!… It's through humility that the Lord allows Himself to be conquered with regard to anything we ask of Him. The first way to see if you have humility? If you do have it, you don't think you deserve these gifts and *gustos* of God, or that you'll receive them in your lifetime."[146]

Teresa is convinced that there is no better way to receive such *gustos* than by not striving for them. It is a common spiritual axiom to live and to pray in a posture of openhanded receiving rather than fruitless grasping, one that might be "proved" simply by her experience, but she still gives five reasons why this is the best way, which seems to demonstrate the frequency with which she faced questions about this. (I have quoted the five reasons here at length to give a fuller sense of her voice on this topic.)

So, why is it best not to strive for such experiences of God's Spirit, such *gustos*?

First, because the most essential thing is that we love God without any motive of self-interest.

Second, because we lack humility by thinking that in return for our pathetic service, we might obtain something so great.

Third, because the true preparation for receiving these gifts is a desire to suffer and to imitate the Lord, not to receive consolations, for we have often offended Him.

Fourth, because His Majesty has not promised to give them to us, as He has [promised] to grant us glory if we keep His commandments. (We don't need these gifts to be saved, and He knows better than we do what is good for us and who among us truly loves Him. This is a certain truth. I also know people who walk along the road of love as they should—*only* in order to serve Christ crucified, and not only do they not ask for *gustos*, but they don't want them, and they even ask God not to give them in this life. This is true.)

Fifth, because we would be laboring in vain: this water doesn't flow through constructed pipes, like the other kind does, so we gain nothing by tiring ourselves out if the spring doesn't want to flow. What I mean is that no matter how much we practice meditation and try to squeeze or press ourselves, even to tears, we can't produce this water in this way. It is given only to those whom God wills to give it, and often when the soul is not thinking of it at all.[147]

"Often when the soul is not thinking of it at all"—this includes not knowing or thinking that such things happen to ordinary, rational people at all.

Lord

One significant difference between what I would call my "fourth dwellings" in prayer and those described by Teresa is the substantial work that had to be done in these fourth dwelling places for me to move closer to Christ, closer to what most people, from the outside, blandly assume it means to be a Christian—that is, to trust that Jesus the Christ is and was more than a prophet of God, more than a great teacher or a moral exemplar. As I described in the first three dwelling places, this was not the nature of my faith. Teresa of Ávila came of age in a different era of teaching in the church and in a society that would have made it difficult for her to even *imagine* my version of Christian piety. Hers was a Christocentric Christianity from beginning to end, as is much of contemporary North American Christianity. I can still get worked up about versions of the church that seem to focus so much on Jesus that they neglect teaching and reflection on God as transcendent Creator and immanent Holy Spirit, but the truth is that my own version of Christianity was really squishy and weak when it came to Jesus, and I knew it. Now, it might be argued that it is better to be uncertain and humble than closed-minded and presumptuous when it comes to what one "knows" about God—and I would still say this is correct. But I also carried an earnest longing to feel just a bit more connected to this figure who was so central to the tradition in which I was seeking God and a fullness of life.

So deep and earnest was my desire that, on the same day I first experienced God's knowledge, love, and presence in ways tinged with "the supernatural," I was not content to rest there. On January 12, in my fourth prayer session of the day, I sat down to pray at 8:30 p.m. with the intent to ask God for forgiveness, because I felt that there was a great gap between my worthiness and the spiritual graces of the day. As I put it then: "I have been so, so lazy—how is it that I am given such a grace as to feel overcome by the Holy Spirit?" I began on this theme but soon moved to my real heart's desire, which was not forgiveness but rather a yearning to experience Jesus.

I had spent much of the afternoon reading James Martin's *My Life with the Saints*, a contemporary rendering of the lives of the saints, which unsurprisingly stoked my desire to have a sense of Jesus present to me. I was aware that this move might be considered "greedy" by some ("As if sensing God's knowledge and love isn't enough!"), but a Marcus Borg sermon I'd heard as a college student echoed once more in my head, from which I gleaned this encouragement: *If you, like Thomas, struggle to believe in Jesus, it's okay to ask to see him.* I had been given permission, and I knew it was an honest struggle and desire.

I began with language that was true but not my own: "I want to see the living Christ" and "Give me eyes to see the living Christ." In repetition, however, as I sank further into prayer, these words became my own: "I want to know Jesus." In the deep silence and attentiveness that developed, in the space that Teresa might call the prayer of recollection, once again something unexpected and powerful came over me—but with new contours. Again, I felt a surge of heat in my body, and, soon thereafter, I felt my heart pounding in my chest; but the most notable feature was something new: the palms of my hands began to feel hot, as if there were a small sphere of warm light resting in them. My hands were cupped in my lap, palms facing up, and as I observed this with both awe and interest, I couldn't understand the meaning. My fingers remained cool, while the centers of my hands were steadily hot. I was so intrigued by this sensation that I even opened my eyes at one point, half expecting to see something resting there. Of course, there was nothing there my eyes could see, and so I closed my eyes and entered into prayer again, repeating my desire to somehow know Jesus.

There came a pause, a space of quiet interrupting my fervor, and then the simple idea of the Eucharist, or receiving the bread of Communion in my hands. I was holding my hands as if I were receiving the bread, and my palms were aflame. I pondered this with some relief and wonder, but also, honestly, some dissatisfaction. (There is some merit to the diagnosis of spiritual greed.) "For now, then," I wrote, "I will continue to seek Christ in the Eucharist, as a mystery of faith—but with a new appreciation for what it means to receive the Host." Do you hear the note of dissatisfaction? "I will continue." I felt as though I had already been seeking knowledge and understanding of Jesus in the practice of Holy Communion for many years. This seemed an affirmation that Christ was indeed mediated though this action, and I was grateful. But we misunderstand gratitude if we think it is impossible to be both grateful and unsatisfied.

As mentioned previously, my own attraction to rationality (and my fear that Jesus would demand extremism of me) kept Jesus far from the center of my faith. I often somewhat clinically referred to him as the "second person of the Trinity," but my life was full of Christians of various persuasions and temperaments, including those who "loved Jesus" a lot, and I was leery but somewhat envious of what I sometimes derisively referred to as the "teddy-bear Jesus." Others seemed to have found a gentle Jesus at first blush, while I stood at a safe distance from the wild-eyed hardliner staring me down from the gospel pages. Yet, each week at church, I stood and listened to a reading from accounts of Jesus' life in the Christian Scriptures, all of which claim to be writings of "good news." I wanted to trust this figure, this person, more or even (one step removed from that) trust the centrality of Christ to my faith tradition so that I might continue to study and grow within it. My foundations were shaky, and I wanted to be released from the angst about the ground beneath me enough to explore the vast house of Christianity. It was a desire that had been present with me from the beginning of the retreat, but on the third day, it moved to the fore.

Wednesday, January 13, 2010

The sister providing me with spiritual direction suggested three different gospel passages to pray with during the day, and a psalm for before bed. She instructed me to read through each passage quietly and slowly, once, twice, three times. "Name the grace that you desire," she repeated, "the longing to know Christ and to meet him. Take a seat, and be drawn into this mystery." It was an invitation to an Ignatian meditation on Scripture, in which you imagine being present in the scene, engaging all your senses. There is a note scribbled in the middle of this "assignment" that causes me to pause to this day: "*At the end of each, be sure you talk to Jesus." It implies an assumed intimacy, closeness, presence that was foreign to me. I notice it still as the obvious evidence of someone else's voice inhabiting the pages of my journal. I talked to God; I didn't talk to Jesus. But God had been present to me in new ways in this Christian retreat house, and I was emboldened to try again on this new day. I commenced my morning prayer by reading the first Scripture passage.

THE SAMARITAN WOMAN AT THE WELL

Now when Jesus learned that the Pharisees had heard, "Jesus is making and baptizing more disciples than John" (although it was not Jesus himself but his disciples who baptized), he left Judea and started back to Galilee. But he had to go through Samaria. So he came to a Samaritan city called Sychar, near the plot of ground that Jacob had given to his son Joseph. Jacob's well was there, and Jesus, tired out by his journey, was sitting by the well. It was about noon.

A Samaritan woman came to draw water, and Jesus said to her, "Give me a drink." (His disciples had gone to the city to buy food.) The Samaritan woman said to him, "How is it that you, a Jew, ask a drink of me, a woman of Samaria?" (Jews do not share things in common with Samaritans.) Jesus answered her, "If you knew the gift of God and who it is that is saying to you, 'Give me a drink,' you would have asked him, and he would have given you living water." The woman said to him, "Sir, you have no bucket, and the well is deep. Where do you get that living water? Are you greater than our ancestor Jacob, who gave us the well and with his sons and his flocks drank from it?" Jesus said to her, "Everyone who drinks of this water will be thirsty again, but those who drink of the water that I will give them will never be thirsty. The water that I will give will become in them a spring of water gushing up to eternal life." The woman said to him, "Sir, give me this water, so that I may never be thirsty or have to keep coming here to draw water."

Jesus said to her, "Go, call your husband, and come back." The woman answered him, "I have no husband." Jesus said to her, "You are right in saying, 'I have no husband,' for you have had five husbands, and the one you have now is not your husband. What you have said is true!" The woman said to him, "Sir, I see that you are a prophet. Our ancestors worshiped on this mountain, but you say that the place where people must worship is in Jerusalem." Jesus said to her, "Woman, believe me, the hour is coming when you will worship the Father neither on this mountain nor in Jerusalem. You worship what you do not know; we worship what we know, for salvation is from the Jews. But the hour is coming and is now here when the true worshipers will worship the Father in spirit and truth, for the Father seeks such as these to worship him. God is spirit, and those who worship him must worship in spirit and truth." The woman said to him, "I know that Messiah is coming" (who is called Christ). "When he comes, he will proclaim all things to us." Jesus said to her, "I am he, the one who is speaking to you."

Just then his disciples came. They were astonished that he was speaking with a woman, but no one said, "What do you want?" or, "Why are you speaking with her?" Then the woman left her water jar and went back to the city. She said to the people, "Come and see a man who told me everything I have ever done! He cannot be the Messiah, can he?"[148]

I began imagining Jesus by the well on a hot day at noon, and I was surprised—and relieved—to find that, in my imagination, in prayer, he was alternately joking and earnest. He said, quite simply, *Would you give me a drink?* And then I watched as the Samaritan woman said something like, *How can you ask me for a drink?* I struggled to see, to imagine, this part because I couldn't intuit its shock value. But then, Jesus said rather playfully, *If you knew who was asking, you would have asked me, and I would have given you living water.* At this point, I imagined the Samaritan woman as haughty and laughing. *Are you better than Jacob?* she goaded. But then Jesus calmly put his hands on her shoulders and looked her in the eyes and said, *Everyone who drinks this will be thirsty again...but the water I give will become a spring gushing up eternally.*

At this point, my attention was drawn from this scene in my mind's eye back to my body, even as my eyes remained closed. I felt water filling my mouth, as if my salivary glands were on overdrive. I noticed this with wonder and curiosity. *Really?* I was still suspicious (is this a gimmick manufactured by my body to support my yearning?), but I had also been enough chastened and humbled to stay with the sensation, to observe and wait for what God might communicate in and through it. And, once again, what came as I waited in prayer was not gimmicky but piercing, truthful: *See? I am already doing this in you; is this not enough?*

Later, as my prayer moved toward the end of the passage, Jesus' deeper conversation with the woman, I too tried to talk with Jesus. I only remember that my attention got caught on the Samaritan woman's phrase, *When the Messiah comes, he will tell us everything.* Once again, I felt my head drawn up, the Spirit's energy focusing my whole self in an inexplicable prayer of recollection, in which I could hear, somehow, *See, God is Spirit, but I TELL you everything. I am he.*

Slowly, I felt released and relaxed, but—shockingly or unsurprisingly—apparently these words had not been enough for me. I reiterated before God my desire to know Jesus. I wrote afterward, "It was almost as if I heard, *Well, this is a start.*" And it was, definitely, a start. *Is this not enough?*

THE WOMAN WHO REACHES FOR JESUS ANONYMOUSLY

Now there was a woman who had been suffering from a flow of blood for twelve years, and though she had spent all she had on physicians, no one could cure her. She came up behind him and touched the fringe of his cloak, and immediately her flow of blood stopped. Then Jesus asked, "Who touched me?" When they all denied it, Peter said, "Master, the crowds are hemming you in and pressing against you." But Jesus said, "Someone touched me, for I noticed that power had gone out from me." When the woman realized that she could not remain hidden, she came trembling, and falling down before him, she declared in the presence of all the people why she had touched him and how she had been immediately healed. He said to her, "Daughter, your faith has made you well; go in peace."[149]

In the afternoon, I went to the small, quiet prayer chapel in the retreat house, a living room intentionally fashioned into a space for individual meditation. There was a simple altar in front of a gray-turquoise wall, a

Bible, a water feature, two white chairs, thick white carpeting, and room dividers to create a sense of privacy. I started again by asking for the presence of the Spirit, the grace to know Jesus. In the earliest moments of quiet, I began, even in asking for these things, to be seized in the same way that I had the day before when I had asked if I was known. My legs trembled, and it quickly became apparent that I was being led, with an energy and interior movement impossible to describe, to the words of my heart's question, but with the tone transformed from an honest question to a slow but steady declaration: *Jesus. Is. Lord.* There was unexpected intensity around the name *Jesus*, which may have startled me into stepping out of this particular prayer. "Well," I seem to have thought, "I'm going to move onto the assignment now." So, I opened my eyes and moved into my gospel reading, but instead of finding academic relief, I found I wasn't even able to make it through a single reading of the passage without being seized with trembling when I came to the part where Jesus first speaks, saying, "Who touched me?"

These words, this moment in the story, brought the most intensity of all: it was as if I was being asked, quite personally, with great power and intensity, to answer the question, to fess up. My trembling body seemed to be a confession in and of itself:

Who touched me?

Me, okay, me!

I paused, settled, and continued reading. But the trembling came again when Jesus said, "Someone touched me." And, as I came to the words, "When the woman realized that she could not remain hidden," I again felt a truth opening up in me with stark clarity: Jesus somehow sees me reaching out. I cannot hide and merely touch his hem. With this realization, as I continued to feel the Spirit's presence (a Spirit I knew as a sign of holy power, yes, but also, on some level, love), I moved my body to a posture I had never taken. Like the woman in the passage, I moved before the altar and genuflected, placing my forehead and hands onto the rug with awe, submission, and gratitude. *It is I, Lord.*

Lord.

I stayed there until the energy of the prayer and encounter subsided, and then went back to the armchair. In the manner in which I was more accustomed to praying (that is, offering words to God), I said, "Thank you"—but again felt that I was not really getting to the depths of gratitude I needed to or ought to.

My fundamental understanding or interpretation of this experience (both at that time and for many years afterward) was that the same God who had come close to me with an affirmation of knowledge and love was present in and through the person of Jesus. It was as if an experiential line drawn from God the Creator and God the Holy Spirit was extended to the person of Jesus, even as that movement made no rational sense to me. Trying to name more particularly the grace I had been seeking, I said that day that it was "to experience the Spirit of God *through* Jesus, or to experience the Spirit of God *in* Jesus."

I don't think that's actually what I had wanted when I sat down to pray. I was just sincerely and desperately grasping, reaching out, for this mysterious and intimidating figure at the center of my faith tradition, wondering if there really was something of God there, like millions of people seemed to believe, or if I should just be honest with everyone (including myself) and convert to Judaism. But those words describe the grace I received: the Spirit of God, which I trusted, aligning itself, speaking through, deeply *in* the words of Jesus, and moving me to acknowledge not only with my lips but also with my whole body that Jesus is Lord. "I don't understand," I wrote, "but I know the Spirit was in those words of Jesus, hitting me with the truth that I had, somehow, touched Jesus…which doesn't make sense." On this day, at least, I was content to receive the gift and leave sense-making aside, acknowledging that the entire encounter wouldn't have made any sense just three days before.

JESUS HEALS AT SUNSET

As the sun was setting, all those caring for any who were sick with various kinds of diseases brought them to him, and he laid his hands on each of them and cured them.[150]

In the evening, I entered my third imaginative Ignatian prayer session of the day with apparent simplicity, asking again for the Spirit's help and the grace to see and know Jesus. Probably because the retreat center where I was staying was a short walk from Sunset Cliffs—a scenic area of San Diego's coastline described well by its name—when I tried to enter this passage, I imagined Jesus sitting on some rocks with the sun setting in the background. In my notes, I describe a movement that is now familiar to me in Ignatian prayer: the way in which one initially enters the scene, often most "logically," most connected to the limits of the text and most removed from the spotlight, will morph into an image or experience that is more truthful and personal. So, in this case, I first imagined taking my sister (who was struggling with her mental health at the time) down to where Jesus sat in order to be healed, but this picture quickly faded.

To my surprise, a new image emerged of all my friends who had been praying for me—my husband, my running partner, a priest mentor, and an old college friend were most prominent—leading me forward to Jesus. He looked up and asked what healing I needed. I said my own pride, my inability to see and respond, my inability to even see what I actually needed. And then, in my mind's eye, I knelt down before him, looking at his feet and his sandals, and he laid his hands on me and said, *Ok, you can go* (or something like that, something that seemed lacking in drama or import). I then asked if I could simply watch from a distance for a while. He must have said yes, but I don't remember this.

After some time, I approached again and said I wanted to ask one more thing: Could I lead people to him? And he said, *Not yet, but you will.* And I clarified, like the sometimes annoyingly persistent student that I am: *Should I pursue becoming a priest?* And he laughed and said an almost begrudging *yes*, but with this implicit warning: Be patient. Remember, you have a long way to go; remember, this is just the beginning, just a start. And then I heard, more distinctly, *Go on; you are well-loved.* It was both a dismissal and a benediction, and, in the wake of it, I smelled something sweet, like lilies or paperwhites, and I knew in a different way that it was true, that I was well-loved and surrounded by much goodness. The prayer wound down from there, and from the notes I made about the experience in my journal, it is obvious that I was intrigued by, but somewhat uncomfortable with, this method of imaginative engagement. "I'm still not sure how I feel about this way of praying the gospel," I wrote, "but I will try to trust the Spirit and try to be discerning." I took comfort in the evident truth of the words offered by Jesus or my subconscious (I couldn't say which, but I could no longer dismiss the possibility of Christ's involvement in my subconscious): *Be patient. Remember, this is just a start.*

Thursday, January 14

The next morning, in the last hours of my retreat, I asked in prayer to know or hear what was most important of all that I had experienced in the silence. I asked and asked, and I tried to clear space, interiorly, for a response, but it took time. It took another reminder to be truly open-handed, another reminder that God cannot be bossed around, that God is not a spiritual candy machine, dispensing answers on our demand. So, I waited and almost gave up, but then a slight trembling came upon me, only enough so that I knew I couldn't have conjured it, and I sensed the affirmation *You are loved.*

Here I am once again embarrassed by my recollections, but I trust the truth of my greed to be more instructive than false gratitude. I remember feeling almost disappointed. It still seemed so simple to me—too simple to be the most important thing I might know from God. I had heard it said so many times in church and in my life without really *hearing* it or believing it. But, and so, the words persisted: *You are loved.*

I asked, "What then shall I do?" (As an aside: I used to think this was a stereotypical Protestant question, a typical American question, obsessed with action, but I now think it is an honest and eternal question asked by human beings who have had a brush with the divine presence. How should I respond? It is what the people said to John the Baptist on the banks of the river Jordan, when they seemed to have seen the less-than-flattering truth about their lives not matching up to God's ways: "What then shall we do?"[151]) In time, in my prayer, the thought that came was, *Keep listening—this will be hard enough for you.* It was almost a joke, or at least I heard and received it with a laugh, for it was piercingly true and funny enough. I think the second part might even have emerged from my questioning, my dissatisfaction with the first part of the answer: *Keep listening.* There was an unarticulated subtext to it, too: we *both* know this will be hard enough for you.

That's all, God? Just like knowing I was loved, it seemed too easy. That's all you want from me? I know I can do more! Where's the call to give away my extra shoes and coats and go live among the poor? No. *Keep listening. This will be hard enough for you.* Tellingly, after I had asked for God's help in loving others, receiving love, and listening after I left the retreat, I wrote that I "tried to hang out with Jesus for awhile in my imagination or in prayer, but eventually I got tired, couldn't focus, and gave up." It was as if I were being shown my own weakness. *This will be hard enough.*

Keep listening. You are loved. "That's what I have after four days," I wrote. It wasn't as flippant or ungrateful as it sounds. I was perplexed. God had graciously brought me into a new landscape, into the borderlands with a country I didn't previously know existed, where the reality of God's presence was not a hypothetical abstraction. I didn't know what this meant or how it would actually change my life, and so I pondered even the simplest words with some confusion, even as another part of me was indeed steeped with gratitude and wonder. As the white-haired nun who had gently walked with me on this journey said in our last session before I left the retreat house, "God has been very good to you." She framed my prayer experiences as healing — a healing of the fear that it was all in my head. "The gift that you received," she said, "is a new understanding of God's love for you." She warned me against striving to keep, repeat, or recreate the good graces given, echoing Teresa without my knowing it: "Trying to keep *anything* going is evidence of *our* effort, not letting God." I really heard this, and, in some ways, through my meager and minimal efforts at such meditation, had already learned this truism, said by Teresa in this manner: "No matter how much we practice meditation and try to squeeze or press ourselves, even to tears, we can't produce this water in this way. It is given only to those whom God wills to give it, and often when the soul is not thinking of it at all."[152] I actually may have taken such warnings too seriously, alongside other observations about such spiritual gifts or experiences being fleeting and relatively inconsequential compared to the actual good work of seeking justice and love in the world. I forgot and neglected the good sister's final word of advice to me. "Tend the graces that you have been given," she said. Be still and know that God is with you. Ask for the grace you desire. Pray and listen!

She invited me to reflect on John 1:35–51, a passage filled with questions about discipleship, Jesus' identity, our ambiguous seeking, our identity in Jesus' eyes, what Jesus knows of us, and what we might say about him:

> The next day John [the Baptist] again was standing with two of his disciples, and as he watched Jesus walk by he exclaimed, "Look, here is the Lamb of God!" The two disciples heard him say this, and they followed Jesus. When Jesus turned and saw them following, he said to them, *"What are you looking for?"* They said to him, "Rabbi" (which translated means Teacher), "where are you staying?" He said to them, *"Come and see."* They came and saw where he was staying, and they remained with him that day. It was about four o'clock in the afternoon. One of the two who heard John speak and followed him was Andrew, Simon Peter's brother. He first found his brother Simon and said to him, "We have found the Messiah" (which is translated Anointed). He brought Simon to Jesus, who looked at him and said, *"You are Simon son of John. You are to be called Cephas"* (which is translated Peter).
>
> The next day Jesus decided to go to Galilee. He found Philip and said to him, *"Follow me."* Now Philip was from Bethsaida, the city of Andrew and Peter. Philip found Nathanael and said to him, "We have found him about whom Moses in the Law and also the Prophets wrote, Jesus son of Joseph from Nazareth." Nathanael said to him, "Can anything good come out of Nazareth?" Philip said to him, "Come and see." When Jesus saw Nathanael coming toward him, he said of him, *"Here is truly an Israelite in whom there is no deceit!"* Nathanael asked him, "Where did you get to know me?" Jesus answered, *"I saw you under the fig tree before Philip called you."* Nathanael replied, "Rabbi, you are the Son of God! You are the King of Israel!" Jesus answered, *"Do you believe because I told you that I saw you under the fig tree? You will see greater things than these."* And he said to him, *"Very truly, I tell you, you will see heaven*

opened and the angels of God ascending and descending upon the Son of Man." (emphasis added)

The truth is, I did not ponder this passage, not in the way that she prompted me to. I largely neglected the disciplines of personal prayer for the next three years. But, in retrospect, I *did* ponder it in my own way, through the inquiries of a seminary education and in the context of community prayer. Teresa writes:

> The will certainly *seems* to be united in some way with God's will, but it's the effects of this prayer—the actions following it—that test the genuineness of the experience. There's no better crucible for testing prayer. It's a great gift from God if the person receiving the gift recognizes it, and a *very* great one if he doesn't turn back.[153]

I did recognize the goodness of the gifts God had given me on this four-day retreat, but what did I do with them? Did I turn back? I have thought about this a lot, and, in the end, I think I was faithful (or responsive) in some important ways (exploring the vast implications of the gifts given with the help of classmates and teachers) and turned back in others (time devoted to personal prayer).

Wrestling with Darkness in Light of Love (or, the Mystery of Suffering)

Toward the end of her section on the fourth dwellings, Teresa notes that with all of her attention focused on the prayer of recollection, she forgot to mention the effects of the prayer of quiet, those spiritual delights that come from God and are received, never caught or grasped. What happens to the souls to whom God gives this kind of prayer? First, she turns to the imagery of "expansion," or "dilation." For her, such expansion of the soul is best understood with this image: "As if the water coming from the spring simply cannot spill over and be lost—as if the fountain had a way of making sure that the more freely the water flows, the more space there is to receive it."[154] She tries to point to a gracious and continual expansion that God enables, not one wrought by our own efforts: "It's like this with this kind of prayer. God works many more wonders in the soul, gradually enabling it to retain everything He gives." This can be challenging language for those of us (myself included) who are not accustomed to thinking of one's soul as a distinct entity. It helps me to think of the soul as that aspect of ourselves, always present to varying degrees of vigor and levels of articulation, that is attentive to matters of ultimate concern, that asks such questions as these: Who are we, really? What is this world, this life, really? Who is God? What is God about? What are we to do? What difference do we understand that our actions make, now or in the future? This is not Teresa's definition of a soul. Indeed, as we discussed in "First Dwellings," for her, *soul* often seems synonymous with *person*.

Maybe, with Teresa's help, we can begin to grasp how much of our personhood is really soulful, affected in ways known and unknown to us by how we relate to those ultimate questions. This concept emerges, at least for me, when she turns to practical markers of a soul, a person, who has been given such *gustos*. (Notably, she says that the "Fourth Dwellings" section is long "since it's the one that more souls enter." She indicates that this place of prayer, where "the natural and supernatural are joined," is not so uncommon.[155])

What do we observe in such a soul? How can "this gentle movement and interior expansion" be "seen," to use Teresa's own terminology? In summary: there is a growth in virtues and in freedom, and a decreasing sense of fear, angst, and attachment to worldly satisfactions. The soul also has a decreased fear of trials and self-sacrifice: "His faith is more alive, and he realizes that if he endures challenges and hardships for God's sake, His Majesty will give him the grace to bear them with patience." The soul retains a strong will to do something for God, and Teresa is confident that this soul will continue to grow if he doesn't "[return] to offending God." She clarifies that all these changes will not be sustained by God granting such spiritual delights once or twice; the soul—in language that suggests the very person—must persevere in receiving them, "for in this perseverance is all our good."[156] She warns strongly against withdrawing from prayer—a warning based on her own experience of abandoning prayer for a time—which she likens to turning away from the "One whom with great love was desiring to give Himself to them as a friend, and proved it through actions."[157]

Yet, there are other times, in this case directly adjacent, in which Teresa's language suggests that the soul is a distinct entity within the person that is on its own course of development in ways that may be very hidden from assessment through the eyes of the world that look only on the "person." Teresa is especially attentive to this ever-present possibility of incongruence based on her experience of being an esteemed nun and offering cherished spiritual advice at a time when she herself was not praying. And so, in her warning against giving up prayer after one has entered the fourth dwelling place(s), she offers this imagery:

> At this point, the soul is not even weaned but is like a child just beginning to suckle at the breast. If it turns away from its mother, what can be expected but death? That, I'm so very afraid, will be the case for anyone to whom God has given this favor who turns away from prayer. Unless he has an exceptional reason, or returns to it quickly, he will go from bad to worse. I know well that this is a legitimate fear.[158]

I am intrigued by these layered descriptions of change—in the soul and potentially known in and to the person—because, in retrospect, I find them to be helpfully descriptive of what I experienced in the wake of my retreat. My prayers in the fourth dwelling place—the first prayers where God gave me the grace of a *gusto*, where there was some evident mingling of the supernatural with the natural—did lead to my having a greater sense of freedom in serving God, much less angst and fear, and a greater desire to "do something" for this God who had created and loved not just me but this world and all therein. (I'll leave the assessment of growth in virtue to those who have to live and work with me.) But it feels important to communicate that this time of change and growth comprised at least seven years, and (I hope) extends even to the present. There has been nothing precisely linear, nothing tidy, about the "progress of my soul," and yet, like a dotted line in the midst of many marks on a scattergraph, Teresa's descriptions do chart a course, a pattern in the midst of the varied changes of the day-to-day metrics.

And what of Teresa's sobering image of the soul at this point as a spiritual babe in need of much more growth? Well, it seems the obvious intent is encouragement, a warning against self-satisfaction and complacency.

(*Strive onward!* she insists again and again.) But I would like to engage the metaphor a bit more directly. Placing my soul in the midst of the image as best as I can, I see a dynamic Teresa didn't anticipate, and my experience as a pastor, friend, and reader tells me I am not alone.

What if the suckling child, like a wary toddler, does not turn away and leave but also does not steadfastly burrow close to God because the scene all around is far too bewildering to focus on feeding? What if the child stands close, drawing near at times but resisting a full embrace, unable to understand or reconcile the reality of such goodness in the midst of our present darkness, and not wanting to turn her back on those who suffer in it? In *The Interior Castle*, Teresa is not particularly interested in the problems of theodicy (i.e., the quandary of a good and loving God as the Creator of a world that contains so much that is not good, so much that is not loving, so much suffering and death). My entire education—both secular and religious—taught me to be attentive to the suffering of others, so my "interest" in the problems of theodicy was nothing new. But to know God's closeness, love, and power in a new way did raise new—or simply more intense—questions. How and why could this world be as it is? I was like the wary toddler, staying close but not fully trusting, not wanting to take her eyes off the world or abandon God, either. I would draw close, and then I would pull back, pointing to the latest injustice or pain that caught my heart or attention. I was not in one continual state. Here, I take comfort that, elsewhere, Teresa teaches that this variation in our souls, in our prayer life, is normal. Constancy is not to be expected: "When someone is continually in a state like this," she writes, "I don't consider them to be spiritually 'safe' at all. I actually don't think it's possible for the Spirit of the Lord to remain in a soul continuously, like this, during our life of exile."[159] Teresa writes of our human condition so simply: as "our life of exile." This perspective came from an entirely different worldview than I had, one that seemed to set life's suffering neatly (but, to me, unsatisfactorily) in place.

For Teresa, our souls are making their way in hostile territory—the world as we know it. I had been schooled in a different understanding: that creation is ultimately good, mirroring the goodness of its Creator. With a revitalized vision of God's goodness and love, I looked on the other side of the mirror, at the created world I inhabited, and wanted to point out every grotesque flaw in the reflection. In some ways, ironically, I had the fervor of a toddler for consistency and perfection, for the graham cracker that is not broken. Of course, it was not crackers that bothered me but broken bodies, broken hearts, broken lives. So much distortion, destruction, decay, and violence. *Our exile* from God's very nature, right here in the very world that God made, and makes. *How? Why?*

It was the fall season on the Cumberland plateau in southeast Tennessee, where my husband and I had moved to attend seminary in preparation for ordained ministry in the Episcopal Church. Autumn is a time of such beauty there that visitors come from Nashville and Chattanooga to enjoy the changing colors, to hike and drink coffee on cool mornings. I was in the last trimester of my first pregnancy, gratefully in good health and awaiting this child's arrival with joyful anticipation. My mother had once told me that there was nothing like being pregnant to make one fall in love with the world all over again, and I remembered her words with some chagrin: this was not quite my experience. Although I was grateful and excited, I was also deeply troubled by the darkness and death and suffering that pierces even our best days on this earth. I walked every day among the trees and saw beauty, yes, but also what seemed to me a disproportionate number of maimed, dead, bloodied squirrels on the roads, lifeless at my feet after brushes with cars whose drivers likely didn't even know they had killed. I could not ignore them, could not glance away. They seemed like a symbol of all senseless suffering, the sort that I had never shied away from but had also never felt so keenly to be in tension with the reality of God's love.

Every life has its own list of grievances, its own share of suffering, and even if your own portion is relatively modest, to be awake to the world is to be a witness to the absence of goodness in countless situations, each day. I have nothing to add to the litanies of atheists and agnostics who count the toll of senseless suffering, weigh it against God's goodness, and declare God's defeat or irrelevance. Although this has never been my position, exactly, I am very sympathetic toward those who want to keep suffering before our eyes for the sake of integrity and compassion. A great teacher on children's spirituality, Gertrude Mueller Nelson, says that a scene, story, or account (e.g., a nativity) has crossed into sentimentality when you cannot imagine the reality of "shit" as part of it, when there is no place or even *possibility* for the offensive odor of natural waste. It is a great temptation in religious teaching, especially (but not limited to) teaching aimed at children, and should be avoided at all costs. A sentimental version of Christianity is fundamentally false to our own story, which could defensibly be said to *center* on the experience of senseless human violence, broken bodies, and broken hearts (see: Jesus' death and resurrection). This was all clear to me, and so my wariness toward God, the tension I felt between God's goodness and the faults of God's creation, was not a move from "sentimental faith" to "realistic faith"—it felt more like a probing of the manure that I already knew full well was part of the picture. How could it still be here? Why?

In addition to pondering the squirrels, I spent the next three years wrestling with these questions in different ways: Approaching the microphone after a lecture by a visiting bishop to ask a variation on that ancient Jewish question "If Jesus is the Messiah, where is the peace, the *shalom*?" Writing almost all of my Old Testament research papers on Job, *particularly* the section where the author points not just to Job's suffering but also to the suffering of the world. ("Does God's answer to Job satisfy you?" my professor astutely asked at the end of her comments.) Driving another bishop to the airport, one who spent a significant portion of his life in Haiti, I pounced, "How do you maintain trust in the goodness of God in places where people are dying unnecessarily from lack of water or food?" He was gentle, thoughtful, quiet. "I can't explain it," he said. "I can only say that it is those people, my friends in Haiti themselves, who will be the first to say, *Le bondieu est bon*. 'God is good.' This is what they say, in the midst of their suffering. The earth shakes, and the rich people take more than they need while children starve, and all of that is bad. But God? God is good."

I continued to press in to the questions with earnestness but also with hubris and futility. As the "common" but searing pain spread through and from my sister's fractured marriage, in my spiritual direction with a retired theology professor, my interest was almost exclusively focused on the topic of theodicy. "I understand the necessity and logic of free will for the possibility of real love," I remember saying, "but why did God create a world in which the boundaries are so broad, in which the pain wrought can be so deep, almost unfathomable?" I wanted a safer world, a less painful world, a world with metaphorical childproofing for the inevitable destructions that human beings would inflict on one another and the planet. "Some wise people say that the Good Friday liturgy is the only answer we have," he said. I paid close attention to the Good Friday liturgy that year, praying for enlightenment about why God would make a world that would need the extraordinary gift of God's presence to us in the first place, especially if we were such wretched creatures as to kill God when he came to visit, which surely could be anticipated. Looking for satisfaction in a two-hour church service, I found none.

In June 2015, in the wake of the Charleston church shootings, when a white gunman killed nine black women and men after they had invited him into their Bible study, I was finally enraged enough, passionate enough, to cry out to God and ask—really ask, as the psalmists do—"Where the hell were you when this happened, God?" In response: *I was there.* God's words were present to me with a clarity and power rare for my prayer life during those days. *Receiving each one into my arms with loving care.* God's goodness in the midst of evil. No answer—then or now—about *why* the deranged perceptions, the guns, the stupidity and hatred might exist in the first place. I do not find any theological explanation I've yet encountered satisfactory. I no longer expect to, though I will keep reading the theories, ever searching. I now expect to spend many more such days of my lifetime in prayer, raging at God with a longing for things to be different, with incomprehension and frustration. But the frustration, tension, and confusion are no longer daily by my side and on my mind; they do not cloud the air every time I think of God, as they once did.

In the years since the *gustos* of Teresa's fourth dwellings began to strengthen my trust in God's love, the intensity of my fixation with the problem of evil has diminished. I suppose, to return to the image of the wary toddler, we are very capable of growing accustomed to jarring juxtapositions if we live with them long enough. That does not mean there cannot be, will not be, bewildering new wounds or scenes that again lead to deep disorientation with God and the world. But I have learned to live with the mystery of suffering, even as the faith I proclaim invites me to reiterate again and again that God's ways are known by love, justice, wholeness, and beauty.

I am still intrigued by Teresa's theology that we are living in a state of exile (and it is not hers alone), but it does not yet satisfy. In the end, I point to three voices who have given me some semblance of rest from my wrestling; they are authors who articulate my own experience in this search for suffering's meaning. The first is Marilynne Robinson, whose intellect I perhaps admire most among the living. She says that there are two areas that simply seem beyond the reach of human understanding, despite all our trying, and those two areas are the problem of suffering and the question of free will versus predestination.[160] I find her candor—and humility—liberating. If humanity, collectively, hasn't been able to figure this out over the ages, why do I think I will be able to?

The second is Francis Spufford, who describes the reality of emotional resolution without rational resolution. He is both matter-of-fact and brilliant in naming the dynamic I experienced: first a brush or few with God's love, then an intensified wrestling with the problem of evil, and then its eventual, inexplicable diminishment, even as the love and the suffering both remain.

> How do we resolve the contradiction between cruel world and loving God? The short answer is that we don't. We don't even try to, mostly…. The question of suffering proves to be one of those questions which is replaced by other questions, rather than being answered…. We take the cruelties of the world as a given, as the known and familiar data of experience, and instead of anguishing about why the world is as it is, we look for comfort in coping with it as it is. We don't ask for a creator who can explain Himself. We ask for a friend in time of grief, a true judge in time of perplexity, a wider hope than we can manage in time of despair. If your child is dying, there is no reason that can ease your sorrow…. The only comfort that can do anything—and probably the most it can do is help you to endure, or if you cannot endure to fail and fold without wholly hating yourself—is the comfort of feeling yourself loved.

Given the cruel world, it's the love song we need, to help us bear what we must; and, if we can, to go on loving.

We don't forget, mind. It doesn't escape us that there seems to be something wrong with any picture in which God's in His heaven and all's well with the world.... The impasse is still there. It's just that we're not in the jaws of it. We're not being actively gripped and chewed by it. Our feelings have moved on elsewhere. Because there is a long answer, too, to the question of suffering; a specifically Christian perception of what God is, which helps us move on.[161]

Finally, there is the author of Job, who brings to our attention the ways we might imagine the Lord of the universe, the Maker of heaven and earth and all the cosmos, actually responding to our charges that the world has not been well made:

> Who is this that darkens counsel by words without knowledge?
> Gird up your loins like a man,
>   I will question you, and you shall declare to me.
> Where were you when I laid the foundation of the earth?
>   Tell me, if you have understanding.
> Who determined its measurements—surely you know!
>   Or who stretched the line upon it?
> On what were its bases sunk,
>   or who laid its cornerstone,
> when the morning stars sang together,
>   and all the heavenly beings shouted for joy?...

  . . .

Then Job answered the LORD:

> "See, I am of small account; what shall I answer you?
>   I lay my hand on my mouth."[162]

There is no reasoning your way into satisfaction with these words, with this image of humility, this image of the vast knowledge and capacity gap between us and the One who is the source of all things. But there is truth in the image, and unexpected freedom in acknowledging that a small account is all we shall ever be, no matter how much we question God.

To Be Called (or, the Mystery of Providence)

> To rise to the dwelling places you'd like to find yourself in, the import-
> ant thing is not to think much but to love much. Do whatever most
> stirs and awakens you to love. Yet maybe we don't know what love
> is. Learning this wouldn't surprise me because love is not found in
> the greatest pleasure or happiness but in the greatest determination
> to please God in everything, and to try in every way possible not to
> offend Him, and to pray that He advances the honor and glory of His
> Son and the Church. These are the signs of love; don't imagine that
> the most important thing is to never think of anything else (and that
> if your mind gets slightly distracted, all is lost!).[163]

By the summer of 2015, I had been out of seminary for two years, working as an associate priest for formation (often known as "Christian Education") at a large Episcopal church in San Diego. My husband also worked there, with a different program emphasis. In our years since ordina-tion, we had welcomed our second child, a chubby-cheeked son with a truly sweet heart, and enjoyed (despite typical frustrations, like sleep depriva-tion) the busy fullness of lives marked by good health, two young children, economic security, meaningful work, and supportive friends and family. Those first years had a certain settled and contented quality to them. I was grateful to be living and working where we were, with doting grandparents for our children enriching our days and a familiar, large church institution allowing us to be one relatively slight part of a large team rather than carry-ing the weight of pastoral ministry on our newly ordained shoulders.

That summer, however, we began to feel the agitation of desire pulling us out of the nest at St. Paul's. Like many such seismic shifts, there were various sources of this pull, but, in time, I would recognize that the most significant strand in my heart was the longing for a home, a place where I could put down the proverbial roots and raise my no-longer-hypothetical children. A place where Colin and I could settle into a church and com-munity for a long time, in Wendell Berry fashion, and witness the rare but beautiful fruits of such countercultural fidelity. From the summer through the fall, I was invigorated by the energy of that desire and its particular vision and scent—all fresh water and pine trees and gray mornings and sun-soaked summer days: Oregon.

Ever since we had driven east out of the state nearly a decade earlier as newlyweds, with me weeping in the passenger seat as we passed through the golden wheat fields of August, I had carried a not-so-secret hope of returning, like a guiding star I carried in my pocket, waiting for its day to lead the way back home. I knew its day would come. As my children grew, and I felt the weight of my mother's absence, it began to burn. I felt its weight, the ways in which its weight was related to the weight of my mother, how she had intentionally given me this star, both beautiful and heavy. Not everyone is given a sense of deep belonging to the land where they live, the land where their ancestors made their way, the land where they now make their own way, but my mother gave her children such a sense of place. Mom was an enthusiast of Oregon's natural history—explaining to us the formation of rock structures on the Columbia George, guiding us through parks and wonders in every corner of the state—and of our familial heritage there. "You're a fifth generation Oregonian!" she would remind me as we visited the grave of our great-great-great-uncle. By the time I was in my early twenties, even after having gone away for college, I felt that the land did not belong to me, was not "mine" or "my home," but went deeper than this typical articulation. It was the other way around: I belonged to this land. I dreamed of sharing this heritage and my mother's passions with my kids in quotidian ways.

I remember one hot October night in San Diego when I was restless with this longing. I wandered over to the bookshelves in our bedroom, rarely visited by me any longer with a one-year-old and four-year-old underfoot, and I took out my mother's copy of The Prophet by Khalil Gibran. I lost my breath as I came upon these words from the introduction: "Now your ship has come," he writes, "and you must needs go. Deep is your longing for the land of your memories, and the dwelling-place of your greater desires."[164] I felt myself under the eye of God; I felt my desire named and seen, though I did not know what it meant.

Colin and I applied to churches in Oregon. One church was in a location where I might have walked the same leafy sidewalks my mother walked with her own mother on the way to school, where I might have preached in the same space where she once sang as a Christmas angel. We were turned down by this place that would have most closely cleaved our lives to my mother's past. I felt a holy and unexpected sense of peace about it, and I did not know what it meant. Then, out of the blue, we got a call from a church in Washington, DC, the church that had been the seedbed of our own vocations in the Episcopal Church: Would we consider applying to lead there? We loved that church, and we had loved our time in that city, but DC was *way* outside the targeted homeland region. Yet it was an obvious fit for our deepest convictions about the way we were meant to live as Christians: a multicultural community committed to social justice. We decided to apply, though, again, we did not know what it meant. Over Thanksgiving, my brother and father warned me about another town in Oregon we were considering, and after discovering more red flags about the church there in the interview process, we withdrew from consideration. Once more, we did not know what it meant to reject, for somewhat fuzzy reasons, a possibility that might have carried me home. In our searching, like so many searchers before, we were disoriented but also attentive. What did it all signify? Where were we heading? Where would we land?

In the midst of this earnest muddling, God once again entered my prayer with a *gusto* full of power but initially short on delight. It was the church season of Advent, the time of preparation for Christmas. On the rainy afternoon of Friday, December 11, 2015, I went to pray in the children's chapel on the third floor of the church building, and I used the following text for my meditation, a text I planned to preach about on Sunday. (In the end, my sermon would have nothing to do with this time of prayer.) I decided to enter the text with the intention of *lectio divina*, listening for which words struck my heart and then meditating and engaging with God from that initial place of insight.

John [the Baptist] said to the crowds coming out to be baptized by him, "You brood of vipers! Who warned you to flee from the coming wrath? Therefore, bear fruits worthy of repentance, and do not begin to say to yourselves, 'We have Abraham as our ancestor,' for I tell you, God is able from these stones to raise up children to Abraham. Even now the ax is lying at the root of the trees; therefore every tree that does not bear good fruit will be cut down and thrown into the fire."

And the crowds asked him, "What, then, should we do?" In reply he said to them, "Whoever has two coats must share with anyone who has none, and whoever has food must do likewise." Even tax collectors came to be baptized, and they asked him, "Teacher, what should we do?" He said to them, "Collect no more than the amount prescribed for you." Soldiers also asked him, "And we, what should we do?" He said to them, "Do not extort money from anyone by threats or false accusation, and be satisfied with your wages."[165]

I sat with those words that echo three times in the passage: "What should we do?" *What should I do?* I felt, I knew, that I had asked this question so often in my life of trying to be a Christian. Maybe I complained, in some inarticulate way. This old question, *again?* In an indirect way, perhaps now what I would call a part of the mystery of recollection, I sensed God's presence responding with affirmation, truth, and humor to my thought of "I've asked this question so often!" *Don't I know it*, God seemed to sigh.

In response, I felt drawn into a space of reflection about what I really was (and was not) doing in my life, and in time I felt led to confess to God that the fruits of my life, my labors, my days, were unsatisfying to me, and, I suspect, to God. Again, I had a sense that "God knows"—less humorous this time, but still not a harsh judgment, just a seeing. I dug deeper into the heart of this dissatisfaction and named, confessed, that I was too drawn to middle-class comforts; I saw the image of the fruits of my life as small and bourgeois and insignificant. There was no response from God then that I could discern; I was left with only a sense of how true this feeling was for me. We are called to "bear fruit," and I did not feel barren, but I did feel that I was offering up light plastic fruits that were not particularly wonderful in my sight or God's. There was release, freedom, as I named this truth, the kind I had felt before to be the real gift of confession. And then I was moved in a new way, with a new depth and vigor, to the same old question: "What would you have me do?"

I waited uncertainly in the silence. I doubted if I would hear; I wasn't sure I wanted to hear. Yet, at this point, I was sitting with the now somewhat familiar sign of the Spirit's presence, a quaking in my legs never predictable or to be taken for granted. So, I waited, trembling, already doubting the answer in some ways because it couldn't ever be so simply received. I felt the question, *Are you ready?* I'm not sure I can honestly say that I was, or even said or felt that I was. But I did not say no, and I waited. After some time, the words seemed to come very slowly: *Saint Stephen and the Incarnation*—the full name of the church in Washington, DC.

Immediately, I registered my resistance, my protesting questions: What about Santa Barbara? What about Portland? What about my joys and desires? I thought you had affirmed them! I pressed back in this way and in others; it was a struggle, and I was increasingly seized, physically, by the energy of that with which I struggled. I became scared and began to doubt this energy, this Spirit. Was it the same Spirit of Christ I had known before? Or a demon? And so, I said the Jesus prayer many times, flailing for safety in a space of exposure: "Lord Jesus Christ, have mercy on me, a sinner. Lord Jesus Christ, have mercy on me, a sinner." Still the Spirit was there, pressing upon me with the words *Saint Stephen's and the Incarnation*. Finally, no longer doubting the words or the presence, I responded with my own truth: "I don't want to go." This cry became piercing. "I don't want to go!" And then it seemed that God said, *I know.* But immediately following this briefest respite of reassurance, of hearing, there was an indescribable intensity that had my heart pounding and turned my face to the sky and exposed my neck, and I heard the clearest words with the greatest force of the encounter: *THIS IS YOUR PRUNING.*

It was as if God had me by the collar, and yet, at this point, I was no longer scared in the way I had been; I was suspended in awe. I whispered aloud, "Okay. Okay." There was some residual conversation, internally, that I no longer remember, but in the midst of this, the rain began to pick up, and soon it was beating against the windows. I tried to ignore it as I continued to register my displeasure with this news, and new words replaced the name of the church as the Spirit's refrain: *You will be fed. You will be fed.* Underneath those words: Do not worry. Do not be afraid. You will have all you need to live. Finally, the rain became so insistent that I opened my eyes to see this unusual downpour, and as soon as I saw the sheets of water running down the red-trimmed windows, I thought of the waters of baptism, the essence I proclaim for my own life and others: you must die to rise to new life. I felt Oregon washing away, and along with it all the dreams I held for my family there. I began to cry and to pray in a different way, with the final quiet questions of one who has already accepted a new truth. I don't want to leave my big brother or my baby sister. And what about our children? "What about the children?" There was no response anymore, not really, but a quiet sense of peace, a sense that it would be all right in this regard. *You will be fed.*

I ended my prayer session with prostration, a posture I had not taken since my silent retreat almost six years earlier. I walked downstairs to my office and typed an email to myself entitled "Prayer Notes" because I did not keep a journal at that time. At the end of the email, I wrote, "I am shaken, and still plagued by some doubt, but also in awe and gratitude." I sent the email to myself and then glanced at my inbox. An email from St. Stephen's and the Incarnation had just come in. It was the latest edition of their monthly newsletter, and it was entitled "Bread."

It's the effects of this prayer—the actions following it—that test the genuineness of the experience. There's no better crucible for testing prayer.[166]

We did not go to St. Stephen's and the Incarnation. Well, we *went*—to visit, to interview as finalists—but my husband and I withdrew from that candidacy, too, about two months after that rainy December morning. What happened? The surface-level facts don't look good (what kind of arrogant fool disregards such a powerful and seemingly rare directive?), but underneath the surface, in what Teresa would call the dwelling place of my soul, it was a time of wonder and expansion. Although it might *seem* that I failed Teresa's wonderfully pragmatic litmus test, I know that the pronouncement of pruning I received is among the most valuable hours of prayer in my life. Because of its intensity and clarity, I really did let Oregon go. The guiding star in my life shifted from returning to the homeland—my dream—to serving and loving God and people in whatever circumstances would best facilitate my participation in the work of the kingdom—which is sometimes called "God's dream." I sat in church a week later and heard the gospel from Matthew 19 read in a way that pierced my heart with its reminder of the radical allegiance I was called to: "Everyone who has left houses or brothers or sisters or father or mother or children or farms for My name's sake, will receive many times as much, and will inherit eternal life."[167] First, it seemed to be St. Stephen's I was called to for Christ's sake; then another gospel-oriented path emerged.

Don't assume that my pious language means this transition was easy and sweet. Indeed, there was nothing facile about this reconversion. The release of my hopes for returning home, held close for ten years, was painful and prolonged. I could not speak of the place for six months without crying, no matter how hard I tried. My husband was understandably dubious that I really did not need or want to go to Oregon every time my eyes welled up: "Are you *sure* you're okay?" "Yes," I'd say. "Just grieving." It's a loss I feel still; I probably always will feel it, as with other deaths in my life. Yet I also felt a sense of adventure and freedom that seems counterintuitive from the world's perspective. With growing trust and attentiveness to God's invitations, a reorientation of my longing toward working with and for the One who knows and loves me better than any other, and a renewed pursuit of a place where our meager efforts to increase justice and love in the world might be best strengthened and sustained, the possibilities for a faithful response to "What should I do?" expanded.

I don't really know how to explain this part tidily. On one very ancient and broad level, it seems obvious that the ways that our actions and choices intersect with "God's will" is a very complex reality (indeed, one might note that it comprises a goodly chunk of anything that has been written about God and human experience since we first developed the capacity to write). Yet I seem to have come of age in a time when that ground of conversation has, in some way, split. One path of the conversation talks about God's will in a way that implies a certain simplicity and straightforwardness: God has a plan; it's part of God's plan or it isn't. The other path only has language for human agency and desire; even in a religious context, this rhetorical space has no place for God's desires, God's will, in a way that moves outside opaque abstraction (God only wants justice and peace). Neither is adequate.

I want to return to the broader place where there is the shared understanding of a dance between divine and human action that is enveloped in holy mystery but also punctuated with moments of insight and understanding. It is rather ridiculous, but I suppose I am trying to admit that I cannot explain divine providence and the way it intersects with free will, even in a simple story of a church call. But the points of insight, change, and surprise in this "simple story" still affect my perception of what it means to "follow God's will." There is meaning, there are points of energizing coherency, even in this tired old theological space where I keep very good company in admitting the obvious: it is inexplicable.

Here's what happened, though, from my small and narrow vantage point.

Colin and I visited St. Stephen's in early January with a very heavy sense that this was where God wanted us to go. In different ways, but to the same end, Colin had been convicted that the church was the right fit due to elements of its identity and work that were not simply surface level "matches" but core aspects of vocation: a multicultural community committed to reconciliation, Hispanic and Latino ministry, and a desire to translate the gospel in an urban neighborhood to young professionals, like us, who had no interest in church or Christianity as they had known it. For me, the days in DC were full of small signs that inspired awe in the truest sense, for it was tinged with fear. We walked through the neighborhood of Mt. Pleasant, and I stopped short in front of a sign that proclaimed it "a village in the city." On the plane ride there, I had talked with Colin at length about how I always thought I was suited to be a village priest, not a city priest. What was God doing?

On our first night of evening prayer, the meditation was on Jesus' obedience and our call to obedience (a rare theme in the Episcopal Church, as its greatest fans and detractors would tell you), and I felt God's eye on me. Would I obey? And then, alone in the church, I stepped behind the altar where the priest says the prayers of thanksgiving for Communion. I held out my hands in the *orans* position, as one does when saying prayers on behalf of the community, and I suddenly heard a quiet *yes* within me, repeating and sounding with every beat of my heart. *Yes. Yes. Yes. Yes.* I stepped back and put my arms down, alarmed. *Enough,* I said back with my body language. I get it.

Yet I was ready to obey, to go. It felt like the clearest "call" of my life; I could not with any integrity say no. But Colin was still wrestling with what all this meant, and his own desire to stay close to his parents as our children were growing led him to form a new proposal: What if we could do all of this work that felt central to our vocations, which had been reidentified and reaffirmed by St. Stephen's, but we could do it in San Diego, not Washington, DC? And so, on the cross-country plane ride home, he crafted a concept paper and proposal for our church leadership at the diocese in San Diego. It was like a Hail Mary pass thrown to the bishop, a desperate and wild attempt at staying close to family while still doing the work we both realized we needed to do. What if we could lead a multicultural, multilingual ministry with an emphasis on justice, relationship, and reconciliation just two miles from our house, at St. Luke's in North Park? It was not a short throw, but a true long shot: we were asking not just for a leap of faith but also for a lot of financial support to revitalize a congregation primarily made up of poor and working-class immigrants and refugees. I remember reviewing and editing the proposal with both interest and wariness. I didn't say so at the time, but this seemed like Colin's final move in the proverbial wrestle with God. And, who knows? Maybe it was.

Shortly after we returned from our visit to Washington, we met with the bishop to discuss the proposal. In an uninspiring conference room, he wrote some big numbers on the back of an envelope, money he'd help us fundraise, and said yes, let's do this. In other words, he caught the Hail Mary pass. This surprising moment and the hours afterward were dramatic enough; but, for me, the real drama, the real story, was what happened to my eyes and my heart, which were transformed in that institutional meeting in ways unknown to me until I stepped out the door.

I am aware that this sounds melodramatic, but *transformation* is the only word I know for what I experienced: I remember that when I walked out the doors of the diocesan office in Ocean Beach on that cool, sunny day, I saw color and vibrancy in the simple landscaping as never before. It...was...beautiful! Suddenly, everything I saw as I walked and as we drove shone: the deep greens in the palms and the pale blue of the sky and the expanse of the water. I had *never* seen San Diego like this before. For six years, I had nodded politely when people would say, "You live in San Diego? What a beautiful place!" "Tell me about that," I wanted to say. "Tell me what you see." I saw too much sunshine and too few trees; I saw brown hills and concrete and tract houses and too many cars and palm fronds that offered a laughable amount of shade. But now, all of the things people said about San Diego that I didn't understand suddenly made sense. I *saw* it. I saw beauty and life and goodness, the world made new around me.

For the next few days, the beauty had an intensity that was invigorating and elating in its own right. Riding in a gondola across the bay with my children, I laughed out loud, shaking my head at the change—not in the water, not in the skyline, but in me. How could I not have seen this beauty before? The initial elation did not last, of course, but the change in sight was not fleeting. Years later, this place is still beautiful to me. I am just like those enthusiasts I used to find annoying and inscrutable. But I tell newcomers, very earnestly, "Don't worry if you don't love it, if you don't even like it. It took six years and an act of God for me to fall in love with San Diego, for the scales to fall from my eyes like Saul's." I'm not sure they are comforted.

Almost immediately, my experience of the prayer of pruning became integrated into my interpretation of what had happened: in a sense, my vision had been obscured by my not-bad-but-inordinate attachment to a future in the Northwest. When I truly let that go by saying yes to the possibility of St. Stephen's, I was freed to see the city where I lived, the city I'd wanted to leave since arriving, in a new light. It was as if God gently but firmly pulled me up from the hook of self-determination for a future oriented around an "ideal life" for me and my children, turned my gaze toward St. Stephen's and the core commitments it represented, and then turned me once more and set me down on the same earth where I had started, but turned completely around. I felt keenly the sense of being *known*: I would not and could not have embraced a new chapter of life in San Diego without the painful but necessary detachment from a vision oriented primarily around family, comfort, and pleasure. And, more to the point, I honestly would not have accepted the challenges of a more entrepreneurial and uncertain ministry at St. Luke's without the intermediary turn to St.

Stephen's. I simply would not have been open to it, or I would have seen only self-sacrifice and self-denial rather than an invitation to a fruitful new life right where I already stood.

On the eve of our decision to pursue St. Luke's and withdraw from St. Stephen's, Colin and I sat and prayed in a way that my spiritual director had suggested, in a way that we've only done a few times in our marriage, always at key points of mutual and necessary decision. In the same vein as the Ignatian meditation on the gospel, it's a prayer practice that employs your imagination and all your senses and asks God to show where Christ is leading you in this decision. You pray for help to see, then pray together in silence. Finally, you share with one another what images or words emerged. That day, as part of our discernment, we had visited St. Luke's, where an elder from Sudan placed her hand on my shoulder as I received Communion. The gesture was unusual, and I remember looking up to see the seemingly stoic face of an older woman; I would later learn that her name was Mama Roda. That evening, in prayer, I recalled that touch, the feeling of the warm hand on my shoulder, and, in my mind's eye, it was now Jesus who touched me, affirming my presence there. *This will be your Jerusalem*, I heard. No need to take up my cross and march across the country, at least this time around.

Almost two years later, I would sit down with Mama Roda over tea and tell her some of this story. I told her that she had mediated Christ for me on that important day in February nearly two years earlier; she probably didn't remember, but I wanted to let her know how she had mysteriously embodied Christ's welcome into St. Luke's for me and my family; how her hand felt like a holy reassurance that Christ traveled with us, invited us, on this adventure. She looked me in the eye across her living room coffee table and nodded. "I remember," she said in Arabic. "I meant it as a blessing. I prayed it would be a blessing."

Mama Roda had lost several children to a brutal civil war. She still worries and prays about one of her daughters, who remains in the Sudan, and one of her sons, who ended up alone in Alberta, Canada, for complicated immigration reasons (her other children are here in the United States). But every word she has ever spoken to me, personally or during a Bible study, reveals her deep trust and deep faith that we are dependably known and loved by God. The strength of this trust fills her life and that of all those in our community who have the privilege of knowing her, with the kind of steady light that changes lives.

T. S. Eliot said, "Teach us to care and not to care."[168] I used to hear this invitation to holy detachment, the kind of detachment that only loves and clings to the most important things, as the province of monks and poets, not common folks with so many things to care for and about. I also used to think of it as a somewhat cold virtue, one I was not sure I wanted or was even "Christian." Yet, in the fourth dwelling places of my soul, God urged necessary detachment in ways I could not ignore. I learned slowly, but I came to see, to trust, a basic element of faith: God knows us and loves us better than we know and love ourselves. Why not hold fast to God, then, and hold everything else (we think would be best) more lightly? As Teresa puts it: "We are His, sisters. May He do with us as He likes and lead us along as He pleases. I'm sure that if any of us achieve *true* humility and detachment, the Lord won't fail to give us this gift [of infused prayer] and many others that we don't even know how to desire. (I say 'true' because it can't be in thought alone. Our thoughts often deceive us; it must be total detachment.)"[169]

I cannot find the small piece of paper where I hastily scribbled down some notes about what happened to me in prayer on February 12, 2016, the Friday after Ash Wednesday, but I have no doubt that it will show up eventually. This battered sheet, which I tore out of my 5.5 x 8.5 steno notebook that I used for work and then tucked away in various books over the next eighteen months, had been both written upon and stored with some ambivalence. The paper would alternately surprise me, comfort me, or disturb me whenever I stumbled upon it during the next year; I obviously didn't care to safeguard its contents or the memory it pointed to. But I would also never throw it away.

It was, it is, a real-time testament to a prayer that my pride might want to forget or deny. Nevertheless, I have not forgotten it. I told only one person—my spiritual director—about it a few weeks later. She said it might be the most important invitation of my life, and I wished she hadn't said that. It seemed likely that I would mess up the response.

At that time, it was my habit to pray up on the third floor of the church campus where I worked. On that Friday, I set the red Ikea chair to face the windows in our children's sanctuary and pulled out the book I was using to prompt prayer and reflection during the pre-Easter season of Lent. It's called *God for Us: Rediscovering the Meaning of Lent and Easter*, and it's filled with beautiful art and well-written meditations by contemporary Christian thinkers: Kathleen Norris, Richard Rohr, Ronald Rolheiser, and others. I'm always much more consistent with this whole "daily reading and prayer" thing at the beginning of Lent than at the end, so it's not so surprising that I was earnestly and somewhat enthusiastically trudging up the stairs to pray. For liturgical Christians intent on self-improvement, the beginning of Lent is like the first few weeks of January: it's a new season! I will be faithful! I will sacrifice! I will draw near to the deep mysteries of God by reading Scripture and praying *every day*.

Yet I was somewhat pressed for time. So, I read the appointed psalm and clipped through the Isaiah passage and the seven verses from the gospel of Matthew that were assigned for that day. Then I turned to Richard Rohr's short reflection essay. "The theme today," he writes, "is clearly fasting itself. Fasting is not something commonly understood, or spiritually practiced in the Western world, so maybe these two readings can give us some good and positive leads. Maybe it is something we can rediscover and recognize that it is much deeper than mere dieting...or any earning of merit." This is bread-and-butter Lenten stuff. But then, Rohr points out that Jesus reframes the question asked him in Matthew's gospel about fasting: "He introduces two lovely new words into the vocabulary, 'wedding guests' and 'bridegroom.'" "Yes, how interesting," I thought. I was still reading as engaged text critic.

But then, as I read the final paragraph, something began to move within me. The words were arresting—entirely, unexpectedly so. I relied on this whole notion of "reading under the eye of God until my heart is struck" for almost all of my personal prayers, but I felt some sense of alarm at the suddenness of this particular striking and the words themselves that were doing the striking. Rohr writes, "In fact, [Jesus] is revealing here his most common metaphor for eternal life or the hereafter. And that metaphor is again and again *a wedding banquet*—at which he himself is God's gracious host or 'groom' and we are the marriage partner. It is daring language, but a worldview that he seems to be entirely comfortable with."[170] I returned to the words that pulled me to them, whispering them with fear: *He himself is God's gracious groom, and we are the marriage partner.* I was not unfamiliar with this metaphor, but it was not one I liked to ponder. I was clearly being asked to meditate upon it now.

I closed my eyes and repeated the words, turning them over and over in my mouth and mind. I was accompanied by the physical trembling that had come to mark an insistent affirmation of the Spirit's presence. In my mind's eye, I saw an image of a black silhouette standing in a small archway, backlit by a yellow-orange sky. The figure was far off, but there was no question who this represented. It was Christ the Bridegroom.

At some point, I began to cry, and I was honest with God: *I don't think I want him as a groom. I do not want to be his wife, whatever that means.* I knew something of what it meant to have a spouse—the intimacy, the closeness—and Jesus did not strike me as a safe partner. He was still too wild-eyed, too scary, for this role. I was comfortable with him as Lord, teacher, boss. I would serve him all of my days in this way. But this groom in the door, this dark silhouette? I wanted him to keep his distance. Do. Not. Approach.

A part of me knew that this was not the right answer; I was not being a trusting and faithful one. I was held in this space for a time, and I made a small, fearful plea: *What do you want me to do?* I had so much fear and uncertainty. And then the most surprising voice came, a voice without sound that made me laugh out loud: *Let me call you.*

It was dating language, piercing my fear with humor. Let *me* call you. Emphasis on *me*, not *call*, not *let*.

In other words, don't fret about responding. Don't worry about responding. *I'll* get back to you. The ball is in my court. When you're ready, let me make the approach from the doorway. I hope you'll let me.

FIFTH DWELLINGS:

BELOVED

"Oh, sisters, how can I ever explain the riches, treasures, and delights found in the fifth dwellings? I think it would be better to say nothing of the dwelling places I haven't yet described because no one can describe them. The intellect is incapable of understanding them, and no comparisons help in explaining them because earthly things are too coarse for this purpose. Send me light from heaven, my Lord, that I might be able to enlighten these your servants—some of whom You are pleased to give these joys to often."[171]

It had been over a year since I had pondered, with fear, the image of Christ the bridegroom standing in a doorway. Life and ministry had roiled on, with certain steady rhythms but also nearly consuming changes: In the summer of 2016, Colin and I moved toward and prepared for new positions in leadership at St. Luke's, a primarily Sudanese-American church in the neighborhood of North Park. In the first week of October, we moved house and also began our work at St. Luke's. We were expected and called to try some new things in this church, to risk doing things differently for the sake of the church's future, even as we cared for the people who were already faithfully present in the pews. It was a season marked by all the intensity and grace and energy of fire, and the ever-present questions about mission, purpose, goals, and strategies (and, more basically, what we should do with our hours, days, and weeks) kept both Colin and me in a posture of desperate attentiveness, constantly seeking discernment. My notebook from those days is scribbled with grand(ious) phrases like this: "Our job— be *cocreators* in heightening the probabilities of redemptive moments of transformation." The question, forever, is *how?*

Each day, we struggled with the how. Yet there was also a lot of normalcy, the steady bread-and-butter work of a parish pastor and contemporary parent: visiting a lovely woman who was slowly dying of cancer, sitting with her in the sun on her front porch; helping our daughter with kindergarten "homework"; reading train books with our locomotive-obsessed two-year-old son; preparing outlines for confirmation classes of teenagers; teaching renewed understanding of the atonement in adult education seminars; cleaning out offices; and wiping toilets and sinks on Sunday mornings as a basic act of hospitality for those who would soon gather to pray in the sanctuary. Honestly, there was nothing notable or dramatic that might provide an adequate explanatory "context" for what happened next in my life of prayer. Similar to the experiences Teresa describes, it arrived as a sheer and surprising gift, like a holy light coming through a worn and peeling plywood door....

Spiritual Union

Teresa begins her writings on the fifth dwelling places with an understandable disclaimer about the inadequacy of any words (including hers) to illuminate these matters, yet she forges on. Her first concern is "how the soul is united to God in prayer" and "how one discerns whether there is any illusion."[172] The entire notion of spiritual union, or being united with God in prayer, can quickly conjure images of spiritual Olympians who achieve this blissful and rare state through years of monastic discipline. Yet, in her treatment of this concept, Teresa continues to place the emphasis on *God's* agency. (This is not to say that our earnest seeking is of no account. Remember? *Strive on!* she implores. But her language discounts any framework that diminishes God's freedom and otherness by implying we can "achieve" union.)

Although this posture aligns naturally with Teresa's language of gifts in prayer, or *gustos*, it seems that union is a particular kind of spiritual delight, almost a subcategory, like the prayer of quiet or even the prayer of recollection. *Union* is a term at once more familiar to and more complicated for most audiences. So: What is union—in *this* part of *The Interior Castle*? (There will be another kind of union later.) How does one know if an experience of God's presence in prayer is "union" or some other gift, or *gusto*? Here I find Teresa's definition, which she seems to have come to late in her life, after much pondering, very liberating. She does not prescribe or delineate the *nature* of the gift of union, which I imagine God can and does give in innumerable ways. What defines union in prayer, its "clear sign,"[173] is simply the certitude that one's soul "was in God, and God was in it." As a point of reference, she says that, in the fourth dwelling places, one remains doubtful it was union, but in the fifth dwelling places, these "little lizards" of doubt and suspicion are shut out, no matter how slender they may be: "Here, our imagination, memory, or intellect can't be an obstacle to the blessings that are given."[174] In her own words, the true sign of union is when this occurs:

> God places Himself in the interior of that soul in such a way that when it returns to itself, it can in no way doubt that it was in God, and God was in it. This truth remains so firmly that even though God may not give this gift again for many years, the soul can't forget or doubt that it was in God, and God was in it. (I'm leaving aside for now the *effects* that stay within the soul, which I'll talk about later).... Afterward, it sees the truth clearly. Not because of a vision but because of a certainty remaining in the soul that only God can put there.... If anyone doesn't have such certainty, I would say that what he has experienced is not union of the whole soul with God but only union of one of the faculties or one of the many other kinds of favors God gives.[175]

Do you see the emphasis on God's action? "God places Himself," "God...[gives] this gift," "a certainty...that only God can put there." It's a fascinating and notable departure from images of union with God that imply the spiritual summit of a strenuously trained soul. Another potential misconception Teresa seems interested in correcting is the assumption that a "vision," or perception of God through our senses (particularly our eyes), somehow ratifies union. No, she says, it is not *seeing* that brings this kind of certainty, though this is often the kind of certainty human beings hunger for when it comes to God's reality or presence. Teresa gets a bit impatient with the discourse of reason as she tries to explain this: "How, you'll ask, can we be so convinced of what we have not seen? I don't know; it's the work of God."[176]

Nevertheless, the kind of union she's describing in the first section of the fifth dwellings (later to be distinguished from "union of conformity to God's will" and the union of marriage) is somehow, in her own words, "delightful," even "delicious."[177] This infused prayer of union is felt, known, appreciated, and loved in a way that she tries to contrast with our delight and love of "vain things," known only through our physical senses. "It's like," she says, "the difference between feeling something on the rough outer covering of the body versus in the very marrow of the bones."[178] She is willing to talk about "feeling something," but it is not in the way that we are accustomed to feeling.

With this topic of union, with language like "It was in God, and God was in it," we are obviously moving into a realm of human experience that some (perhaps many, perhaps most) find simply unbelievable. Both the stolidly traditional religious crowd and the vaguely spiritually seeking crowd are much more comfortable when we are talking about gifts of "infusion," "quiet," "recollection," and the like than when we venture into talk of "union." This is nothing new. From the outset, Teresa addresses our reluctance to believe in the possibility of such a gift, and she does so on the grounds (once again) of God's agency, freedom, and wisdom beyond our understanding in giving such gifts. She writes, "My own opinion is that anyone who doesn't believe that God can do much more than this... has closed the door shut to receiving [such gifts]."[179] It is a subtle rhetorical move, slyly asking those who acknowledge the possibility, reality, and desirability of certain spiritual gifts why they might arbitrarily close the door on others. "[God] has been pleased and sometimes still *is* pleased to give His creatures such gifts," she gently states. Who are we to deny these good gifts? "Sisters," she adds—reminding us that at least some of these doubters are Carmelite nuns!—"never let this be true of you. Instead, trust God more and more."[180]

Teresa offers a wonderful little story that points to the inexplicable, unpredictable, transformative, and lasting nature of the gift of an experience of union in prayer. Speaking of herself in the third person, she writes, "I know someone who was unaware that God was in all things by presence, power, and essence. God gave her a gift of this kind, and it...firmly convinced her of this truth."[181] I love this line alone for its semi-humorous and rightly wild outline: There once was a person who didn't really understand or accept God's omnipresence, but then God changed that. She trusted, forever afterward, that God was in all things. For Teresa, however, the most telling detail of "this woman's" experience came later. So great was her conviction, her certitude, born of God's gift and presence to her "that even when she asked one of those half-learned men...*how* God was in us, and he told her that God was only in us by grace, she did not believe him—because she had the truth so firmly implanted within her."[182]

We might read this account as a quaint story about a sixteenth-century woman who refused to submit to patriarchal authority, but then we would be missing the point. It seems to me that this is the same divine power and presence, communicated in various ways, that has led so many African American women, such as Jarena Lee, Sojourner Truth, Zilpha Elaw, and Rebecca Cox Jackson (nineteenth-century activists and preachers) to proclaim, to know, to fully understand themselves as beloved of God when absolutely *everything* else in their world denied the possibility of such favor in word and deed.[183] The strength, the blessing, is lasting. *The soul can neither forget nor deny God's presence to it.*

The Wine Cellar (or, Forget Your People)

> Take note, daughters: for what we're talking about [union], He would have you hold nothing back. Whether little or great, He will have it all....

> ...For the short time that the condition lasts, the soul is left as though without its senses, unable to think even if it wanted to. There is no need for devising any method for suspending thoughts. Even in loving, if it is able to love, it can't understand how or who it loves, or what it wants.

> Ultimately, it's like one who has died in every respect to the world so that it may live more fully than ever in God. Thus it is a delicious death, an uprooting of the soul...while in the body.[184]

On March 7, 2017, the first Tuesday in Lent, I went into the vesting sacristy to pray, as had become my custom. I sat down in the burgundy wingback chair in the corner of the small yellow room and got out my

Lenten devotional, *God for Us*, to catch up to the day's readings. It's possible I hadn't yet picked up the book during this Lenten season or hadn't looked at it since Ash Wednesday. In a semi-sincere way, I read through the essays by Richard Rohr that corresponded to these days; this kind of "catch-up" reading can be, for me, a procrastination from the actual day's readings, essays, and time in prayer. I took note of the essay for the first Friday in Lent, the one that had so moved me the year before, and it reminded me briefly of this notion of Jesus as the bridegroom, the image of a wedding banquet, but I didn't dwell on it or ponder it much. This time, I felt no sense of being struck by these words or images, and it had been so long since then that I think I even felt a little wistful, as in, "That was my invitation before, but I didn't respond well enough"—or, more basically, "That was that." There was nothing memorable or noteworthy about my emotional state, nothing going on that made me feel particularly open to God or prayerful, or humble or repentant or needy, which had so often been the grounds for my deepest prayer experiences. I was in a state of steadiness, earnestly setting off on my Lenten journey, as I had the year before, with good intentions and a good student's desire to do a bit better this year than the year before (which is always the hope).

So, I finally got to the page for the first Tuesday in Lent, and I thought that, for this day, I should do the Bible readings—and not just cut straight to the essay—so that I could engage more deeply in the essay, and maybe I would do some *lectio divina* with the Scripture passages. For some reason, very unusually, I decided to start with the psalm, the first one listed. Usually, I skip the psalm and move directly to the Hebrew Scripture reading and the gospel lesson. Afterward, this struck me as a relatively blatant example of providence; it spoke to me again of how little we know or see of the ways in which God is moving with us and in us through our days.

On that March morning, this psalm brought a surprise that I, echoing Teresa, could never fully describe. Later that day, when I penned notes about my experience, I felt—and still feel again as I type now—that my efforts to explain it make a pathetic plastic something out of sheer beauty. But I attempt to do so for the sake of those who might be healed in some way by knowing that such wonders do happen, and for those who have experienced such things and might have felt ashamed or alone.

Psalms 45, 47, and 48 were all assigned for that day. I turned the pages to find Psalm 45, and I recognized it immediately as one of the "court psalms." Not my favorite. The feminist in me has so many objections to the objectification of these women presented to kings and princes; I spent many days in seminary chapel wondering about their agency and experience as we read through these psalms in Morning Prayer. Nevertheless, I decided to read the psalm out loud to focus my attention. It begins with these two verses:

> My heart is stirring with a noble song;
> let me recite what I have fashioned for the king;
> > my tongue shall be the pen of a skilled writer.
>
> You are the fairest of men;
> > grace flows from your lips,
> > because God has blessed you for ever.

I read the psalm all the way through, but I did not then go on to the next psalm. Something was changing within me as I read verse two, so much so that I paused and read it twice: "You are the fairest of men;... God has blessed you for ever." I was embarrassed to pause here because the cynic in me finds the words cheesy, un-relatable. But, the truth is, I suddenly heard and felt these words as they pertain to Christ. I began to feel a quickening of energy, attention, focus, and curiosity, and I thought— still detached, still observing—"This is interesting...." And so, I began to follow the thought, the feeling, in a way I never had before. I read through the rest of the verses with openness and attentiveness:

> Strap your sword upon your thigh, O mighty warrior,
> > in your pride and in your majesty.
>
> Ride out and conquer in the cause of truth
> > and for the sake of justice.
>
> Your right hand will show you marvelous things;
> > your arrows are very sharp, O mighty warrior.
>
> The peoples are falling at your feet,
> > and the king's enemies are losing heart.

Your throne, O God, endures for ever and ever,
    a scepter of righteousness is the scepter of your kingdom;
    you love righteousness and hate iniquity.

Therefore God, your God, has anointed you
    with the oil of gladness above your fellows.

All your garments are fragrant with myrrh, aloes, and cassia,
    and the music of strings from ivory palaces makes you glad.[185]

The figure being described here was suddenly, in a way I could not explain, Christ. Christ was unexpectedly, inexplicably real to me and very compelling, very desirable. "Ride out and conquer in the cause of truth and for the sake of justice." The goodness, the justice, of this figure was meeting my own yearning for the cause of truth and the defense of what is right. "A scepter of righteousness is the scepter of your kingdom; you love righteousness and hate iniquity." And yet, this stoked desire for goodness above all goodness comingled with an image of strength and power that was nevertheless beautiful, the garments fragrant with myrrh, aloes, and cassia—scents I probably couldn't identify blind but have enough familiarity with to imagine. "God, your God, has anointed you with the oil of gladness."

Although it was the line my rational and culturally conditioned self was most averse to, most allergic to, I could not deny the phrase that had first struck my heart: "You are the handsomest of men." Following the "rules" of *lectio divina*, I allowed myself to submit and surrender to a meditation that began with that phrase. Unsurprisingly, the parts of my body that were most attuned to experiences of physical union begin to engage: warmth, presence, intensified pulsing—but not in any way I'd previously experienced. Part of me instantly doubted that this was of God, wondered if I were not psychologically cultivating desire in a sort of autoerotic delusion. But almost as quickly as this thought came, it was silenced by a powerful sensation that can only be described as penetration, but one of spaciousness, breath, life, and not encumbered or defined by my own or any other anatomy. It was as real and as present as the breath coming into my lungs, but the expansion and movement was not defined by my breathing. It came in its own timing and intensity as I allowed it to, filling me, inviting me in time to relax, extend my gut, make more room for this presence that

I would define most simply as incredible, inexplicable energy, but it was not so impersonal or foreign. It wasn't "energy"; it was Christ, unseen but present, identified by something in my own soul upon its entry into the room. On a day and in a place and in a way I never could have anticipated, the old sacristy with its fading maroon carpet was suddenly a simple court chamber where I was undeniably and completely consumed by Christ as lover, Christ the bridegroom.

At some point, even in the midst of this encounter, as in my handful of other experiences of God's Spirit being present to me or with me with striking intensity, my first response was, "What do you want from me?"

It was an instinctual response, not a trained one. The sense was this: "What do you want me to *do?*" The subtext: "Okay, you have my attention! What is this divine shaking-by-the-shoulders [metaphorically speaking] *for?*" Although, as previously, such a question might strike some people as hopelessly American, hopelessly Protestant, it was heartfelt, not duty bound. I was grateful and overwhelmed by the holy. In awe and thanksgiving, I glimpsed, even if fleetingly, my willingness to do anything for this God—or at least the most sincere desire to know what he was asking of me.

There was, conspicuously, no answer to this question. Only silence, movement, presence. And some part of me was still grasping at the why, still able to think, and I responded with, "The writing? It must be the writing," alluding to more subtle experiences in prayer when I had felt God inviting me to dedicate more time to writing again. Once more, my query didn't find any traction; there was no resonance, and then it was as if Christ said, within, *Forget that now.* I was reluctant to let it go, but I was also flattered, surprised, overcome. *Really? Okay, then.* That was it, I realized. I didn't know what this was for or about, but I was grateful for this expression of love. So, as the intensity waned, I knelt down and put my face to the ground and simply said thank you, resting in that thanks until I was at peace. Then I returned to the chair, thinking I might just recover there, pray quietly there, but I started to read the psalm again, my attention called and fixed this time to the next portion, verses 11–18:

"Hear, O daughter; consider and listen closely;
    forget your people and your father's house.

The king will have pleasure in your beauty;
　　he is your master; therefore do him honor.

The people of Tyre are here with a gift;
　　the rich among the people seek your favor."

All glorious is the princess as she enters;
　　her gown is cloth-of-gold.

In embroidered apparel she is brought to the king;
　　after her the bridesmaids follow in procession.

With joy and gladness they are brought,
　　and enter into the palace of the king.

"In place of fathers, O king, you shall have sons;
　　you shall make them princes over all the earth.

I will make your name to be remembered
from one generation to another;
　　therefore nations will praise you for ever and ever."

Once again, so much of this imagery was foreign to me and ratio-nally unappealing. But this was not the time or place for historical-critical method and feminist objections to earthly subjection by patriarchal sys-tems. There is a time and a place for those things, certainly. But, at this moment, I was attuned to the words on a different level; they struck my heart and moved me toward this loving presence once more: "Hear, O daughter; consider and listen closely; forget your people and your father's house." I heard in these words a personal invitation to intimacy, to detach more fully from the family systems that had shaped and defined me, to attend to and move forward into, with trust and abandon, Christ's invita-tion to know him, love him, and be loved by him.

"The king will have pleasure in your beauty." I was gently and per-sistently moved into another round of ecstasy, and I allowed and welcomed this movement of power and presence into my body—my intellect still capable, at times, of marveling and doubting and wondering when and if it would all abruptly end. Other times, I was able to simply surrender; as if moving through the mirror image of the early contractions I knew in child-birth, I felt the Spirit's presence to be most potent when I was able to find utter stillness and release. "I will make your name [O Lord] to be remembered from one generation to another." The power was shocking, breathtaking; but, this time, I was not afraid. My awareness of my body gave way to an internal space where all of that feeling was suspended and, in my mind's eye, I was held in a fiery, luminous darkness, subject to, caught up in, and facing a great light that was the source and essence of the divine presence. A gradual release, letting down. Then, once more, I was mindful of my body and of the time. When I looked at the clock, knowing I had a meeting at 10:00 a.m., I heard Christ's voice, in some way, tenderly, knowingly, humorously: *Stay with me a bit longer. I know you have a few minutes.*

In another moment of quiet, overcome and disoriented but also abounding in gratitude and teary with joy, I opened my eyes, looked at the sunlit yellow walls, and heard, *Turn to Teresa. She will guide you.* I remembered the Bernini statue and laughed aloud. "It is time to actually read her work," I thought. Maybe some Sarah Coakley, too, who I vaguely knew talked about *eros* and God, holy desire at the heart of the Trinity.

It is impossible to do justice to the goodness of this gift I received, and I pray for your mercy as a reader in interpretation or judgment. In that moment, I knew it to be a gift, and I have continued to know it ever since, without any intellectual instruction—an unmerited gift, holy and inexplicable. That day, I wrote, "I obviously still do not understand what one is to do with a gift like this. And I know I am not alone in receiving it, not special; and yet...I have been given this gift, which feels beyond my status as a human being."

Now, having read Teresa, I look back and think about the whole Christian story anew, and I conclude that, yes, of course, it is beyond my human status. It absolutely is. This is the heart of the Christian story— that God reaches out to us across lines we thought impassable, that God in Christ "condescends" to love and be in relationship with such simple and humble creatures as ourselves, that God is completely other but is not confined to heaven. What I experienced is so very strange, but in a way that is also familiar to anyone who has listened to other stories about God: On a particular, ordinary day, in a particular, ordinary place, Christ came to me as the lover, the groom, the king I didn't even know or think I longed for. I didn't know why. But I also felt the Spirit in the short prayer from the Lenten devotional I read that day after concluding the essay and daily devotion that had gently led me into this unforeseen place. I think I picked up the book again as a means of trying to ground myself in something more ordinary, more familiar, but this is what I found. It spoke directly to my heart in the wake of a gift I really didn't know how to receive:

> You alone are good, you alone are sacred and holy, loving God,
>
> yet you have chosen to invite us into this promised land, into this household of God,
>
> into the temple that is your body, where we are not yet fully at home.
>
> Show us how to live here with conscious gratitude and confidence.
>
> We know it is your gift, but we still do not know how to receive free gifts.[186]

Almost six months after this day, I read Teresa's *Interior Castle* seriously for the first time. It was a reading unlike any other in my life, although the difference came more in intensity and frequency than nature. For me, the text was full of those thrilling moments every reader knows, usually quite rarely, when a voice from another time or place illuminates a previously unutterable truth from your own heart or life, one you didn't know anyone else actually shared. There was so much I couldn't say about how God had moved in my life, so much I didn't know how to express. But then, in her own way, Teresa was saying it, and I felt the Spirit of truth practically shouting at me from across the centuries: *Yes! This. This!* In a reading with many such moments of being dramatically caught short, a few still stand out. One of those passages is the following short section from the fifth dwellings, which, for Teresa, is almost an afterthought to describing our relative lack of agency in this kind of union. Basically, she says, the way we find ourselves in this type of prayer makes me think of this line from the Song of Songs (that great Hebrew love poem of the Bible):

"He brought me into the wine cellar" (or "*placed* me there," I think it says). It doesn't say that she *went*. It says that she was wandering around in all directions, seeking her Beloved. As I understand it, this is the cellar where the Lord is pleased to place us, when He wills and as He wills. But we can't enter by any of our own efforts; His Majesty must put us right into the center of our soul, and enter there Himself.[187]

The edition I was reading had a footnote after the first line pointing to Song of Songs 2:4. I looked up the full verse: "He has brought me to his banquet hall [literally, "house of wine"], and his banner over me is love."[188] I was typing notes and quotes as I read, and I placed this one in bold, sixteen-point font. The shouting on the page echoed the shouting in my soul, for this is what I had known that first day when I was praying Psalm 45 and have known in other times of prayer since. *He brought me into the wine cellar, and his banner over me was love.* I had looked for Christ in so many places, never seeming to catch more than a glimpse of him as he went around the corner, or only seeing his silhouette from a distance. But then, unexpectedly, he came; he drew me to a place I trusted existed—for others, the truly devout—but thought I'd never see. After all, my pursuit of God's company or ways had never been wholehearted. And yet, Christ came, shattering the boxes for God my intellect had constructed and renewing the most ancient and basic teachings of my faith tradition: God is real. God is near and is made known to us in Christ. God loves this creation, including you. God is *good*.

Once again, I am fully aware of the many factors in this image from Song of Songs—and even in Teresa's interpretive language, focused on God's agency—that point toward problematic places for contemporary readers: the line between seduction and coercion, questions of sexual consent, patriarchal romance, and a reiteration of God as an essentially male power. I can see and feel all of these matters in the background, manifesting themselves in a very simple way. The wine cellar image is, on some level, embarrassing. And yet, it is essential to my understanding of my experience, and (perhaps) a potentially helpful image to others, too. It is just that—an image, a metaphor, not the fullness of the thing itself, as full of cracks and distortions and limitations as any other descriptive words would be. I fight the embarrassment in the same way I would fight to acknowledge the integrity and goodness of anyone's story of being unexpectedly, fully well-known and well-loved, regardless of whether that goodness came though "hopelessly" traditional or conventional channels.

Upon my first reading of the fifth dwelling places, I didn't recognize everything Teresa described as a precise overlay of my own experiences. There were many places where Teresa's descriptions and imagery felt foreign to my initial experience and the way I understood it. Particularly, her main image of these fifth dwellings—a silkworm building a cocoon, dying, and reemerging as a butterfly—was an enigma. However, I was not, and am not, troubled by the places I could not "relate to"; I was intrigued, and I hoped then, as I hope now, to understand more as I age. Yet the points of resonance were strong enough for me to know that Teresa was an important conversation partner and teacher, even if I couldn't grasp all that she was saying, like a three-year-old at the feet of a wise grandmother. The overarching metaphor of increased (and unexpected) intimacy and knowledge, betrothal, and commitment still came through like a lightning rod of shared truth (even as I might have wished for a metaphor that was more modern, more hip). I am somewhat consoled that Teresa herself seems to struggle with this metaphor but can think of nothing better:

> I'm only making a rough comparison to the sacrament of marriage—though the two work differently, I can't find another metaphor that will better explain what I'm trying to say.... (Bodily union is a far-distant experience: the spiritual joys that the Lord gives and the pleasures that those who marry must have are a thousand leagues from each other.) Because it's all a union of love with love, and the actions of love are pure; so delicate and gentle that there's no way of describing them...but the Lord knows how to make them very clearly felt.[189]

Teresa draws out the comparison to betrothal, which was an elaborate sequence in her day. After the initial agreement to be committed, "His Majesty" grants this mercy:

> [He wants the soul] to know Him better, and for them to meet together (as they say), and joins her with Himself.... All giving and

receiving of gifts has come to an end, and in a secret way the soul sees *who this Spouse is* that she's going to take. Using her faculties and senses, she couldn't understand in a thousand years what she now understands in the shortest period of time.... The soul is left so in love that she does everything she can to not mess up this divine engagement. If she's careless, though, and sets her affections elsewhere, she loses everything.[190]

Perhaps because I don't share Teresa's social formation around marriage and betrothal, I didn't initially have the sense of anxiety and care that this passage suggests. On the contrary, formed as I was in a social landscape of fleeting passions and divorces, I subconsciously assumed the lasting *impression* of this time of being beloved in prayer would not be accompanied by a lasting companionship. It was a gift of a lifetime— and for a lifetime—I thought. Much to my surprise and amazement, it didn't turn out that way. Although not of the same intensity as the first nine months, much of the work of my soul's transformation and change (as I would self-diagnose it, at least) has, for years, fit in this section of Teresa's spiritual landscape, with echoes of Christ as the unbidden but welcome lover and companion who takes much more than a lifetime to really know. Yet I have *never* known how long this intermittent awareness of presence and companionship will be with me; I am utterly convinced of God's mysterious but absolute freedom and my own potential for defiant departure.

Teresa also includes other movements and metaphors in this section that are very different from the wine cellar or betrothal, and there are many ways the soul might be transformed in the spiritual landscape of the fifth dwellings. And so, very helpfully, Rowan Williams describes this fifth-dwellings phase in a broad way that could apply to those who have experienced dramatic and warm encounters with Christ, as I have, as well as for those who come to know union and commitment to God in very different ways. He writes (my emphasis),

Yet this phase can also be called the *beginning* of "spiritual betrothal"—when God and the human spirit make a conscious mutual commitment. We know with new clarity *who it is with whom we have to do*—though this knowing is certainly not a matter of expressible conceptual clarity. Perhaps it is simply the stubbornness of our conviction that, *whatever else is going on, we are at least no longer in danger of mistaking ideas and words about God for God, or confusing our own sense of doing well with the grace of God. We have been brought up against that sheer difference of the creator from the creature, about which we can finally say nothing satisfactory.* But [in Teresa's analogy] the betrothal is not yet formalized and finalized (we should remember that Teresa's society treated betrothal as a major ceremony): all we have is a declaring of intentions. Our *sense* of stubborn adherence is still deeply vulnerable; it is not itself the reality of lasting union, and we may still deceive ourselves, especially as the devil is now more than ever eager to hold us back.[191]

In the first few days of Christ being present to me in this new way, drawing me into a place of encounter whenever my life allowed it, I had a secret but abounding joy, a quiet joy with a strength I'd never known to accompany that emotion. Whatever else was going on, I was at least no longer in danger of "mistaking ideas and words about God for God," or "confusing my own sense of 'doing well' with the grace of God." *The soul can neither forget nor deny God's presence to it.* I knew whatever else happened in my life, I could not forget this, and my soul was imprinted not just with a general sense of "God's presence" but more particularly of God's *goodness*.

One night, I dreamed that I was in a dark place, entirely alone, surrounded by black nothingness. A man with a gun approached, faceless but clearly communicating, and informed me calmly that he was going to kill me. I did not flinch. "I am ready to meet the Lord," I said steadily, not with bravado but with true fearlessness and peace; this response was not based on any retrospective evaluation of my own life but on considering what, or who, was ahead. I had seen that the Lord was good. I did not know what was beyond life except for the presence of this Holy One, and that was enough. Love awaited. The man shot, and I woke up with a start, my heart pounding—not with fear, but with wonder. It was true, I knew. I was ready to meet the Lord. But how would such certainty of God's goodness, this pillar inside me, change my life before death? Had some part of me died? Was some part of me in the process of dying? Jungian theologians and dream interpreters would say yes, obviously. I did not know this at the time, though. That awareness simply came to me, a fruit and extension of how God was being made known to me in the daylight hours. I did not know this at the time, either, but if there is a scriptural "theme" to Teresa's fifth dwellings section, it is probably this text from the third chapter of Colossians: "You have died, and your life is hidden with Christ in God."[192]

Around the edges of this pool of deep joy and gratitude, I was plagued by questions that I deemed, as expressed in my journal, "wretched and fool-ish…but on my mind nevertheless." Some of these questions were: What's the point? (Not so much "Why is this happening to me?" but rather "What good will it do?") Where am I being led? What am I to do with this expe-rience? What is the lesson? How do I appropriately respond? It was so very clear to me that I could say "nothing satisfactory" about what was happening, to use Rowan Williams' phrase, that I confided in only one person: my spiritual director. As a retired professor of ascetic theology, she knew (and knows) more about the breadth of prayer experiences than I ever will, and her presence and words were great moorings in the weeks and years to come. She insisted, against all of my economical and transac-tional instincts, that this was simply a gift of love. I didn't have to figure out what the gift was "for" or try to intellectually integrate it into my day-to-day life. Christ would lead in those movements of integration and even understanding in ways I could not.

The primary danger, as I suspected, would simply be a narcissistic con-flation with what was happening (i.e., "I am special!") when Christ's way is *always* humility. And, my spiritual director asked, "What will you do when he no longer comes?" I knew this question was on the horizon; I had been trained in every way to not expect such overwhelming grace to last forever. But, for once, I resisted this quick movement to the seemingly inevitable "dark night of the soul," when God withdraws and we must find a new way of relating—although not because I doubted its eventual arrival. "Do I have to think about that now?" I asked. She paused, seeming to regret her own question, and her face softened. "No," she said. "Don't worry about when it will end; simply delight in the moments you have now."

A Seal on the Heart (or, Let Me Love You)

I tried to do this, especially in those first weeks and months, when Christ's presence seemed to be waiting in the wings of my quotidian life, teaching me anew about the false barriers we put up between the holy and the mundane. I was led and loved with persistence, generosity, and extravagance. Because I didn't yet know or understand what this was "for" (and because everything within me struggled against the notion of a gift without purpose), I followed the advice of my spiritual director and tried to surrender to this persistent, generous, extravagant love without losing my attentiveness to a more demanding directive, praying that my heart was being transformed through this time, through this mysterious process, in a way that God wanted. I did trust that the love was *for* something, *doing* something, even if that something was well beyond my comprehension.

Teresa alludes to this semi-passive work of allowing Christ to shape the soul, somehow *imprint* the soul in prayer, through the image of a wax seal placed on the heart. This picture is connected to the image of the wine cellar, which may be primarily about hiddenness: this work of sealing our hearts is done in the quiet places of our inner lives, our prayers—"a tilting / within myself"[193]—in ways that are hidden from others. It is an intimate work and connection between the human and the Holy One, but, once again (and not surprisingly, when you consider the participants), the lead agent is God. This is how Teresa describes the metaphor of sealing wax:

> God brought her into the inner wine cellar and put love in her.... This soul has now delivered itself into His hands, and His great love causes such complete surrender that it doesn't know or want anything more than what He wants with her. (In my judgment, God will never give this favor except to a soul He takes as His very own.) God desires that the soul may go forth from this union impressed with His seal, without understanding how. Indeed, the soul doesn't do any more in this union than the wax when a seal is impressed upon it.... And it doesn't even soften itself in order to be prepared; it merely remains still and gives its consent. Oh, goodness of God, that all of this is done at Your cost! You only want our will, and that there be no impediment in the wax.[194]

Although I didn't read the above passage in *The Interior Castle* until September of 2017, the prayer notes in my journal from March to September are full of reflections that match this description of being led to stillness, giving consent, and letting Christ love me in ways that seemed aimed at my heart, that seemed to be for the "purpose" of grounding me more deeply in love, that seemed to be somehow *about* that previously baffling scriptural language of being "filled with the fullness of God"—all things that had always seemed exclusively metaphorical and yet suddenly included the tangible, too. Take this passage from Ephesians, which always felt soaring, fantastical, and inspiring in the way of big images and big words that are beyond the capacity of the human race but were nevertheless set forth to comfort us or stretch us toward goodness or understanding of divine mysteries:

> [May God] grant you to be strengthened with power through his
> Spirit in your inner being,
> so that Christ may dwell in your hearts through faith—that you,
> being rooted and grounded in love, may have strength
> to comprehend with all the saints
> what is the breadth and width and height and depth,
> and to know the love of Christ that surpasses knowledge,
> that you may be filled
> with all the fullness of God.[195]

Suddenly, my little life, my obscure body, waking and sleeping and eating like any other person, felt like a living text of this prayer, partially but distinctly answered. The only part of this famous biblical passage that at first glance runs counter to Teresa's narrative, that runs counter to what I have observed of "the love of Christ that surpasses knowledge," is the notion that it is *our* power to know—that we might somehow possess the "strength to comprehend." To use Teresa's metaphor, the sealing wax does not have great power in and of itself to form an image: it *consents* to being imprinted. Receiving, or knowing, the love of God is more like a gift we open our hands to than a prize we snatch with all our might.

But, then again, maybe this notion of "strength" depends on how you read the clause afterward: "with all the saints." Does it suggest we have the power to comprehend, to know, the love of Christ *like* all the saints (meaning, in this case, faithful people), in the company of all the saints? This seems to grant us too much credit, too much agency. (Although, if one reads the power as coming "through his Spirit," as the previous verse says, our credit seems appropriately diminished.) Or, does this language suggest we have the power to comprehend, to know, the love of Christ *together*, with *the help* of all the saints, with the collective voices of all the saints speaking to the breadth and width and height and depth of Christ's love? If it's read in that way—with people sharing the imprint of Christ in their own lives, that we may *together* have the power to comprehend the breadth and width and height and depth of that love—then I see that. I have known that. It speaks to the ways in which I have been learning about the love of Christ my whole life from wise mentors and friends of all ages, with or without dramatic prayer encounters (on my part or theirs), with or without even the name of Christ being invoked. And I certainly felt, when I came upon Teresa's writings, a new depth of comprehending God's presence in my own life, a stronger and more expanded vision of where God's love reached and how I, too, might talk about it. It's why I'm revealing these tender and personal moments at all, taking elements of them out from their hidden place, with the same essential prayer as the author to the Ephesians: that you may "be strengthened," that you "may have strength to comprehend with [the help of] all the saints what is the breadth and width and height and depth" of God's love in Christ.

On the morning of March 9, I entered my time of prayer with excitement and a sense of wonder and unknowing, perfectly aware that the particular gift I had received two days earlier might not be present this day or ever again. I sat to pray in the sacristy and began with the *God for Us* lectionary readings again, praying the psalm appointed for the day; but then, comically, my husband (and co-pastor) and the church treasurer came bustling into the sacristy to get the keys to the safe while I was praying the appointed psalm out loud, and the whole scene seemed so normal and bland. Oh, here I am, reading the Psalms with the Bible in my lap. What old-fashioned piety! The ironic disconnect between the assumed dryness of this stereotypical devotional image and the elation of the past two days in that place was not lost on me, though it was a joke I could not yet share.

Almost as soon as they left, it was as if I was called back to Psalm 45, and I read it only once before being invited to cast my book aside and close my eyes. And, once again, he came, the Spirit moving into me in a way that intensified until it embodied, more and more, the very notion of powerful and expansive entry: Christ filling me. The experience was mediated by the boundaries of my body, as sometimes I became aware of where the movement stopped or reached its limits, as my lungs and ribs and hips and neck and even sometimes the top of my skull became part of this very limitation. After a time, the intensity subsided, and I moved into a more "traditional" prayer of questioning, relating. Two ideas or points of dialogue stood out from this colloquy: "What do I call you?" I asked. Never had God's presence through the figure of Christ been so close, so sustained, and it seemed an important question. *Am I getting this right?* In response, there was silence, a sense that this question was irrelevant or superfluous. But something in me was shifting around this question. I kept returning to it as if I needed more affirmation of what I thought I knew, perhaps because the answer still felt so foreign to my accustomed piety. Finally, it came to a point of knowing, of clarity, so that I discerned: *I am the Christ, the bridegroom* [but you already knew that].

I also couldn't help but return to the first question. "What's the point of all this?" Again, as I had gathered from the past couple of days but still couldn't absorb, I had a sense that this was not the right question—it was off the mark. Instead, a response emerged from *beside* my point of inquiry about purpose: *Let me love you.* Beneath this, in another layer of understanding, I detected a sense of acknowledgement: "Yes, you're right, this season won't last forever, but stop worrying about that now. Let us have this time." At some point during this encounter, I came to a place of expressing my unworthiness, knowing all too well my own laziness and inattentiveness to prayer, my stubborn love of comfort and unwillingness to make any deep material sacrifices for the good of others, but there was a strong and yet gentle rebuke: *Isn't that for me to decide?* It came coupled with the knowledge that he knew my limitations just as well as I did but didn't want to waste time in the bridal chamber on lamentations of unworthiness. And so, we took all the time we could get, until a church meeting at 9:30 called me away. Later that day, I journaled this "conclusion": "I am trying to simply delight and rejoice and savor this gift of being the beloved while it lasts. With wonder, and gratitude…and a little confusion about how to attend to normal life in the midst of it."

"Annunciation"

Even if I don't see it again—nor ever feel it
I know it is—and that if once it hailed me
it ever does—

And so it is myself I want to turn in that direction
not as towards a place, but it was a tilting
within myself,

as one turns a mirror to flash the light to where
it isn't—I was blinded like that—and swam
in what shone at me

only able to endure it by being no one and so
specifically myself I thought I'd die
from being loved like that.[196]

"*And…if once it hailed me / it ever does.*" In that first week after March 7, I was made aware of Christ's presence to me and in me with a persistent expansiveness of context that shattered all my previous assumptions about where and how God is close to us. I never would have admitted that I kept God in any boxes, but I did indeed assume that if we were to know something, anything, of God's presence to us, closeness to us, love for us, then it would be in the intense quiet and concerted effort of prayer. What I observed, instead, with great curiosity and wonder, was that this invitation to recall Christ's presence with me, in me, came not only during prayer but also at so many surprising times, a delightfully bewildering demonstration of the abstract theological idea that our life with God doesn't go on hold when we are parenting, shopping, working, talking with friends or parishioners, or otherwise engaged in the world—Christ is very much still there, a part of it.

On the afternoon of March 9, I went to a homey coffee shop across the street from our church to get some work done apart from the interruptions of the office. I sat perched on a bar stool with my laptop resting on the gnarled wooden table, typing up notes from a book about renewed atonement theory into slides for an adult education class. I searched the Internet for images that would help illuminate the ideas, formatted quotes, considered timing, and looked out past the warm glow of the table lamp reflecting off the red wall to the other patrons in the shop. I must have appeared quite the fool, though, like someone reading a love letter on the screen instead of explication of Jewish temple practice, because I was being filled in a way that I could not ignore, and I was feeling the surprised and playful lightheartedness of someone being loved while in the midst of trying to get some work done. The physicality of the reminder of what I'd known in prayer that morning, the expansion within, was less intense but still apart from my control, the obvious echo of the more arresting encounters. At times, I would briefly close my eyes to rest in this unaccountable delight, but I spent most of those hours actually working, looking at my computer screen with a slight smile on my face, enjoying the company of the (most unexpected and unseen) lover who would not leave my side. I finished the presentation, packed up my backpack, and said hello to some colleagues on the way out the door.

That same afternoon, my husband, children, and I went to the North Park farmers market. My six-year-old daughter and I wandered off to get some of the produce on the grocery list and got distracted by some early season strawberries, which were practically glowing in their jeweled reds. She wanted them, and I wanted them, and we bought them, in addition to the kale and lettuce or whatever other responsible items were on the list. On the way back to the car, Colin and I got into a tiff about the strawberries. "They were how much?" he asked. "They weren't on the list," he added. "That's part of the fun of farmers markets!" I exclaimed, my temperature rising as I opened the door to our hot car. "That's why I hate them," he said. "They're just endless opportunities for unplanned spending." As we drove home, rehashing this new variation on an old theme, I thought to myself, "What is the point of all this wonder and love in prayer if I'm still arguing with my husband about *strawberries?*"

That evening, I went to my book club. Sitting on a gray sectional couch with a group of middle-aged counselors and pastors and professors, the invitation to internally acknowledge, notice, attend to Christ's presence kept returning, and it was almost as if the unspoken message was, "Whenever you do not *need* to be focused, in work or other relationships, I will be here (in this season, anyway)." I looked at the women talking, and I heard them on some level, but I was simultaneously distracted, this unseen and more interesting presence clamoring for my attention. "What should I do? Should I even be here?" I thought. Somehow, though, I knew the answer was not to stop my life, to run off to a cave in the mountains east of San Diego where I could be alone with Christ. So, I stayed the course. I remained on the gray couch and engaged with the group; and, actually, as I reported blithely in my journal, "It was a very good discussion," although now I have no idea what it was about.

As I lay in bed that night, with my husband on my left and the open window on my right, Christ drew me to encounter, again, but I was more leery, more cautious, needed more assurance that I was not now delusional, because I was *in my bed*. It's one thing to consent to the overwhelming imprint of God's love while sitting in the church sacristy, where it seems wild but still safely within the bounds of the tradition, and another thing to lie in your marriage bed, where it seems the possibilities for distortion, delusion, and unhealthy overlays with earthly experiences of *eros* could increase exponentially. Christ seemed sympathetic to these concerns in that the approach of the Spirit was different then. I was not consumed (even in that wondrous way); rather, I felt a series of very gentle invitations to acknowledge Christ's presence to me (*I am here; it is I*), a series of subtle moments to draw my attention to the reality and goodness of the encounter (*Is this really you?* I pressed, *The same one I have known?*). I did not have a rigorous philosophy of spiritual counterfeits but remained vaguely aware of the possibility. *Yes, yes, yes,* I was reassured, through many layers of questioning and waiting and prayer. I stayed extra still, internally and physically, in my initial caution. This was not me taking action, doing anything but saying, *Yes, okay; come unto me.* Christ's presence, unbidden but welcome. "[The soul] doesn't even soften itself in order to be prepared; it merely remains still and gives its consent," Teresa says. "You only want our will and that there be no impediment."[197]

For the past few years, in the course of my life of parenting and working and praying, I have been trying to learn to be with God, to be in relationship with God, in a new way, one informed and formed by this surprisingly close and persistent love. The old model of my faith, quite well-suited to the skeptic, the agnostic, the deist, the perfectionist, or the meritocrat of any stripe, shaped me to think of myself as an actor, a performer, a laborer, when or if considering God at all. "Go out and do a good thing!" this model of God says. "Show me (or, if you don't believe in me, show the world) what you've got! I'll help if you really, really, *really* need it." Again, with the breaking in of such intimacy, such goodness, such extravagant love, I've had to learn—and am still learning—a new way of being with Christ, one guided by the revolutionary posture of some passivity and stillness, by trust that another is acting, and will act, in this world that I perceive but also still invites my participation, response, action, still honors my person and agency. In retrospect, with God's help, I have been learning "the middle voice," a linguistic term that Eugene Peterson describes as the language of friendship, the language of marriage and love—and, yes, the language of prayer.

Although I took Greek in seminary, I was not attentive to the implications of the middle voice beyond a new verb tense to memorize. Peterson brilliantly makes those deeper connections for both Greek students and those who have never learned the language as he writes in *The Contemplative Pastor* about his own dawning understanding of the middle voice:

> I was the slowest in my class but by no means the only person to have difficulty coming to terms with the middle voice. Active and passive voices I understood, but middle was a new kid on the block. When I speak in the active voice, I initiate an action that goes someplace else: "I counsel my friend." When I speak in the passive voice, I receive the action that another initiates: "I am counseled by my friend." When I speak in the middle voice, I actively participate in the results of an action that another initiates: "I take counsel." Most of our speech is divided between active and passive; either I

act or I am acted upon. But there are moments, and they are those in which we are most distinctively human, when such a contrast is not satisfactory: two wills operate, neither to the exclusion of the other, neither canceling out the other, each respecting the other.

My grammar book said, "The middle voice is that use of the verb which describes the subjects as participating in the results of the action." I read that now, and it reads like a description of Christian prayer—"the subject as participating in the results of the action."...

Prayer and spirituality feature participation, the complex participation of God and the human, his will and our wills. We do not abandon ourselves to the stream of grace and drown in the ocean of love, losing identity. We do not pull the strings that activate God's operations in our lives, subjecting God to our assertive identity. We neither manipulate God (active voice) nor are manipulated by God (passive voice). We are involved in the action and participate in its results but do not control or define it (middle voice). Prayer takes place in the middle voice....

...[And] no friendship, no love affair, no marriage can exist with only active and passive voices. Something else is required, a mode of willingness that radiates into a thousand subtleties of participation and intimacy, trust and forgiveness and grace.[198]

This "mode of willingness" cannot be learned overnight in any of the contexts mentioned, and Teresa of Ávila's writings, in *The Interior Castle's* fifth dwellings and elsewhere, abound with this paradox of what Peterson calls "willed passivity."[199] I did not have this language as I wrestled with this new (and yet ancient) reality, but I wrote down notes after my times of prayer, in part for the reason anyone journals—to remember, to clarify—but also because I felt like an amateur scientist, interested in what I was noticing, discovering, about how this prayer was "working" or happening.

One day, about five months into these new encounters with Christ, I felt moved to write a more detailed description of the sequence of these experiences. I had begun to read *The Interior Castle* at the beginning of August, so I did have some language from Teresa regarding "passive" prayer, but I had not yet read the Eugene Peterson description of prayer as a space of "the subject participating in the results of the action." Nevertheless, I share this untidy-but-real journal entry of an untidy-but-real prayer experience because it depicts the working out, in real time, of my *learning*, slowly, to be a subject participating in the results of an action, learning to give of my will, learning to "turn a mirror to flash the light."

Journal Notes from Prayer—August 29, 2017

I once again sit in the yellow and maroon sacristy, which is not just a closed room but also one where I feel very safe, very sure that I will not be interrupted. I lock the doors. I sit in the chair and pull out my phone. I get distracted for a couple of minutes, looking at the weather and then basic news coverage of the horrible flooding in Texas due to Hurricane Harvey. After I finish the article, I draw myself back to the Mission St. Clare app and begin morning prayer, starting with a Welsh hymn. I really have little sense of expectation: at this point, it is "pure" discipline, saying the prayers because I trust that it will help orient my heart and head toward God as I begin my day. I am, on some level, aware that "today is the day(!)" I said I would begin the new pattern of prayer, writing, and reading, but I am (just) seasoned enough in such new patterns (and the often quick-to-come failures) that I am pragmatically trying not to make too much of it. So I sit, and read, and half-expect that I will go through this whole morning prayer session with no experience of what Teresa calls "passive prayer." I am prepared, in other words, to simply try to align my thoughts with the Scriptures. But then, about halfway through the psalm, I feel that subtle stirring in my body and my soul, an invitation of sorts. There is still waiting: today I had the sense that it was not yet time to set aside the phone and the set prayers; I was to continue with them for a bit. But then, as Christ's presence grew stronger, more pressing, it became clear that it was time.

I set the phone aside and begin to simply breathe, sometimes trying to keep centered with the Jesus prayer ["Lord Jesus Christ, have mercy on me, a sinner"]. Sometimes, like today, I am tempted to—and do—try to jump into sharing other concerns or things on my heart. Like today, it was almost as if an immature (but under-standable) part of me was saying, "Jesus is here! Time to talk to him about your guilt over not connecting well with [my son] or your worries about [my sister and her husband and their kids]. But there is often (as there was today) a gentle response that invites me to leave those thoughts for a moment, for a while. It is the phrase that has come around, off and on, since March: *Just let me love you.* I am tempted to add a time element, and I think sometimes that is there (…"for a while." …"for a moment.") But I think there is something that is dishonest about these additions. The heart of the phrase is: Stop. Wait. (Those are unsaid.) *Just let me love you* (at least for a while). And so I try to leave space, to focus on what is happening in my body, unbidden but welcome.

This was a dynamic I was especially attentive to today, and I felt God drawing my attention to: I am so careful, still, to not do any-thing that might move in the direction of trying to conjure or even actively encourage these visits from Christ and their development (different each time) because I want to be able to trust that this is indeed [still] Christ and not a game I then think I can take into my own hands. I have been shown in many ways that this element of doubt (the lingering shadow of a question from my postmod-ern and materialistic formation that tells me this could just be an experience conjured by my psyche) is invalid, not true at all to my experience of the power and *otherness* of God, but it remains in the corner nevertheless. I don't think it is all bad, either, because, as I said, it keeps me careful to remain in the position of the one following and responding.

And so, this was the image of Christ's presence: unbidden but welcome. I go to prayer (now!) open to the possibility of Christ's presence but not expecting this presence to come in any particular way. And then I try my best to pay attention to the physical man-ifestations of his presence as they change, go away, come again, trying to be attentive to other signals or words from the Spirit in this space. But also trusting the framing of "Just let me love you," knowing there is nothing in particular I need to do *in that moment* and knowing I will be led in love. I feel there is something here I am forgetting; I will let it go.

It was in this space today that I felt the reminder of "Let me remind you how this works." It has been some time, since early August when we got back, since there had been a fuller experience of union or ecstasy. So, it was as if I were slowly being led through the steps, the motions, the dynamics, and at each turn, there was this essential element of "WAIT." *Stop, pause, wait for me. Let me show you it is me, it is I; I come on my own time and my own ways. You welcome me, you are open to receiving me, but I am OTHER— you cannot predict or manage this experience. You can only respond as you are willing to engage (or not).* And so, in time, I heard the encouragement to move to the floor; check the doors as you need so you feel safe; I checked the doors. And then, in the new posture, lying on the floor, in some ways (at least today) the most pivotal moment of trust. Christ had been deeply present, but now there is a [quiet] space. It is time to wait, passively, with quiet and also the possibility that nothing further will happen. Today, it felt like a long pause, but so helpful and essential, this time of waiting— *Wait for me. Let me come to you.* And then, it begins—so subtle, and today an unexpected sort of physical change, more expansion from within rather than a sense of penetration, and there is then a progression that I do not direct but still participate in. This felt like the other deep reminder, gleaned before and in so many ways: I am not "in control," but God still desires my participation, my hand. The power of what happens is from God, but I am invited to participate; I continue to connect this lesson to my writing and what may or may not come of it. And then, there is the reminder (also heard in early August and other times) that this is all about my *heart*; it's transformation, change, growth. This is the point, the end of these experiences—a change of heart, a strengthening of heart.

Then, after I moved back up to the chair, it was interesting and good to feel that I still had my worries with me, and I felt more open in praying about [my sister] and also my parenting. I felt God gently remind me to hold [my son] more lightly; not to try to control as much; keep him safe and fed and love him but don't worry so much over his every action—simply an image of loosening the grip. I prayed about Hurricane Harvey, questioned the meaning of these experiences of love in the midst of such suffering, and again heard a phrase that has been with me a lot since August: "Not your work, not right now." It sounds flip, but it is not; it is matter-of-fact. And it is so liberating and empowering to hear in various times and places these days—though not now.

This messy struggle, this gracious training, this formation of a new understanding of who we are to and before and with God is part of what I think Teresa is talking about when she writes, "When those receiving these gifts from God prepare themselves, there's a lot to be said about what the Lord then works in them."[200] The metaphor she then dives into is that of the shocking transformation of a silkworm into a butterfly, a change so dramatic that it is disorienting even to the subject:

> Truly, the soul doesn't recognize itself.... The soul can't think how it could have deserved so much good—or, rather, where this good might have come from, I mean, because it knows full well that it hasn't "earned" or deserved such goodness at all. The soul wants to praise the Lord, feels that it would gladly sacrifice itself and die a thousand deaths for His sake.... It's even less impressed with what the saints endured, knowing through experience how the Lord can help and transform a soul—so much so it seems no longer like itself.[201]

In that first six months or so, I thought about the experiences of Christ's presence in me, with me, that kept cropping up apart from these intentional prayer spaces as "echoes of encounter" because, in some ways, they were (and are) a more subdued version of the deeper, more intense encounters I experienced during my times of quiet prayer. Now I understand them differently, in a more layered way: When this expansion inside my body comes, unbidden but welcome, it is not just an arrow pointing backward.

It is a wonderful signal of Christ's presence to me in that moment, too, strengthening me or raising my level of attentiveness to what is happening or to the people I am with, *and* it is as if Christ is speaking to me in a language most often without words, a language based in, and indeed echoing, the more intense experience of union, a language rooted in the knowledge of God as love, moving into this world and acting upon this world with the Spirit. So, I trust this unpredictable presence of Christ "outside" of prayer much more now. It is really, simply, God as Other and yet in me, with me, helping me through this life and trying to teach me, lead me, encourage me into the particular ways I might participate in sharing this love with other human travelers, equally beloved and yet struggling mightily for lack of knowing this or remembering it.

The gift of these reminders, which, of course, may leave me forever yet (and often do already for long stretches at a time), do not make me a perfect love-er by any means: I still get impatient with my children; neglect to extend self-sacrificial care to my husband, my friends, my parishioners; walk by many of the homeless men and women sprawled outside the courtyard leading to my office building with a calloused heart; ignore the ruin of the earth and all therein as I drive less than a mile to go to an exercise class. Yet God is with me, even in my obvious imperfections, my obvious humanness, urging me to greater love, to do the work that I can do in this humble frame, even given all my weaknesses. My spiritual director told me, after I confessed to arguing with Colin over the strawberries, that Teresa writes about having an argument with another nun, slamming the door shut, and finding that Christ was still waiting for her within as she sat to pray. It is the gospel writ small: our perfection is not required for God's presence. It is a live reminder of that old aphorism "God loves you just the way you are, and too much to let you stay that way." You are enough, and you will be transformed by Christ if you say— and mean—*yes*.

God gently prods me: sometimes I am taken aback by the startling reminder of God's presence to me when I have fallen asleep to that reality; other times, I am drawn to notice how deeply Christ has been invited to dwell in the soul of another person. I do not, cannot, control these expansions within, but I believe I could close them out, shut the door. There is freedom and unpredictability in this love, coming from an agency that is clearly distinct from my own; but its persistent presence, urging me on even when I have failed, is slowly changing my heart, transforming a soul that really believed perfection in action and spirit was a prerequisite for knowing God's love—a soul that was shaped inordinately by the myth of works righteousness, that old lie that work sets free or makes one worthy. "Again and again we must abandon the illusion that we must first prove ourselves and earn God's love."[202] For some people, like me, that illusion runs deep. Many layers of paint would be needed to fully cover it; many winds would be needed to clear it out; many times, the butterfly would be startled, yet again, not to see a silkworm in the mirror. Regardless of the metaphor: it takes time.

And, over time, I have simultaneously come to perceive another invitation from Christ—to a different sort of union. What I had suspected from the beginning of Christ-the-bridegroom's appearance was true. *Let me love you*, though revolutionary, beautiful, essential, is indeed not the end of the story. The beloved is also invited to seek, with that paradoxical mix of passivity and willfulness, "the union of conformity to God's will"—what I first thought of, upon reading about it, as the union of obedience. This *other* union Teresa talks about in the fifth dwelling places[203] is one that makes more sense to me, intellectually, but one I still have to learn how to respond to in a different way than I tried to for the first three decades of my life. Say the word *obedience*, and I have usually been ready to ride off on my steed, doing "good things for God" (or at least trying to), but then have also usually found myself knocked off the horse and alone on the plain, exhausted and confused. Perhaps this is why God kept calling me back to the simple chamber room of intimate presence both within and outside of prayer. First: *Let me love you*. Again, and again, until this foundation is sure, until the imprint is deep. Because if I am to pursue conformity to God's will in the long run, in a sustainable way, I must learn how to do so *not* with a heart shaped by my childlike desire to run off ahead, eager to prove worthiness and earn easily frayed gold-star stickers, but rather with a heart transformed by Christ's imprint, a heart that acknowledges God's closeness when I am walking, running, or daring to ride at full gallop toward an earthly end I know not.

The Union of Conformity (or, Put Your Hand to the Work)

For those readers with inclinations like mine, who find too much talk of romance tiresome, who want to remain grounded in tangible human action even as the center of conversation shifts toward the work God does in us, the final section of the fifth dwelling places offers invigorating reassurance that we are not alone. Here we find teachings that shine with Teresa's honest-and-hard-earned humility and her keen eye for human folly, never lost amid her insistence that God nevertheless *can* do wondrous things in us. After discussing the "delightful"[204] prayer of union that results in the soul's certainty that "it was in God, and God was in it,"[205] elaborating on the effects of this union through the image of a silkworm dying in order to birth a butterfly, and observing the initial state of this new creature, Teresa then (re)turns her attention to the more prosaic theme of striving and action:

> Always understand that she must strive to move forward in the service of our Lord and in self-knowledge. Because if she acts like she now has complete security and doesn't do anything beyond receiving this favor, growing careless with her life and abandoning the heavenly path (which consists of keeping the commandments)...it "gives the seed" for the creation of more silkworms and then dies forever.[206]

Forever?! Thankfully, God's mercy exceeds Teresa's rhetorical flourishes, as her own life and experience testifies. She counts herself as one who received this gift of union in her early twenties but then turned away from striving to know God and from sincere obedience. Even so, as she instructed others in prayer, she "did them *a lot* of good," and, "later, the Lord again gave her light."[207] In the end, the fire didn't go out "forever." Still, out of this experience, Teresa wants to speak candidly with a word of warning and clarification to those whom God has given "similar favors"[208] in prayer, and also to those whom God has not: she offers a word about a kind of union that is for "everybody."[209]

> This dwelling place seems a little obscure to me, despite all I've said about it. There's a lot to gain by entering it, and yet I want to avoid the impression that there is no hope for those from whom the Lord

withholds such supernatural gifts. For true union can be reached, with God's help, if we try to attain it by keeping our wills fixed on whatever is God's will. Oh, how many of us are there who *say* we do this and *think* we want nothing more, and would die for this truth.... If this is really true, then you have *already* obtained this gift from God, and you don't need to care about the other gracious union that was mentioned. Because the most valuable thing about it actually *comes in and through this union* I'm now describing. We can't reach the heights I've talked about if the union in which we resign *our* wills to the will of *God* is uncertain. Oh, this union is so desirable![210]

In short, there are many ways in which the soul might be united to God. Don't worry if the "supernatural" is not part of your experience. At the outset of "Fifth Dwellings," Teresa suggests that, in her opinion, "there are really very *few* who fail to enter these dwelling places that I'm about to describe. Some get farther than others, but the majority do manage to get inside."[211] This is not the realm of the spiritual elite. Although she believes "very few" experience "some of the things *in* this room,"[212] toward the end, Teresa returns her attention to describing the spiritual dwelling that *many* of us feel drawn toward, even from childhood: that place where we are doing what is right and true and good in the deepest sense (not superficial conformity), where we are living in alignment with a greater purpose for our life in ways that benefit others—in other words, the place of union with God's will.

This is the kind of union with God that is the root of all of Teresa's spiritual desires and longings; the surprisingly gracious "delights" of prayer are real, but they are not the real point; they are helpful in offering strength for the journey but are not essential. As she stated in the fourth dwelling places, this desire to live and be in congruence with God's intentions and desires is the foundation of her prayer life and, she firmly believes, the wisest path in the spiritual life as a whole for all people, no matter where you are or what is happening (or not happening) in your prayer life: "This is the union I have desired all my life," she writes at the age of sixty-two, after she considers herself quite well-established in a permanent state of union with Christ, which she describes through the metaphor of marriage. But here she reminds her readers of the persistent foundation of that relationship: "It's this union [with God's will] that I continually ask of the Lord, and the one that is clearest and safest."[213]

Part of the clarity and relative accessibility of this union comes from the fact that "we don't need to receive great favors from God before we can achieve this. He's given us everything we need in giving us His Son to show us the way.... The Lord only asks two things of us: love of [God] and love of our neighbor. This is what we must work on."[214] Teresa is returning to the shorthand navigating point that Christians (and Jews before them) have used to measure a holy life, a good life, a life lived in accordance with "God's will," for thousands of years: *love God, love your neighbor.* For Jesus, it is the summary of God's law (often referred to as "the greatest commandment" where it appears in the Gospels), and it is a word of distilled wisdom that had been offered to the people of Israel before Jesus, too, in various ways and places. Teresa is walking on ancient and well-established ground, then, when she reminds readers of *The Interior Castle* that aspiring to do these "two things" is the most important work of all, the movement of our wills that is behind and within every worthy moment of prayer or action or life itself.

Yet for people of all times, the experience of pursuing these "two things" is that the commandments may be clear, but they are not easy. Furthermore, if we are interested in self-assessment, in improvement, in simply being honest with ourselves when we know that we are notoriously self-delusional creatures, then how do we *know* if we really love God, really love our neighbors? We can all think of people who we think don't live up to their own rhetoric about such things (oh, those religious hypocrites!), but this ease of finger-pointing merely points out how difficult the work is for all of us. There is some humor in this self-delusion, as Teresa points out:

> The wiles of the adversary are terrible—he'll run around hell a thousand times if doing so will make us believe that we have a single virtue that we actually don't have....

> It's amusing to me how, when they are praying, some people think that they would like to be humiliated and publicly insulted, for God's sake—and then they try to hide a very small failure. Oh,

and if they're accused of anything that they haven't done!—God save us from having to listen to their protests![215]

Teresa approaches the desire for honest self-assessment with a practical tip: first look at how well you love your neighbor. It's a bit harder to fool ourselves that way. "In my opinion," she writes, "the most certain sign as to whether or not we are observing these two laws is whether we observe the love of neighbor well. We can't really know if we love God, even though we may have strong reasons for thinking that we do—but we *can* know if we love our neighbor."[216] Or, put otherwise, "If we have great perfection here [in loving our neighbor], we've done everything."[217]

Again, it is with writing like this that Teresa of Ávila surprised and delighted me upon my first reading of *The Interior Castle*, with her characteristic blend of hard-nosed realism and determination and frank assessments of the many pitfalls on the road to deeper relationship with God—yet all of this stridency is found within the context of a text seeking to illuminate the features of supernatural gifts and graces that God can and does give in prayer, those unearned spiritual delights that might also play a role in our transformation, strengthening our hearts for the work of love. It is this amalgam of contemplation and action that makes her the quintessential "grounded mystic," although, the more I read about other saints of the faith, the more I realize that this is not as rare as I once thought. Popular culture tells us that "mystics" (when it considers them at all) are fuzzy-headed people with their feet off the ground, detached from the world and human realities; historical renderings of actual spiritual luminaries say otherwise. There is a certain sort of detachment to Teresa and other great souls, as mentioned before, but it usually doesn't include the neglect or abandonment of earthly relationships[218] or of work and action with the bodies we have been given.

She actually points out that excessive attention to the nuances of prayer or the interior life without proportionate attention to the nuances of how life is lived in community makes it more difficult to move into the union of conformity to God's will:

When I see souls very diligently trying to understand the prayer they have, and so completely and seriously wrapped up in their prayers that they're afraid to move or indulge in a moment's thought (because they're afraid of losing even a touch of the tenderness and devotion they've been feeling), I realize how little they understand the road to attaining union. They think it's all about this [interior experience]. But no, sisters, no! The Lord wants *works*."[219]

The "works" she offers as examples include compassion, empathy, self-sacrifice, and the very prosaic but telling virtue of feeling joy when someone else is praised (and, conversely, wanting to hide the faults of others as if they were our own, rather than exposing them for the smug satisfaction of communal consumption).

There's a certain artificial grandiosity of spirit in prayer that Teresa wants her readers to be aware of (and beware), one I don't think is confined to religious communities or even people of faith; it's a grandstanding before God and/or ourselves that says, "I will go forth and be so good; I will save this other person, or this situation, in some way or another." These are "beautiful plans" that sometimes come to us suddenly, and we "[imagine] we will carry them out for the good of our neighbors."[220] On the whole, I don't believe Teresa would deny that God might and does communicate to us certain significant "works" that we might fulfill for the good of our neighbor; indeed, her own life of active reform of the Carmelite order in the face of severe political and religious opposition evidences her trust in the validity of certain big and "beautiful plans." But, again, that old theme of our capacity for self-delusion emerges. She simply wants pray-ers to pay "careful attention to how [they] are [actually] proceeding in this matter."[221] With cold water that both shocks and enlivens, she wakes the virtuous daydreamer from her stupor: "If our later *actions* don't match up with these plans, there's no reason to believe we will accomplish them."[222]

When my dad walked out of my family's household for a woman who was not my mother, he kept saying, "But I still love *you*." There was a deep dissonance that his kindly meant words could not cover. From this and other experiences and my natural proclivities, I learned—and held tightly to—the belief that love is best known in action, not emotion. In many ways, my life was shaped around this tenet, even when it got buried beneath other truisms. So, although I have never reached the perfection, the maturity, the *ideals* of self-giving love that Teresa refers to as an essential part of the "union of conformity," these kinds of actions were not the difficult sort of works for me. I tried, and still try, to act with compassion and self-sacrifice in my various communities and roles: as a mother, a spouse, a priest, a friend, a sister, and a daughter. The will for this sort of "work" of love is well-conditioned, though not (obviously!) unfailing. The more challenging sort of work, the more challenging "union of conformity to God's will"— what I have sometimes thought of as the union of "obedience"—in my life has proved to be the sort of work that does not immediately benefit the bodies closest to mine but is instead an earthly act in response to God's love that may benefit souls and bodies I may never see: the work of writing.

Now: writing about writing is almost always boring for people who don't feel the need to write, and often even for those of us who do. But I have come to trust that the *kind* of movement I've known from the Spirit in my life as relates to writing comes to other people as *other*-but-similarly-persistent-invitations to work yet unrealized, the kinds of nudges and themes that simply refuse to disappear over the years, though the precise form may shape-shift, and the intensity of the prompting may ebb and flow. God speaks into our lives with answers to that deeply personal and yet universal seeking of purpose: "What is mine to do?" With this in mind, I share pieces of my story toward greater obedience—which, as any frustrated parent or Greek scholar will tell you, comes first from hearing, perceiving, and listening. But then, as Teresa reminds us, it involves concrete action, too.

As I did the typical college and early-twenties articulation of self-definition and self-discovery and gifts assessments, seeking that magical place where my "deep gladness and the world's deep hunger"[223] might meet, writing often appeared as part of the equation. But in my late twenties, I decided that writing would be part of my work in the world, but not primary. I lost sight of this work almost entirely as I became a mother of babies and toddlers and entered ordained ministry. Then, just after my middle child turned two years old, in March of 2016, it came back to me. I was praying after receiving Communion on the Tuesday before Easter, at a service where clergy renew their vows, and so perhaps I was listening a bit more closely than usual for anything God might want to bring to my attention, for anything I ought to do. When the notion of writing emerged, seemingly from nowhere, I questioned it, doubted it. "How do I know this is not just a manifestation of my own desires?" I probed. "I want to write, so how do I know this isn't just my subconscious telling me what I want to hear?" Without pause, the Word came back, piercing but not cruel: *You don't want to* write. *You want to be famous!* Um, ouch. But also: caught. I laughed and took note.

A few weeks later, on a prayer retreat in Santa Barbara, I wrestled further with this persistent nudge. "What will happen if I *don't* write?" I asked testingly. Underneath was this deeper question: Is this like a life-or-death matter, a heaven-or-hell matter, a God-will-forsake-me-otherwise matter? Or is it optional, like extra credit? What's at stake? In response, God seemed to sigh this weary word of love and wisdom, in various ways: *All would not be lost, but it would be like choosing not to dive into a part of yourself where there are treasures to uncover and behold. Your life is—would be—diminished.* Almost a year passed, and I focused on other aspects of listening and obedience as I let go of my Oregonian dreams and said yes to the parish work at St. Luke's, trying to love the neighbors in my life earnestly though imperfectly. But I didn't forget these holy nudges to this other vocation, which is one of the reasons why, when Christ the bridegroom first came, my first instinct was works-oriented—namely, with an eye to that area where *inaction* glowed, and I guiltily asked, "What do you want from me? What is this for? The writing?"

For the first couple of months of Christ being present to me in this new way, within and outside of prayer, any "work assignment" was clearly secondary, and the reorientation of my relationship to God —reshaped around this close love—was primary. By June of 2017, however, a theme emerged from prayer to prayer, day to day, week to week: *pray and write.* "Every day?!" I pressed. *Well… You'll get there.* My restless energy was in many ways understandable, logical: God's goodness and closeness to humanity had never been clearer to me, and I lived in, worked in, drove through a world that largely didn't trust such goodness was possible, real, alive. I listened to mindfulness apps with friends and felt sad and frustrated; mindfulness is fine, but there's so much more! It felt like stopping prematurely on the path. Ah, mindfulness. Peaceful meditation. Breathwork. Being present to the body. Good, good, good—but there's more! There's a *relationship* possible, a source of love, goodness, truth that is Other and yet as close as your breath. I was repeatedly struck by the challenge of Psalm 40:11: "Your righteousness have I not hidden in my heart;…I have not concealed your love and faithfulness from the great congregation." I could not hide this righteousness, this goodness; I had to share it somehow. *Pray and write.* I didn't know what, where, or when I would write. But there was this invitation to write, returning with rhythm and insistence, a drumbeat I wanted to follow.

When God had been so good, what kind of lout would delay in following, would struggle to walk in the direction of the call? I would, it turns out. The stumbling blocks were both obvious (scheduling, space, priorities) and hidden (fear, cynicism, spiritual indolence). Teresa herself is clear that souls who have experienced the dwelling places of union in the fifth dwellings, through conformity of will and/or via the "shortcut" God sometimes gives in prayer, can then still be lost. Those forces that oppose God's goodness might be even more eager to detract such an individual. Here's how, Teresa says:

> But the adversary comes along with very skillful deceptions, and under the claim or illusion of doing good, begins confusing her in small ways, convincing the soul to get involved in things he makes her think are "not bad." Little by little, he darkens the understanding, weakens the will, causes self-love to increase, until, one way or another, he gradually withdraws it from the love of God and persuades it to follow its own desires.[224]

"Vigilance! Don't assume security!" Teresa says once again. Watch out for the crooked voice that "[confuses us] in small ways, convincing [us] to get involved in things" that are "not *bad*."[225] Distraction and temptation under the guise of good. An ancient theme in novels and religious texts alike, but seemingly not age-worn. "I can do other things that would be good for God (and the world) than write," my fear, cynicism, and indolence said. Maybe the devil, too—but I'm not sure about that yet.

What I do know is that healing those hidden sources of resistance took more time and attention from God than I'd like to admit, but Christ's faithfulness and persistence in the face of my slow-walking stands as its own testament to mercy and grace. An early scene of fear: At a conference in Washington, DC, for Christian activism, I signed up for a spiritual direction session, imagining I'd have a cut-and-dried intellectual conversation about "balancing vocations." Instead, as I begin to describe the calls I wanted to integrate, I started to cry, my failure to be responsive before me anew. The man across the table asked what I felt called to write, and I told him, vaguely: God's presence to us, God's love for us, etc., etc. But then he asked, "What are you feeling in your body when you describe that?" I stopped, searched, and found a surprising word: *fear*. I was afraid of looking the fool, of being mocked as simpleminded and delusional, a privileged white girl meditating on God's love. Eye rolls. *Who cares?* The world has bigger problems. But then again: I cannot, cannot, cannot deny the invitation placed on my life to tell out the goodness of God to the "greater congregation." In the midst of broken political systems and injustice and chemical weapons attacks, I realized, I am still called to write about God's goodness, even if some would—will—mock and reject. As Teresa would remind me, such responses should not be out of the question, but probably expected, for those who want to walk in Jesus' way.

Living in a world that values the concrete, and due to my own valuing of the concrete, I wanted work from God that was more obviously substantive. Couldn't I get an assignment to do something that the world would recognize as good, something American sensibilities would say was worth the time and effort, like designing a better water-filtration system or building a school for under-resourced children? Christ revealed to me the depth of my cynicism, the groundwater of "nothing I write will make any difference in the world" that poisoned any potential harvest. As an antidote, this word came forth in prayerful reflection: *you did not choose me, but I chose you, and appointed you that you should go and bear fruit—fruit that will last.*[226] There was a part of me still disgusted with and leery of this kind of personal, self-focused piety, which seemed so presumptuous and potentially egotistical. Who are we—any of us humans—to think that God chooses us? Appoints us to go and bear fruit—fruit that will last! Who do we think we are? Who do I think I am?

Again and again, Christ keeps answering these questions in me with a presence that says what the Christian faith has always said on behalf of God: *You are right. You are nobody special. You are but a speck of dust, a creature, a human. Yet I come into this creation, into you, asking you to live in response to this divine gift of my loving presence, not just your creatureliness (though there is nothing to be ashamed of there, essentially, because I made you). You may find it absurd, you may secretly want the line between human and holy to be sharper, but I invite you to a higher purpose, a more intimate relationship: to work with me, through your very human body, in your very limited life, in all the mess of the world. Bear the love that I give you into the world, in the name of Jesus—the name of the One who condescends to be with humanity.*

For many months, I was given this image in prayer, this experience of God's invitation for our participation. I was being filled with the fullness of Christ, yet I was still only passive, receiving. The chamber was warmly lit, and I felt Christ's loving presence. At some point, however, he made clear that I must participate in the smallest, simplest, way: *Put your hand to the work*—an instruction to labor and participate akin to "put your hand to the plow." I reached forth, quietly, and extended my hand, setting it down. With a simple touch, practically resting in its insignificance, this one small bodily sign of consent ushered in an overwhelming, hyperbolically powerful movement in which I was blinded, paralyzed, taken up into the luminous darkness and then pressed back down with this voice of Love pounding in my heart: *Do you see? So little is required of you. I can do so much.*

The One who came to life on earth in Mary is present to us still through the Holy Spirit, and this Christ bids our own consent, though you may draw courage from the reasonable presumption that your task will be (much) more humble than hers was.[227] I used to not care a whit for the supernatural elements of the nativity story: the church I was raised in didn't make much of the miraculous, and this element of "traditional" faith soon found itself on the "irrelevant" shelf. I took the big-picture view, as I was wont to do: What were the Gospels trying to *communicate* through telling us that Mary had not "known" a man? That Jesus, of divine parentage, is for everyone. I was satisfied with that. I read about other religious myths of virgin/divine births without worry. If Mary had indeed been raped by a Roman soldier, as one of my seminary professors suggested, it didn't really affect my faith in Jesus as the Way of God, the Truth of God, the Life of God. Who's to limit God's power? I thought. Who's to say God couldn't come to earth in this way, in a way that would be redemptive and full of forgiveness for humanity's wretchedness from beginning to end? Today, perhaps not surprisingly, I see the annunciation differently.[228] Although the world has long not believed Mary, as it often doesn't believe women when it comes to the truths related to their sexuality, I believe her: "How shall this be," she says to the angel, "seeing I know not a man?"[229] I now understand—as so many billions have realized before me—that she, in her *Yes*, is an icon of the Christian faith, the faith that proclaims that we, too, are invited to bear Christ into the world through our bodies, our minds, our hands; that the Holy Spirit is present to us and that we are invited to participate in God's reconciling mission. Christ can, and does, come into us when we are yet unmarried, to God or to anyone else. What will we say—and what will we do—when we are loved like that?

SIXTH DWELLINGS:

PARTNERSHIP

"Now, with the help of the Holy Spirit, let's talk about the sixth dwelling places, where the soul has been wounded with love for the Spouse. It looks for more opportunity to be alone, trying as much as possible to renounce everything that disturbs this solitude."[230]

On November 13, 2017, about a month after I began work on this manuscript, feeling called to write a book that might illuminate elements of Teresa's castle for a contemporary audience, something different happened to me in prayer. For eight months, intermittently, and only when God wanted, Christ had drawn me into the wine cellar with the primary intention, it seemed, of engendering trust and love. Yet, as noted before, it relatively quickly also became about obedience and encouragement in writing. On this particular day, feeling uncertain and experiencing a general lack of energy, I sat down on the sofa to pray, starting with a morning prayer app on my smartphone, after which I planned to move to the desk to write. Nothing was striking me about the prayer passages; but, at the same time, I began to experience fairly intense markers of Christ's presence with me. I soon put down the phone.

There was a rather long time of silence with this quiet presence as I sat, trying to move within to the truth of my situation. I acknowledged to Christ my general feeling of passion and energy for this book project, and yet I also admitted to slothfulness and slowness and a general sense that my body resisted the pace at which my mind and spirit would like to live—the gap between my holy, high-powered aspirations and my slow-as-molasses reality! It was the ancient sadness: the spirit is willing; the flesh is weak.[231] It was a weary admission, not a sharp outcry—how could it be so with a theme so tired and worn? But I saw and acknowledged that it was there.

When prompted, I lay down on the floor, and I waited in silence and stillness to be led. What started as a feeling of neutral expansion within me changed to something different. Eventually, what I thought was merely increased intensity became unmistakably hot, like fire. It was a persistent heat, a penetrating heat, expanding—but not like the expansion of air that had become almost familiar. The sensation of fire happened many times, and, each time, I would wait quietly in between; there would be an obvious movement introducing the arrival of fire initiated by Christ.

As with all the other times, something new had happened, and a part of me became a bit scared; was this still, indeed, Christ? Whose power was this? I did not want to be deceived, misled. And so I pulled back, recollecting my mind. I prayed the Jesus prayer and moved my mind over the words of the Gloria, a hymn we sing or say most Sundays.[232] In time, I felt reassured, though not entirely "safe." Eventually, I surrendered again, responding to the invitation in order to demonstrate my willingness to trust the dynamic I was learning: it is God who beckons, and yet my active response is required. What I heard in prayer was *Put your hand to the book*—similar to previous messages I had received to "Put your hand to the work," but, this time, more specific to my writing work. Absorbed in Christ's energy, I once more reached out my hand as a sign of assent that I, too, must act. Yet again the ensuing power overwhelmed the small gesture. As in times before, the voice of Love pounded in my heart, impressing upon me different words at different times. One time: *All that doubt? The burden on your shoulders, shoulder to plow. That's the old you. We are doing something wonderful* together.

The wondrous thing, the important thing, was not the infusion of affirmation (though that was beautiful, too) but this concept of doing it together: *We are doing something wonderful* together. I would forget this in the days and months ahead—not the words themselves, but in my heart, my behavior—and then God would remind me of it again, over and over, with actions of love that initially centered on fortification and encouragement but increasingly took on the emotional tenor of awakening to a necessary *movement* in order to more fully embody and trust this togetherness, this union of integrity between me and God-in-me, Christ. In such diversity and with such nuance that seems impossible to explain, these gifts of Christ's love told my soul a truth that was often difficult, even anguishing, for me to receive because I didn't know (and still don't, really) *how* to answer with my very life. Christ seemed to be saying, "You still have a way to go until you rest in me. Taste and see! Wake up! Come after me. There is more."

Teresa's section on the sixth dwelling places is a daunting place of conversation with her for many reasons—most simply, because it is the longest section of the book by far, containing eleven chapters that together account for nearly a third of *The Interior Castle* text. It is also more deeply challenging because, in this section, as Rowan Williams points out so bluntly, "Teresa seems to bundle…her reflections on nearly all the most controversial topics in the life of prayer."[233] Hearing from God? Experiencing raptures of many kinds? Having trouble sorting out the veracity of different kinds of visions? Wounded by God's love in a paradoxical blend of pleasure and pain? Well, it is here, in the sixth dwellings, that Teresa might be your guide.

This rather flip introduction reflects my own post-enlightenment unease with so *many* "supernatural" phenomena (I can handle pondering a few) and detracts from what I see when I take a deep breath: the gift of Teresa's work in these spaces, which is her great care and thoughtfulness in addressing such phenomena with so much possibility for misunderstanding, confusion, and ridicule. Beneath her attention to detail and terms and cautions is her trust that because others, like her, may be given such experiences (even if it is only one person), they might benefit from her mature reflections. And underneath all of these seemingly remarkable experiences is something very common: a sustained, urgent longing for an even closer connection to God, and the sustained work of God in continuing to draw us nearer.

So, let me try again, walking with the respectful caution these spaces deserve. I will attempt to summarize and illuminate essential aspects of Teresa's sixth dwelling places, including the three basic categories of "supernatural" phenomena (locutions, ecstasies, and visions). The treatment will not be comprehensive. I enter this part of the castle with some trepidation, with awareness of my limitations as an interpreter and guide. There are a great many *moradas* and experiences Teresa describes here with which I have no familiarity, either personally or relationally. I can and will say little about them, allowing her expert sixteenth-century voice to stand alone. There are a few experiences, other "rooms," here that I *have* known and that were part of my great comfort from and attraction to *The Interior Castle* in the first place. I found in Teresa a voice speaking thoughtfully, humbly, and yet courageously about spiritual experiences no one else in my world was directly addressing. She helped me feel grounded and put in perspective for me the unexpected ways God kept showing up in my prayers and in my very body: I am just one more human pilgrim, like her, wanting to know and love the One at the center of us all, one more daughter of the Church trying to walk in God's ways, one more traveler unexpectedly met by Christ Jesus on the road.

I look in the mirror at my creaturely body and laugh: "Who are we that God might be mindful of us?"[234] And yet he is, still, thousands of years after the psalmist penned that question and nearly half a millennium after Teresa walked, ate, slept, and wrote in Spain. I already knew that the best response to any divine gift was not to obsess over it but to thank God for it and then get on with the earthly work given to us to do. Teresa's writing work, including the vivid and varied wildness of the sixth dwellings, helped me to accept certain divine gifts with greater equanimity and courage. My prayer is that this current text meets readers with similar needs.

Trials, Misunderstandings, and Hearing from God

In chapter one, Teresa brings the reader into the sixth dwellings through a door with a giant warning sign over it: *Greater favors, greater trials!*[235] She might as well say, *All who enter, beware.* The basis for all of these trials (apart from the mysterious purposes of God, about which we can say nothing) is the reality behind the image of transformation offered in the fifth dwellings: a butterfly has emerged from the cocoon, but it does not yet have a lasting home or resting place. It is somewhat "vulnerable, restless, confused."[236] (To make matters worse, others are nervous or angry about what this soul says or does in conformity with the ongoing transformation.) Or, to use the other metaphor that Teresa employs from the outset, it is as if there has been a betrothal but no marriage, with all the suffering that implies.

The soul is now completely determined to take no other spouse. But the Spouse disregards its yearnings for the completion of the engagement, wanting the desire to deepen even more, and wanting this greatest of all blessings to be won by the soul at some cost to itself.[237]

The metaphor of prolonged engagement is an astute one. Fairy tales skip from proposal to marriage in the blink of an eye, perhaps because engagement is actually a very fraught and disorienting time—full of joy and anticipation, yes, but also loss, change, confusion, and powerful social/ familial projections and judgments. It's something we either talk about jokingly or not at all: we must give up a great deal to marry. Not all the voices in our lives or hearts are able to cross the threshold with us, and some will resent and cast aspersions on the whole affair. Though the "greatest of blessings," our most serious unions take place at a high cost. Teresa reminds us we shouldn't expect a union with God to be any different. We may even need to remember the gifts of engagement (the "sign or token of the engagement"[238]) for a long while—like a fiancée, separated for a time from her intended spouse, enduring the trials of an extended transcontinental journey in part through the promise of the ring on her hand. Williams names this as the "profound union of will" that took place in the fifth dwellings and says it might be the "hidden sustainer of the soul in the vicissitudes of the sixth."[239] Teresa implies we will need this commitment more than we could guess in our initial betrothal bliss. "Oh, my God," she says, "these trials the soul will suffer before entering the seventh dwelling place are great, both within and without!"[240]

One of the more well-known "interior trials" that has often been overlaid on the sixth dwelling places by theologians is the famous "passive night of the spirit" or "dark night of the soul" described at length by St. John of the Cross.[241] The nature of this trial has been brilliantly illuminated elsewhere, but it is worth reading just a few of Teresa's words, in retrospect, about the effects of this famously dry and doubt-filled state, when the senses and intellect are of no use and there seem to be no words about God or even assurances from past memories of divine presence:

In this state, we don't need [intentional] reflection to understand [our weakness without God's help]. The soul's experience of enduring it, and finding itself completely powerless, has made it realize how utterly helpless we are—impoverished creatures. Because, although the soul can't be lacking *all* grace (despite all this torment, it doesn't offend God and wouldn't do so for anything on earth), this grace is buried so deeply that the soul doesn't seem to feel the smallest spark of any love for God. It doesn't feel that it ever has. If the soul has done anything good, or His Majesty has given it any gift, the whole thing seems like a dream or work of the imagination; all it knows for certain is that it has sinned.[242]

After explaining that worldly riches and delights only "increase the torments"[243] of souls in these states, how prayer feels meaningless, how it is painful to be alone or with others, she admits that it is impossible for this state to not affect one's outward demeanor, no matter how determined the sufferer: "Thus, despite all her efforts to hide what's happening, she becomes very noticeably upset and despondent."[244] She admits that words ultimately fail everything about such states, and that we shouldn't expect explanations from those afflicted in these ways. Ever the pragmatist, she does have a few words of wisdom for those beset by these sorts of internal trials of deep dryness and disorientation: "The best medicine to help the soul endure it is to occupy oneself with external tasks and works of love for others—and to hope in God's mercy, which never fails those who place their hope in Him."[245] In short: Keep loving others in practical ways, as best you can. Wait for God's mercy.

There is similarly little that can be "done" about the external trials she mentions, which include detracting gossip, unwelcome praise, anxious and fearful spiritual directors, and physical maladies. The task is to endure as steadfastly as possible. If Teresa's experience is any indicator, it seems gossip hasn't changed much through the centuries. Her examples focus on the twin targets of arrogance and self-deceit, and she indicates such talk can have real, sometimes lifelong, repercussions of distrust and avoidance. The words she quotes as coming from the gossips, such as the following, seem fresh in her mind, even in her sixties: "She's trying to act like a saint"; "She's only going to these extremes to deceive the world and to make other people look bad, when they are actually better Christians than she is without this outward show!"[246] Teresa adds, "There's so much more that I could say about this [gossiping and ridicule], but I won't stop to get into it here."[247] Worse, however, than the unfriendly, denigrating gossipers are the few who inordinately *praise* the person (which, again, we can gather even without picking up a biography that Teresa knows from experience): "But to find oneself publicly and undeservingly described as good is incomparably harder than the negative gossip...."[248] Over many decades, Teresa has learned to deal with every double-dealing social layer of projected gossip and praise—from her fellow impoverished Carmelite nuns to the once-doting and then vengeful princess who made sure her autobiography was reviewed and withheld by the Inquisition. She shares some of the perspective that was helpful to her along the way ("People will speak well of others as readily as they will speak poorly of them, and so [the soul] takes no more notice of the praise than of the harsh gossip[249]") before pointing to the eventual hope of sage detachment: "Once the soul has learned to pay little attention to praise, it cares even less about disapproval. On the contrary, it now sounds like sweet music and brings rejoicing."[250] I do wonder, sometimes, when she reached this sweet lack of solicitude!

Although so much of Teresa's social and religious world is foreign to twenty-first-century readers, there is at least one "spiritual phenomenon" of the sixth dwelling places that still wedges its way into conversations and gossip, even in our primarily secular society: hearing from God, or locutions. The word *locution* comes from the Latin *loqui*, "to speak," and refers in this context to those times we experience God speaking to us—to our soul—in a word or a phrase. Like the costs of marriage, this reality of divine communication is one that our popular culture seems capable of talking about only mockingly or not at all: with nervous or vicious laughs and jokes, or with the silent solitude of those who feel they have been spoken to by God in this way, left to wonder if they are crazy or the only one who has experienced something like this. (I know this is not true in other subsets of Christian and religious culture than the ones I have inhabited; there are many parishioners in my current church who talk about the relief of being in a community where one is not expected to have a "word from God" for every day and every circumstance.)

Yet because of the continued controversy about the notion, Teresa's reminder about external "trials" and misunderstandings seems an appropriate bridge to her teaching on locutions. For what it's worth, "practical guidance about how you might know the words heard in prayer are from God and what to do about it" is on the short list of lessons I think every Christian should at least *hear* from her, whether or not they ultimately agree. (Rounding out the top three: "Teresa's basic approach to how to pray with and through constant distractions" and "What are extraordinary experiences in prayer *for*?") God is still speaking, in many ways, but it is as tricky now as it was then to know what—or whose—voice we are hearing when we find ourselves grappling with actual words. Where did they come from? Our subconscious? The built-up residue of marketing campaigns? Or the Holy One, from without and from within?

First, Teresa wants to be very clear about the dangers of this topic. Our preoccupation with the potential for someone's claim of hearing "the voice of God" to be crazy talk is not as postmodern as we think: "God awakens the souls in another way, one that *seems* a greater gift than the others in some respects—but may also be more perilous." She spends time considering how "the soul is awakened by words or phrases that come in many ways: some seem to come from outside, others from the very interior of the soul, others from its higher part, others so completely outside the soul that they are heard with the ears and seem to be from an actual voice."[251] There is frank acknowledgment that some locutions are simply illusions—and, in fact, that may "often" be the case for individuals who are hypersensitive and imaginative.[252] But even for the "healthy," there is reason to be cautious and maybe even to prescribe a break from contemplative prayer for a time, just to wait and see. For "these may come from God, in any of the ways I've mentioned," she says, "or they may equally well come from the adversary or our own imagination."[253] And, just in case we might have forgotten, there is always the secondary danger of hubris: "Even if you hear words or phrases from God, don't think that you are somehow superior to others," she chides. "Any benefit depends on how you respond to what you hear. And unless it agrees strictly with the Scriptures, don't pay any more attention to it than you would if the words came from the adversary himself."[254]

Thankfully, Teresa does not leave us in a state of neurotic anxiety about where the words we have heard come from but instead strides onward to three pragmatic signs we might look for to help discern if they are authentically from God. First and foremost "is the sense of power and authority they carry with them, both in themselves and in the actions that follow"[255]; they bear power and authority in and of themselves. For example, she says:

> Consider a soul experiencing all the interior tumult and hardships that have been described, and all the spiritual dryness and darkened understanding. A single word of this kind [from God]—just a "Don't be troubled"—is enough to calm him. No other word needs to be spoken; a great light comes, and all his trouble is lifted. Even though he had been thinking that if the whole world and all the smartest people in the world were to come together to give reasons why he should not be troubled, they couldn't bring relief, no matter how hard they tried. Or consider a soul distressed because its confessor and others have told her that she has a spirit sent by the devil, and she's full of fear. Yet that single word she hears, "It is I; don't be afraid," takes all the fear away. She is wonderfully comforted and trusts that no one will ever be able to make her feel otherwise.[256]

The second sign is like unto the first: even if the words are not directly ones of peace and comfort, but ones of conviction about missteps or even an unwanted truth revealed, "a great quiet is left in the soul, along with a devout and peaceful sense of recollection, and a readiness to sing praises to God."[257] Finally, the third sign is this:

> These words stay in the memory for a very long time. Indeed, some are never forgotten. Those we hear on earth—I mean from people, however important and wise they might be—are not so deeply engraved in our memories. And if they refer to the future, we don't give weight to them in the same way we do these [divine] words, which impress us with *such* certainty.[258]

It is not just that we remember these words, though we do; it is that we trust them in a way we cannot shake. Though "our mind hesitates to believe it" and may doubt their veracity if the core truth of what we heard from God has not yet come to pass or been fully realized, "within the soul itself there's a certainty that cannot be overcome.... There *still* remains a living spark of conviction that they *will* come true. (Where this comes from, I can't say.) Though all other hopes may be dead, this spark of certainty cannot die, even if the soul wanted it to."[259] That is, even if it would be more convenient, psychologically and otherwise, to tell ourselves the words were all in our heads, were not from God, we can't snuff them out; they persist within us until, at last, in God's time, they are fulfilled.

In this last part, Teresa has clearly crept into pondering locutions that involve outward action, not just interior temperament. She has shifted from examples effecting a change in disposition—"Don't be afraid"—to examples that seem to imply the working out of an exterior change (of an ambiguous nature, but still...one in which we clearly see or experience the fulfillment of a word of God to us). Here we tread onto "the Lord said unto me!" prophetic territory that every mature religious community has fences around, for good reason. Sure enough, Teresa swiftly brings in the caution tape herself. Even if a person can identify the three signs she's mentioned as being present with the locution, and feels pretty darn certain the words are from God, "this confidence is not extreme: if what is said is of great importance and involves the hearer taking action, or includes matters affecting someone else, we shouldn't do anything about it—or consider doing anything—without taking the advice of a wise mentor, a person of clear insight and a servant of God."[260] In other words, don't sell the family farm and hit the road for a hut in the Alps "because God told you to" without seriously and earnestly consulting a mentor or someone in authority with good judgment. And then—here's Teresa's catch for any individually minded soul hell-bent on following "the Lord's commands"—you actually have to listen to and heed the advice given!

Fear not, Teresa says: if it is truly God's will, then, "if our Lord wants to, He will speak to the confessor and make him recognize the work of His spirit."[261] If not, then you are released from obligation to act. To follow nothing but your own opinion "is a very dangerous thing." "And so, sisters, on behalf of our Lord," Teresa continues, in such important matters to self or community, "never let this happen to you."[262] For those of us not under strict obedience in a monastic community, it might not be immediately clear how this precaution applies, but surely we can creatively interpret and heed the spirit behind it: action resulting from locutions still requires caution and layers of discernment, even if we know, in some mysterious depth we can't explain, that we are walking with the words of God ringing in our hearts, souls, ears. We are still small creatures with limited vision. In her vast work of reform and development, Teresa was no stranger to hearing "no" from authorities. But she also knew how to wait and pray until, somehow, through various means, including political pressure, letter writing, and the Holy Spirit, the naysayer changed his mind or changed his post, and the path was opened. You could say that it is a disingenuous sort of obedience, but I also see it as humility: if God is really in it, the way will be made, the posts rearranged. No need to jump the fence.

I do wish someone had laid out a bit of this teaching for me earlier in my life. I grew up with a mind as literal as most children's, thinking that if God were to deign to communicate with us, it would be very clear, words heard through our ears. (I've tried to teach my own children to listen for God in the quiet of their hearts; I don't know if this will prove helpful to them as they grow, but it's my attempt at a course correction.) This perspective later shifted to the assumption and implication that God didn't speak to us anymore like that, if he ever did, except vaguely through Scripture, nature, teachings at church, and acts of love. To think that God was still speaking, to think that God might speak directly to us—dangerous hubris! The stuff of terrorists! Of course, there is danger and the potential for hubris in it, as Teresa knows. But when the idea of God speaking more personally and directly is completely eliminated from the vocabulary of society, even communities of faith, then the impulse, the desire, to hear from God, to communicate with God, is still there, but there is no language for the conversation. What are the different ways in which God speaks? How might one discern the imaginative responses of our ego's desires from the voice of God? The questions are still there; they are simply unspoken, beneath the surface. Thomas Merton told one of his novices that "the problem today is not that people suppress the sexual instinct, as Freud said; now, people suppress the spiritual self and keep it repressed."[263]

As a pastor, I have seen the fear and wonder in people's eyes when their spiritual self suddenly broke out and onto the scene. One young woman leaned toward me across the table at a coffee shop, telling me about her risky and precarious labor and delivery, a scary but not uncommon tale of fear and uncertainty as she was rushed into an emergency procedure. She paused, looked around, and whispered the words, "Then God spoke to me. I don't know how. I didn't hear it with my ears, but it was inside, clear as day: *Everything will be okay*. And the fear was gone. I knew it was God, and I knew it would be all right." She looked around again. "Does that sound crazy? That's crazy, isn't it?" Teresa would say no, not crazy. It meets the criteria for genuine divine communication: the words carried power and authority, both in themselves and the actions that followed, leaving peace and praise and gratitude, and a mind that cannot forget. But we all need guidance, reassurance, teaching to sift through what we hear in our heads and our hearts, both within and outside of intentional prayer time.

This "outside of prayer" piece is the last part of Teresa's teaching on locutions that I'd like to hold up for consideration. Although, initially, and most often, we discern God speaking to us in and through intentional prayer, or an intentional turning inward to seek the truth about ourselves and God (see the first five dwelling places), eventually and occasionally, "there's another way the Lord speaks to the soul."[264] The onetime experiences like that of the woman in labor described above are one such example, but Teresa spends more time tending to a different dynamic, wherein an individual is given the gift of a more pervasive knowledge of Christ's presence in the day-to-day movements of life. She calls this gift an "intellectual vision,"[265] but the term is a bit misleading because the eyes have no part to play. Even she says, "I don't know why" it's called this.[266] The knowledge of Christ's presence is not given in response to prayer: "It might happen this way: while the soul is not in the least expecting this gift, and even though it's never even *thought* that it deserved such a thing, it will feel our Lord Jesus Christ near, though it can't see Him with the eyes of the body or soul."[267] It is, simply put, one of "the ways and means that His Majesty communicates Himself to us, revealing His love for us."[268] Teresa writes that when this happened to her,

> since she was afraid about this vision, she went to her confessor, very worried. (This isn't like an imaginary vision that quickly passes; it can last for many days and sometimes even more than a year.)... And even though people stirred up serious doubts in her about it, she felt again and again that she couldn't doubt it

was genuine, especially when He said to her, "Don't be afraid; it is I." These words had such power that when she heard them, she couldn't doubt—and was deeply strengthened by and happy about such good company.[269]

This experience is distinct from an intellectual, theological understanding that Christ is always with us. By God's grace—and with all the lack of striving or earning that implies—there is a presence as real as the grass itself. There is no controlling this gift: "The Lord gives this when He wants, and it can't be acquired."[270] And, dovetailing with, or out of, this acute awareness of Christ's presence, a different sort of locution may arise.

This contact takes places so far down in the soul's depths, in such secret, and the words spoken by the Lord seem to be heard so clearly with the ears of the soul: the very way in which they are heard, combined with the effects of the vision, convinces and assures the person that the adversary has no part to play in this. The wonderful effects produced are enough to make us trust this, or at least we can be sure that such words and phrases don't come from our imagination.[271]

There are other sources of assurance, too: the clarity of the locution, which is "so clear that even if a single syllable is missing from what the person heard, or if it was said in one style or another, he remembers—even if it's a whole sentence."[272] The words we make up for God in our imagination are fuzzier, half dreamed. Also, these locutions can be a sort of "interruption" of our own thoughts, though not necessarily disconnected from the context of the moment. There is often—though again, not always—a future orientation to the words, and the word or phrase arrives as if we are hearing it, not engaging in the slower process of mental composition. The words cannot be ignored. Finally, there is a depth to the words and the knowledge they bear that our own intellect cannot manufacture.[273]

Perhaps most telling of all, when we remember the fundamental lesson about God's freedom and agency and otherness, just because one has been given the gift of this acute awareness of Christ's presence doesn't mean that Jesus is suddenly captive to conversation. We have a confidence that Christ hears us, but we have no control over when He speaks to us. He retains all the freedom, agency, and element of the unexpected we would imagine from accounts of the risen Christ in Scripture. It's a characteristic of this kind of locution that applies quite nicely to all divine communications. As Teresa puts it: "She *wasn't* able to hear Him speaking to her whenever she wanted to, but only unexpectedly, when the words were necessary."[274]

Drawn by Fire: The Wound of Love, Longing, and Ridding Ourselves of Obstacles to Solitude

His be the bravery of all those Bright things.
The glowing cheeks, the glistering wings;
The Rosy hand, the radiant DART;
Leave HER alone THE FLAMING HEART.
     Leave her that; and you shall leave her
Not one loose shaft but love's whole quiver.
For in love's field was never found
A nobler weapon than a WOUND.
Love's passives are his activ'st part,
The wounded is the wounding heart.
O HEART! the equal poise of love's both parts
Big alike with wound and darts.
Live in these conquering leaves; live all the same;
And walk through all tongues one triumphant FLAME.[275]

We have reached the place in the castle where, ostensibly, the greatest drama lies, or at least the greatest place of popular interest in Teresa's life is found. In chapter 2 of the sixth dwellings, we find, as Williams writes, "the language of the 'wound of love,' so important in the imagery of John of the Cross: the deeper touch of God creates a sense of longing that is excruciatingly painful, yet also a source of pleasure."[276] It is the section that aligns most obviously with the image of Teresa's prayer experiences and theology that you might run across after the short inspirational quotes but before anything else. If you are unfamiliar with this most iconic Teresa moment, as I was—apart from viewing Bernini's famous rendition of the scene in Rome's church of Santa Maria della Vittoria—here is the short section in Teresa's autobiography that has sparked so much theological, literary, and artistic passion. Again, this passage is not found in *The Interior Castle*, but elements of this experience clearly echo therein:

> I saw close to me toward my left side an angel in bodily form.... I saw in his hands a large golden dart and at the end of the iron tip there appeared to be a little fire. It seemed to me this angel plunged the dart several times into my heart and that it reached deep within me. When he drew it out, I thought he was carrying off with him the deepest part of me; and he left me all on fire with great love of God. The pain was so great that it made me moan, and the sweetness this greatest pain caused me was so superabundant that there is no desire capable of taking it away; nor is the soul content with less than God. The pain is not bodily but spiritual, although the body doesn't fail to share in some of it, and even a great deal. The loving exchange that takes place between the soul and God is so sweet that I beg Him in His goodness to give a taste of this love to anyone who thinks I am lying.[277]

When Teresa writes the *Moradas*, later in life and using a different narrative voice (one that takes care to couch every extraordinary gift of God in prayer in the third person), she makes no mention of the angel and downplays the language that caused her the greatest trouble.[278] Yet all of the essential elements are still there in the sixth dwellings: it is still the place of fiery arrows, where that paradoxical blend of pleasure and pain leads some people to a simplistically sexual interpretation, leaving casual onlookers either scandalously scared or briefly scintillated.

A more serious student of Teresa, and a more sincere seeker of God, must be willing to courageously contemplate the ways in which "the body shares" in the pain, fire, and love of God while not getting fixated there. What is it all *about*, as much as we can say? What is it all for? What work are these sorts of gifts of poignant fire *doing* in the body and soul? Where do they lead? Although the English poet Richard Crashaw wrote his Teresa poems after reading her autobiography, not *The Interior Castle*, he still captures the thrust of Teresa's point, and God's point, too, it seems:

> For in love's field was never found
> A nobler weapon than a WOUND.

Love's passives are his activ'st part,
The wounded is the wounding heart.

To be touched by love but lack complete fulfillment or rest in that love enkindles greater desire and love.

As Teresa herself puts it, broadly and simply, when introducing these kinds of enkindling spiritual delights, she is dealing with "some of the ways in which our Lord *awakens* the soul." (Emphasis added.) Don't worry, she preemptively reassures the reader: "It seems that there is nothing in these awakenings to fear even though the experience is sublime and the favors are great."[279] She is describing the sort of fire that makes the little dove or butterfly "fly higher."[280] The love of God is a drawing flame. What might be considered her thesis statement to the section boldly identifies how a deeper and distinctive touch of God's love for us, felt as surely as fire within us, is meant to create a sense of longing that drives us forward in our pursuit of God's company above all others, even if our progress is painful and halting: "Before [the soul is] completely one with Him, He fills it with a strong desire. This happens in ways so delicate that the soul itself doesn't understand the means. (I don't think I'll be able to describe them in an understandable way, except for those who have experienced this.)"[281]

It is, as people have long suspected, about desire: about God's desire for the soul to "fly higher," away from interior and exterior attachments that compromise our God-given integrity and identity, and about the soul's desire to belong fully to the One who made it and knows it better than any other. We know something of this from earthly love affairs, yes, but also other realms of great desire and halting progress, of glorious arrivals awakened in our consciousness but not yet fully realized. For Williams, this relates to the "restlessness" of the sixth dwellings in general: "There is a pervasive awareness of something begun, something promised, and the requirement to wait for it to come to fruition is agony."[282] There are things that must be worked out in the betrothal period, even if it takes many years.[283]

Often, when a person is quite unprepared and isn't even thinking about God, he's awakened by His Majesty—as if by a streaming comet or a clap of thunder. Although no sound is heard, the soul is very well aware that it has been called by God. [The call is so clear] that sometimes he begins to tremble and complain, even though he doesn't feel anything that causes pain. The soul feels it has been wounded in a wonderful way, but it doesn't understand how, or by whom. It *is* certain that this is a precious experience and would be happy if the wound never healed. It complains to its Spouse with loving words, even out loud (not being able to refrain from doing so). It realizes that He is present yet will not manifest Himself in a way that allows the soul to enjoy Him. This is painful, although also delightful and sweet. Even if the soul didn't want to suffer this wound, it wouldn't have a choice—but anyway, it wouldn't want to refuse. It's much more satisfying to a soul than the delightful and painless absorption that happens in the prayer of quiet.[284]

Intriguingly, Teresa is uncharacteristically calm and confident about the provenance of this delightful, sweet pain, especially since it is a type of gift in prayer that has made the rest of the world so very nervous. "There are no grounds for thinking this experience comes from any natural cause, or is caused by mental illness, or that it's an illusion of the adversary or the imagination,"[285] she writes. If the Lord has granted you this favor in any form, she says, you'll know it by the description, and you should thank God for this precious gift without fear of deception. (However, as always, don't prove ungrateful for such a generous favor, and strive to live a better life of service. You might continue to receive.)[286]

Teresa has thoughts on "why there is greater security in this experience than in other things." Basically, she thinks the paradoxical blend of pain and peace is inimitable by tempters to a false way, but it seems this sort of spiritual delight also draws security from the effects on, or benefits to, the soul: "as a general rule" (which seems such a surprising and yet comforting term from her here!), one feels determined to serve and suffer for God whatever the cost, and simultaneously more determined to "[withdraw] from the satisfactions and entanglements of this world."[287] More security of authenticity: no matter how the soul may strive to experience this spiritual delight, it absolutely defies counterfeit attempts. There is no way to grasp it, fake it, create it, or fancy it from or in your imagination. This gift, which proceeds "from the interior part of the soul," is "felt as clearly as we hear a loud voice with our ears."[288] She recognizes that this is an unusual amount of assurance, but she stands behind it: "I know of a person," she writes—ahem, herself—"who was terribly anxious about being deceived in prayer, and yet never had any fears about this kind of prayer."[289]

For Teresa, the place of struggle here is explaining "this act of love." She admits, "I don't know how,"[290] for she can see all the logical contradictions the descriptions she has offered include. Rowan Williams generalizes this struggle as one that characterizes the sixth dwelling places as a whole: the soul doesn't know how to communicate its experiences; there is "an absolute lack of convincing, honest-sounding religious language for what is going on."[291] For example: How can the Spouse, or Beloved, be "making it very clear that He *is* with the soul and yet [at the same time]…giving it such a clear, undoubtable sign that He's *calling*; that the call is so penetrating that the soul can't fail to hear it"?[292] In other words, how can the Beloved be *with* the soul and yet *calling* the soul? How can this act of love powerfully dissolve the soul with desire for God and yet also leave the soul stupefied as to what to ask for, "because it clearly seems to her that God is [already] with her"?[293] She anticipates the questions: If the soul knows God is present to it, what more—what "greater good"—could it possibly want? What pains it? "I don't know," Teresa says again.[294] There is something, or there are many things, going on here that cannot be explained but can only be described—sort of. Perhaps it could be best described in baroque poetry, though I think Teresa does a better job than she gives herself credit for: "I know that this pain seems to reach her entrails—her very depths—and that when the One who wounds her takes the arrow out of them, it truly seems that *He draws out these inmost depths after Him*, following the deep feeling of love."[295]

Teresa continues with the visual metaphor of fire, now dropping the arrow and concentrating instead on the relationship between the source and the spark. In order to glimpse, if not grasp, the tension she is pointing to, the reader needs to keep in mind that the soul yearns to be set on fire, to be consumed, by the presence of God, even as God's presence is not comfortable:

I've just been wondering if my God might be described as the fire in a lighted firepit; it's as though a spark flies out and touches the soul. It can feel the burning heat, but the fire is not hot enough to set the soul on fire, and the experience is so delectable that the soul is left with that pain; the spark merely touching the soul creates this effect. This seems the best comparison that I've been able to find, because this delectable pain—which isn't really pain—isn't continuous. Sometimes it lasts for a long time, and sometimes it suddenly comes to an end, according to how the Lord wants to give it, because it's something that can't be procured or obtained in any human way. Even though sometimes it's felt for a long while, it comes and goes. In short, it's never permanent. So it never completely sets the soul on fire; just as the soul is about to ignite, the spark dies, leaving the soul yearning again to suffer the loving pain.[296]

Lest we think that Teresa is describing an attachment to the spark, not God—and picturing a languorous soul left and waiting with desire to be touched again by holy fire, addicted—recall again this saint's impatience with fixations on any gracious gift. It is always about awakening, forming, strengthening, drawing us toward the fire "that is my God."[297] We never "aim" for any grace of prayer, seeking to grasp or acquire it. There is a surprise twist at the end of this chapter, too, an important one for readers who may not resonate with Teresa's emphasis on pain or the "wound of love" but know they have at least once been set on fire—enkindled—with love for God in a way for which there are no suitable words to describe:

Our Lord has other ways of awakening the soul, too: quite unexpectedly, when it is praying aloud and not thinking of anything interior, it suddenly seems to catch fire in a wonderful way. It's as if a fragrance were suddenly to become so powerful that it spreads through all the senses, only in order to convey to the soul an awareness that the Spouse is there. (I'm not saying it *is* a fragrance; it's only a comparison.) The soul is moved by a delectable desire to enjoy Him, and thus the soul is prepared to do great acts and make praises to our Lord. The source of this gift is the one already referred to [the Lord, "very deep within the soul"[298]], but in this case there's nothing that causes pain, and the soul's desires to enjoy God aren't painful in any way—this is actually how the soul *usually* experiences it. For many of the reasons already mentioned, I don't think there's much cause for fear here; one should try to receive this gift with gratitude and give thanks for it.[299]

In this experience, there is no pain but plenteous enjoyment of the Spouse. What's the result? Much the same: preparation for action, and praise. And, surprise, ye masochists! This painless version is actually the *usual* form of this merciful gift. Nothing to fear here, either. Just be grateful. There will still be plenty of angst and longing to work through outside of prayer. Teresa's beloved Augustine said it so well: "You made us for Yourself, and our hearts are restless until they rest in You."[300] The often-unspoken good news alongside this idea is that Christ will keep beckoning, especially if our hearts are trying to rest, accustomed to resting, elsewhere.

When my husband, Colin, and I were engaged, we were lucky enough to have a wicked-smart, funny, and wise pastor lead us though our premarital conversations. I remember sitting on the scratchy brown couch across from our pastor in the church office, feeling pretty smug about some of my answers concerning what I had learned from my own parents' marriage and divorce. I had thought about this *a lot*, I explained. I listed many pitfalls that I hoped to avoid, but I remember having extra certainty and conviction about what my mother had named as one of her fatal mistakes: she had made an idol of my dad. She had made him her world, and no human can bear to be the center like that: they know the other person will be crushed when they fall. I had witnessed my mother's pain, and I did not want the lesson she had learned to be in vain; I would never make that mistake, I said. Colin would be my partner, my spouse, my husband, but never my idol, never my lord. I was a good student of the premarital sessions, and, again, I felt pretty good about my answers—especially this one. God, and not any person, would be at the center.

What I didn't know when I got married at age twenty-three is how subtle these things sometimes are. Our incisive pastor may have seen this before I did. "One thing to be careful of," he said at our final session, "is a certain functioning that's more responsive to your personalities than your theology. In your families of origin, Colin is an older brother, and you are a younger sister; make sure you're on guard to that dynamic creeping in. You want the mutual respect of two equal adults." "Ah, yes!" I said with youthful enthusiasm. "I know all about *that* false romantic trap. No person can complete you. Two halves don't make a whole. Each person must come to the marriage in wholeness." *Got it.* I realize now that there were still layers unseen. What if the two oranges roll along, but their progress is more like a set of unequal magnets? Happy and whole, but with one having the stronger pull? The way you defer to an older brother is more subtle than idol worship. It's harder to see, especially if you're comfortable tagging along, and never lacking in love or respect.

Colin and I strove for the true and practical equality that, from the beginning, we both thought of as the ideal. Thankfully, God arranged our calls to ordained ministry in such a way that we never had to wrestle over whether one of us was "following" the other: he first felt an invitation to the priesthood when he was still a Roman Catholic, while living among Jesuit priests in El Salvador. On Valentine's Day of my junior year at Stanford, I cried the tragic tears of a girl "dumped for God," sensing that I couldn't even complain about this. But then Colin discerned that he was emotionally healthier when he was in a relationship and that, ergo, the priesthood was not for him. He threw himself into community organizing. Three years later, when we were newlyweds living in Washington, DC, I began to sense a call to ordained ministry. Then, two years after this, when it was finally time for me to start the "official" process in the Episcopal Church, a mentor asked Colin, "Have *you* ever thought about becoming a priest?" Why, yes, he had. And now he could do so, though married, and would. So it was that we went off to seminary together, were ordained together, and were assigned to serve in the same church together as associates. Because we could see the way our different gifts complemented one another, and because we wanted to serve in the same church while our children were young, when it was time to venture forth from the mother ship, we then pursued a joint position as co-pastors. We arrived at St. Luke's in San Diego in October of 2016 and shared the yoke of a challenging but blessed entrepreneurial ministry, restarting a small Sudanese-American church.

We often expressed our earnest gratitude out loud, to each other and to others, that we were not solo pastors. It was so much better to not be alone in this sometimes-consuming work.

From the beginning of our time at St. Luke's, though, it was clear that it was a different thing to lead together than to serve under someone else's leadership together. We struggled, conscientiously, to find our way into a dynamic that worked at our place of employment. We knew how to parent together, run a household together—surely, we could figure out how to lead a congregation together, especially with the help of a church-planting coach and a therapist. You'll notice, I'm sure, that we had a lot of togetherness, and many people expressed worry about this: "Is it too much?" "No," we'd reply, "though we can see how you might think that! We barely see each other at the office. We're busy doing our own things. And, don't worry, we figured out quickly that having two desks in the same office did not work. We're rolling along like two compatible oranges, similar but different. We're cool."

Until I wasn't cool with things. Over a year after Christ the bridegroom first came to me, and eighteen months after our arrival at St. Luke's, on an April evening, Colin and I sat together in our living room, and I said things that were honest but scary: "It's not working for me, the way we are working together. At home, it's good. At work, it's not. *We can do better.*" That night, I had a dream that I was leaving Colin for my "animus," a man whom I had long ago identified as the symbolic bearer of creativity and wholeness in my dreams. Representationally, I think he is related to Christ, but I can't explain how. In the dream, I was running away with him, flying on an airplane and landing on a mountaintop where there was a cozy home. I was excited and relieved and joyful but also questioning and uncertain. I kept asking, "Is this real?" The subtext: "Do you [the man] really know me and love me?" Underneath my excitement and questioning, a terrifying realization came to me: *This is how mothers and wives do this. This is how they leave their children, their husbands, their families.* I never before understood how they could, but I did then.

I take dreams seriously but never literally. I was intrigued by this sequence but couldn't quite grasp what God was telling me through my subconscious until the meaning came to me in a different form, more bluntly, during a time of prayer. Four days later, my heart was struck by this Scripture from Matthew 6:24: "No one can serve two masters." In contemplative silence, I began to experience what felt like a dividing line in the center of my body, which the Lord drew my attention to. At first, it was just a line, but I sensed what tension it depicted: that between "serving" Colin and serving Christ. This was part of my tension, my discomfort, at St. Luke's. Christ pressed in with greater clarity, enlarging my heart with this pounding truth: *For joy, serve me.* My prayer had begun with Psalm 51, that ancient psalm of renewal, which includes these words: "Give me the joy of your saving help again."[301] It ended with a directive on joy that was simultaneously a rudiment of Christian catechism and a piercing internal critique: *For* [more] *joy, serve me*—not whoever or whatever else you're actually responding to. Simple, but not easy, just like the gospel as a whole. Four days after this, I journaled these short fragments:

> Two months' turmoil
> taking me to this place
> still without a path forward.
> You shall not serve two masters
> but I, like others
> do not yet know how
> to fully serve the One.

I made human-paced progress. I consulted with a female clergy mentor; I paid closer attention to my daily prayer practice, trying to a find a word from Scripture that would help me navigate the day from within, not without. Colin and I were both more careful about how we talked to each other at work, with more respectful professionalism and fewer casual assumptions (and accusations). I leaned in to the idea—the truth—that God and the bishop were my boss. Still, it felt essential to me to recognize that Colin's behavior was not the problem; he was rolling along without malice, never insisting I stay close. It was *I* who needed to shift the alignment on my magnet, away from him and toward God at the center. It's an inside job—and not an overnight one. Seven months later, I would be convicted by the day's psalm: "I have gone astray like a lost sheep."[302] Again? Again. In prayer, I saw an image of myself leaving Christ's presence in a sunny room to go outside on the patio to pour water for the people sitting there. Not a bad thing, pouring water for other people, but still clearly an act of avoidance, of wandering. *Return to me. You can do it*, I sensed God saying. We laughed together.

A couple of months later, after ten months of conscious struggling to reorient my center of gravity, I had a dream that I was remarrying Colin. It was clear that I was marrying the same man again but on different terms. When I asked him in the golden-hour light of the dream if he was okay with this, he said, very tenderly, "Yes—you have been unhappy as long as I have known you, and this way will be better." I was surprised, even in my dreaming mind, by his observation, but also comforted. We could move forward in a different way, and he would want that, too. Once more, my waking mind wanted to scream corrections: *I have not been unhappy!* But dreams sometimes paint in technicolor and rude symbols what we will not examine without the help of the Spirit. *For joy, serve me.*

At the very beginning of "Sixth Dwellings," Teresa says that this is the place where "the soul has been wounded with love for the Spouse. It looks for more opportunity to be alone, trying as much as possible to renounce everything that disturbs this solitude."[303] The wisdom of this summary expands for me nearly by the day. Just as before, when Teresa talked about what it would take to progress from the first dwelling place to the second (getting rid of "*unnecessary* affairs and business"[304]), she makes room to accommodate seekers of many states. I hear in this an invitation to each of us—married or single, parents or not, leaders or low-key followers, priests and dentists and teachers and security guards—to rid ourselves of everything that can be an obstacle to "this solitude." The wise particularity of each person's "renouncing" rings out for me here: "as much as possible." Given your actual life, the holy responsibilities you carry, and the vows you have already made, what does it look like to "renounce everything that disturbs this solitude"? I hear resonances of a solitude that is not as much about being physically alone (although, sometimes, of course, that is helpful and necessary), but more about a solid individuality growing like a blade of grass toward the light of God even as others grow around you, close and in community.

My life is not as silent as Teresa's; it is not my state. But still, when we are wounded by God's love, and long to draw nearer to him in a way that goes much deeper than our moments in prayer, extending into every corner of our lives, finding strength in "this solitude" with God even in our social states, then we will have to rid ourselves of the subtle, sometimes unseen, obstacles to this solitude. Where are we otherwise too closely attached? Who, or what, have we been rolling along behind? It is often said that, in spiritual maturity, we must basically shift from self-regard to seeing God as the center of the universe and of ourselves. That's probably true for many people. But, for some of us, as we make that shift, we will find that the center of our universe and the center of ourselves is crowded. We must clear it out, leaving God alone. Then we can love others from a place of greater wholeness and stability, with a balance that comes from the integrity given through the weight of the One in our center who knows just who we are, and who and how we are meant to be.

I wish I were more like the energetic soul Rowan Williams seems to imagine in the sixth dwelling places, driven "forward in urgent longing that is more and more consumed and determined by its object—the God at the center whose presence has become irreversibly pervasive in us and compelling to us."[305] Or, maybe it is just that he has forgotten to highlight the struggle that accompanies this longing, the ways that we are caught up in webs even as feel compelled toward God at the center. I relate much more to Teresa's frustrated butterfly:

> Oh, poor little butterfly, tied up with so many chains that prevent you from flying wherever you would like! Have pity on her, my God! Ordain and arrange her path so that she might be able to accomplish some of her desires for Your honor and glory! Don't take into account how undeserving she is or her lowly nature. You have the power, Lord, to make the vast ocean pull back, and the Jordan river open wide, to allow the children of Israel to pass through. And yet—You don't need to take pity on her. Because, with the help of Your strength, she *is* capable of enduring many challenging works; she's determined to do so and wants to suffer through them. Stretch out Your mighty arm, O Lord, and don't let her life be spent in such lowly things! Let Your greatness appear in her, feminine and base though she may be, so that the world might understand that none of it comes from *her*, and might give *You*

praise. No matter what it costs, this is what she wants. She would give a thousand lives, if she had them, so one soul might praise You a little more. She would consider them well spent.[306]

Even in what she asks of God, Teresa is uneven, and yet wanting, wanting, to spend her life in a way that draws more love to the light, more moths to the flame.

A Brief Interlude on Raptures

In this dwelling place, raptures happen very frequently, and they can't be resisted, even in public. As a result: persecutions and criticisms. And even though she wants to be fearless about this, it's not entirely possible because there are many people who lay fears *on* her....

As a tour guide through Teresa's sprawling *Interior Castle*, I have little to say about "God suspending the soul in prayer with rapture or ecstasy or transport, which are all the same," in her opinion.[307] For those with experiences that you think may fall into these rooms, or those who simply have a deeper curiosity about the terms and what Teresa describes, chapters four, five, and six of the sixth dwellings, as well as the twentieth chapter of her autobiography, are good places to start. These descriptions include what might be called levitation and a more sudden rapture she calls the swift "flight of the spirit."[308] Teresa is pretty comprehensive, though understandably not crystal clear, about these areas. She's well into the rooms of the castle that are just plain hard to describe. Both sections of writing have drawn what Williams chasteningly says is "rather disproportionate attention."[309] Oh, but not everyone can be as reasonably constituted as the brilliant former Archbishop of Canterbury! We are human beings, notably fascinated by the dramatic and unusual. It was a weakness that Jesus pointed out,[310] and one he famously denied the temptation to lead with when invited to jump off the temple into an angel's arms.[311] Yet what is more wondrous than the resurrection? God is clearly not opposed to signs and wonders; we just don't get to expect them, demand them, or declare them necessary for our trust and love.

Therefore, here are some rapture basics, according to Teresa. Raptures draw the soul out of its senses, for good reason: to draw closer to God's glory *in* our senses would probably kill us. (Frankly, she points out, some people are probably so weak in their constitutions that even the relatively tame but still divinely given "prayer of quiet" would be enough to put their lives in jeopardy.[312]) There are different kinds of rapture: Some raptures take place during prayer. In another sort, a soul that has been suffering from a long spiritual drought with a painfully dim "spark" of light is touched, unexpectedly and outside of prayer, by "some word it remembers or hears from God."[313] In a phoenixlike renewal, "God unites [the soul] with Himself" in a way that only "the two of them" understand.[314] Although this experience sounds fairly sudden, it must be gradual and gentle compared to the kind Teresa describes later as the "flight of the spirit," which is "*experienced* within the soul in a very different way" from the others: "sometimes, suddenly, the soul feels a movement that is so fast it seems the spirit is being carried away—and at a scary speed, especially in the beginning[315]… as quickly as a bullet leaves a gun when the trigger is pulled."[316] There is no means of resisting; it is like a giant snatching up a piece of straw, or, returning to the water metaphors of the fourth dwellings, like a piece of bark being lifted on an enormous and forcefully swelling wave.[317]

Despite our rhetorical implications that levitation or raptures are the work of the saint ("Apparently, she could levitate!"), Teresa always keeps the agency in God's hands; the soul is pulled up or toward God by the power of the Spirit, not by flying through physics-distorting contemplative acumen. Raptures, like all "extraordinary" gifts, are not given for raptures' sake, like some simultaneously jolly and sobering cosmic ride. As with all that Teresa describes, the work of revelation, teaching, empowerment, and formation is accomplished through them. And, "when the soul is in this suspension, the Lord sees fit to reveal some mysteries, things about heaven, and imaginative visions."[318] Some of the things "revealed" are seen by the imagination, with images attached, and some are not seen but somehow known (as by that same difficult term, "intellectual vision"). Though unexplainable, the things "seen" in either way "are still clearly imprinted in the very depths of the soul, and never forgotten."[319] Teresa offers the earthly comparison of being led into a room filled with treasures: you may not remember in detail any of the fine things you saw there or understand how any of the things were actually made, but you could still in general remember seeing everything, and the beauty of it all. And it's not just about being "impressed" with holy grandeur (although that reifies a beneficial humility, too): there is something essentially fortifying about the experience. She uses Moses of an example of this:

> Moses also didn't know how to describe everything that he saw in the [burning] bush, but only as much as God wanted him to. Yet if God hadn't revealed mysteries to his soul in such a way that he became *sure* of their truth—recognizing and trusting Him to be God indeed—he wouldn't have taken up so many works, and such difficult ones! Amid the thorns of that bush, he *must* have understood profound truths, things that gave him the courage to do what he did for the people of Israel.[320]

There is nothing "exceptional" about raptures in terms of how Teresa understands them to *function* within a life of faith: they give greater understanding of God's grandeur; they make us more aware of who we are as limited creatures and less wont to offend or defy our Creator; and they realign our vision and priorities—leaving less "value for earthly things, except those that can be used in the service of such a great God."[321] Granted, a rapture is a powerful tool for the teaching and imprinting of these lessons, but one can see the continuity of a theologically simple idea: one needs to deeply understand that God is God and we are not in order to bring about, with humility, ways of being on earth that are truly *of* God. We can even see raptures as grand journeys of love, deepening our understanding of the Other. Paradoxically, raptures leave the physical body temporarily weakened even as the soul is strengthened by what it has seen or known by God's invitation. It mirrors this lesson: there is something more lasting than what we know through our senses. To "see" it is to be strengthened to work for it and toward it more steadily and confidently, even in our frail, uneven, unpredictable bodies.

Wretched Tears, Invitatory Joy, and Staying Close to Jesus

> The soul wants to be completely occupied in love, and doesn't want to be engaged with anything else. But this can't be, even if the soul

wants it to be so. For [imagine this], even though the will is not dead, the fire that usually kindles and reignites it *is* gone; someone needs to blow on it if it's going to produce heat. Would it be good for the soul to stay in this state of dryness, waiting for fire to come down from heaven like our father Elijah did, burning this sacrifice it's making of itself to God? No, certainly not; it's not right to expect miracles. The Lord will perform them for this soul when *He* sees fit to do so, as I've said and will say again. But His Majesty wants us to consider ourselves undeserving of them because of our ordinariness, and to do everything we possibly can to help ourselves. I myself believe that such an attitude is necessary until we die, no matter how sublime our prayer might be.[322]

On March 4, 2019, I arrived at the Spiritual Ministry Center in Ocean Beach, San Diego, in a state of deep tiredness. I could name all the surface-level reasons for my fatigue, visible on the calendar: out-of-town visitors followed by the festivities of my son's fifth birthday (and anyone who has been to Chuck E. Cheese with a group of children can testify that it's enervating to even the most vigorous of spirits), the side hustle of preparing our house to rent out on Airbnb, filling in as a part-time chaplain for two months at a private Episcopal school on top of my parish ministry work, and the recent near-deportation of the father of seven children who were part of our church family. On the calendar, it was a classic case of overextension. After all that, any soul would be deeply tired, close to burnout, right? But I was aware, somehow, that it wasn't just rest I needed. I knew, somehow, that the monk who offered counsel to David Whyte was right: the antidote to exhaustion wasn't rest, it was wholeheartedness.[323] The Christian world is full of invitations to self-giving, to service, to personal sacrifice. Rightly so, considering the life of Jesus. But in all this language of "pouring ourselves out" like Jesus did, a crucial step is often left out, silent except in the copious passages of Jesus' own time in solitary prayer and rest: it turns out you cannot pour from an empty cup. One must know oneself as a distinct vessel before God, filled by the love and power of God, to be able to pour oneself out for more than a day.

I had begun to know that shape, that distinction, the necessity of being filled up in order to rightly pour out, but now I felt the vessel cracking.

Water was seeping out. I resented all the bodies around me soaking up my life but was at a loss to stop the sprawling cracks in my vessel, the persistent leaks. I could sense that I was losing my deeper grounding in God. Thankfully, the wisdom of the church and the prodigious organizational skills of my husband meant that a two-night Lenten retreat was already in the books. Otherwise, I might have kept walking in dryness, foolishly waiting for "fire to come down from heaven" to light up this sacrifice that I was making of myself. To go on retreat was a simple way of "helping myself" in my yearning for God to rekindle the kind of fire that cures and sets, forging the vessel anew. As always, I really didn't know what God would give me, even though I thought I knew what I was looking for. Our eyes see only so far.

After a brief orientation from a RSCJ sister and a quiet lunch, I finished writing my Ash Wednesday homily on my laptop so I could experience more freedom and spaciousness during my remaining time. I felt carried by and close to Christ as I wrote this offering I had no energy for; but, as I closed my computer, the exhaustion welled up, carrying me upstairs to the bedroom, where I collapsed on the comforter in tears before God. I cried like a child nuzzling into its mother's chest, overwhelmed and pressing all the weight of my burdens into this presence that was bigger than myself. It felt so good to cry and receive Christ's comfort. To express aloud how tired and at a loss I felt, not on the surface but deep down. To be met in that place with palpable love, allowing me to fall asleep as a grateful child, spent.

In sleep, and as I was waking up hours later, the words "Psalm 113" repeatedly came into my mind. I was not biblically steeped enough to know the content of that particular psalm, so I looked it up:

Who is like the LORD our God…?

He raises the poor from the dust,
And lifts the needy from the ash heap,

To make them sit with princes,
With the princes of his people.

He gives the barren woman a home,
Making her the joyous mother of children.[324]

I was curious about this passage, struck by the promise and imagery of help for the needy. On the surface, I was gliding along, but within I needed "lifting." The term "ash heap" was a bit much, I thought with some detachment—not the word *I* would have chosen; still, I could not deny that the image spoke to me. Knowing so many people who were materially poor and repeatedly battered by the world, I was still loath to allow myself to acknowledge my own places of poverty. "I am a bit burned up and burned out," I conceded in my journal. "I need God's help to both be raised and find joy anew in motherhood, wifehood, and priesthood."

Later, I carried out the exercises prescribed by my spiritual director—recalling patterns of my current rule of life that were most life-giving, making a gratitude list ("I am the mother of two heart-wrenchingly beautiful children who want to play with me; I have a supportive, loving, intelligent, attractive husband who wants to spend time with me; I am in a flexible ministry role;" etc., etc.)—but then, ironically, right on the heels of this earnest practice of thanksgiving, I felt compelled to write an amateur poem that seems like a cliché of the midlife woman but is still pulsing with honest desire:

I dream of traveling lighter
    Heading out the door with one bag
    Rather than three.
    Some dream of Mary Tyler Moore,
    Established in the corner office,
    But I can only see
    The way she steps out,
    Unencumbered,
    Walking with vigor,
    And one small handbag.

Will I ever carry just one bag?
    Or is this what I've taken on
    As mother
    Wife
    Pastor
    Writer?

Can I learn to be these things,
    In turn and altogether,

> In a way that also allows me
> To walk with a lighter load?

More spring in my step
> More wind in my hair
> Moving, not plodding
> With joy.

As I finished the poem, a bit embarrassed but still relieved to have the truth on the page, I thought of the Amy Grant song that I had hated and made fun of at age ten: "Hats"(!) That song is also about the burdens of multiple responsibilities and identities in the world—and was penned by a woman who, at the time she wrote it, was about my age. Suddenly, I had compassion for Amy and all the women who felt the angst of that song: *Why do I have to feel the weight of so many things on my head?* How can we walk with all these hats, all these bags? Where would a freedom that was still loving and responsible come from, and what would it look like?

The next morning, in the sober light of early day, I returned to prayer with Psalm 113. It was a quiet and muted prayer session, which was honestly not what I had expected after the warm overtures of the Spirit the previous day in my exhausted despair. I realized I expected Christ to meet me in a way that was more passionate, more intense. I was again chastened, reminded of God's ultimate agency and ever-surprising ways. Drama and knowledge of Christ's presence are never required for grace or growth, and so, in the quiet, as I meditated on the psalm, I began to draw close to two lines, forming an amalgam from my heart: "Raise me up from the ashy heap, making me a joyful mother." I realized that I longed not only for renewal in general, but also renewal in the joy I had with and for my children. I tried to probe the patterns of the past months: when and why had I allowed myself to interiorly degrade them, losing their timelessness to the pressures of the calendar? I think of the days when I felt more generous in love toward them, free to see and be present to them, released from the fog of generalized modern malaise—*overwhelm*. The days and weeks of greater clarity and joy all had one thing in common: I had taken time to pray and write. I had honored the call God had placed on my life. Somehow, out of that essential work, the other work had all looked different.

I think that many retreats would have ended there, and it would have been fine. But the transformation Christ wants to work in us goes deeper than this surface-level tweaking and scratching and rearranging. Our healer is not content with prescribing a new program to manage our symptoms. "Give me more time," our loving physician says. "Take off your shoes. Disrobe. What's really going on here?"

Sister Regina, petite and soft-voiced, spoke to me from across the small room that had been set aside for spiritual direction. "I have been praying about what you said," she began. "At first I thought you were being too hard on yourself, but then I decided to really listen. And I wonder…do you really *see* your children? *See* the people in your parish? Can you be juggling slowly enough that you don't lose the ability to see? (Oh, and don't add any more balls to your life anytime soon!)"

I was quiet, and I could not hold back my tears from this near stranger. I began to cry, not out of exhaustion or embarrassment but from real sadness. She had touched a nerve—not one of vanity but of pain: I had not been the fully present, steadfast, joyful mother, wife, and priest I would like to be. That I felt I could be, should be. She reminded me gently that I was human, but I could see not just a general human frailty but all the particularities of my failings. I had grasped for control of my children, losing sight of their own humanity as I nagged them to clean and move and hustle. I recognized my lack of faithfulness in small things at the church, my laziness around connecting with people instead of tending to the building or ideas. It took no effort to see it all; the vision of my internal failings had been with me all along, a dull pain I had ignored because I thought I wasn't supposed to feel it anymore, that I had ostensibly been cured of my works-righteousness perfectionism by Christ's gracious love. "This old thing?" I thought. But it wasn't quite the same. This was not about performance; it was about deep desire. Maybe it always had been, but I couldn't see it until some of the other layers had been stripped away.

About midway through her writings on the sixth dwelling places, Teresa says this:

Sisters, you'll probably think that these souls—with whom the Lord communicates Himself in this unusual way—will be so sure of enjoying Him forever that they don't have any reason to fear, or weep for their sins. (I'm talking in particular to those who *haven't* had these gifts, because if they *have* been granted enjoyment of such gifts from God, they'll know what I'm about to say.) This assumption would be a big mistake; for the more they receive from our God, the *more* their sorrow for sin grows. I myself believe that this never leaves us until we reach that place where nothing can cause us pain.[325]

Her analysis offers no false hope: no matter how fully we know God's presence in us and His love for us, we will always suffer somewhat over our sins—the gap between the image of God placed in us and our human frailty. There will always be sins to weep over. "[To the soul,] it's very distressing to find that she can't avoid committing a great many [sins], unknowingly."[326] To some people, this might seem like a classic case of overly scrupulous religiosity, the whole reason not to get caught up in this quest for "true goodness," but that would be to miss the locus of the pain: it's a lack of alignment—not from without but from within.

After the weepy spiritual-direction session, I went upstairs to my room, where I decided to pray in the imaginative, Ignatian way with the song of Zechariah. It's a canticle from the gospel of Luke (1:68–79), the prophetic song of praise offered by John the Baptist's father when he is finally able to speak again:

> Blessed be the Lord, the God of Israel;
>> he has come to his people and set them free.
> He has raised up for us a mighty savior,
>> born of the house of his servant David.
> Through his holy prophets he promised of old,
> that he would save us from our enemies,
>> from the hands of all who hate us.
> He promised to show mercy to our fathers
>> and to remember his holy covenant.
> This was the oath he swore to our father Abraham,
>> to set us free from the hands of our enemies,

Free to worship him without fear,
   holy and righteous in his sight
   all the days of our life.
You, my child, shall be called the prophet of the Most High,
   for you will go before the Lord to prepare his way,
To give his people knowledge of salvation
   by the forgiveness of their sins.
In the tender compassion of our God
   the dawn from on high shall break upon us,
To shine on those who dwell in darkness and the shadow of death,
   and to guide our feet into the way of peace.[327]

In my mind's eye, I see Zechariah looking at baby John, who turns into John-in-the-desert, forever pointing to Jesus in the icons of the church, an icon of every Christian called to point to Christ in the midst of repentance. "You, my child, shall be called the prophet of the Most High." Who do you think you are? What do you think you're responsible for? In the image of this prayer, it is so clear: I'm not the one who will guide *anyone's* feet into the way of peace. That is for Jesus the Christ. And so, I turn to Christ anew, in a more focused way, asking him to guide my feet into the way of peace, and I spiral further and further down in my probing until I reach the bottom of my tears. The simple answer to "What am I crying about?" is that I want to do better, *be* better, as a wife and mother and priest and writer and overall human being; I'm not doing well enough in *any* of my vocations.

But then, the question of the prayer practice comes back to life. Where are you in this story? And, gently, eyebrows raised, Christ points to where I am, crying with pitiful shame against the temple wall, crumpled up in a ball, lamenting my sins. I laugh at the truth of it. Oh, I see. That's not my intended role. *You, my child, shall be called the prophet of the Most High, for you will go before the Lord to prepare his way.* Like every Christian minister before me, I have been called to imitate John the Baptist: *To give his people knowledge of salvation by the forgiveness of their sins.* Like every Christian before and beside me, I am meant to be a prophet of forgiveness, of God's *tender compassion*, pointing to Jesus the Christ. It's a role not well-fulfilled when weeping over one's own sins.

Suddenly, a line from an old Advent hymn, "Comfort, Comfort Ye My People," came into my prayer in a personalized way: "Your sins I cover." It was all there in a flash as Christ came closer to my weepy mess: *Yes, of course, you don't measure up in these things. But that's what the story is all about. Did you forget? Your sins I cover. That is the goodness you are called to proclaim, but you can't do it if you are crying about your own anxieties on the steps of the temple.*

> Comfort, comfort ye my people,
> speak ye peace, thus saith our God;
> comfort those who sit in darkness
> mourning 'neath their sorrow's load.
> Speak ye to Jerusalem
> of the peace that waits for them;
> tell her that her sins I cover,
> and her warfare now is over.[328]

There was still more to see in the corners of the rooms I couldn't seem to bring light to on my own. After this wondrous time of Ignatian prayer—I already felt that God had been so good, unlocking unnamed problems with the timeless reminder of the simple gospel—I took some journal notes. However, shortly after I set down my pen, I began to cry again, not knowing why, really, since hadn't we just addressed the source of all shame? Yet, in my quiet tears, I began to feel the prayer of recollection, that inimitable and unconjurable awareness of Christ's presence close at hand. Words emerged: *Why are you crying?* The tone was not harsh. There was space as I waited. I didn't really know. An answer emerged: *These are the tears of a woman who has forgotten how deeply she is loved.* This truth was not without an accompanying loving judgment, and a long and awkward conversation commenced from there, a sense of honest probing about why I had not sought or even invited Christ's presence in prayer during the last year, why I had avoided even the areas of the castle where I might potentially be called into the wine cellar. I had given no real space or time for God to act in prayer, though I was praying regularly in the most basic ways.

I saw my own shame in a different light and at new depths: the shame I felt for lack of progress on the book, the shame of all those old inadequacies around righteous productivity—it doesn't just lead to sadness; it leads to avoidance of God, a self-righteous desire to soldier on, once again, until I am really up to standard, worthy of this great love. *Sigh.*

These were the fragments of truth that emerged as God led me through a slow and stilted progression, my soul unaccustomed to the more nuanced notes of spiritual delights after a long season of marching, song-less, through the desert. It was as Emily Dickinson says:

> He fumbles at your spirit
>   As players at the keys
> Before they drop full music on;
>   He stuns you by degrees,
>
> Prepares your brittle substance
>   For the ethereal blow,
> By fainter hammers, further heard,
>   Then nearer, then so slow[329]

Somewhere in the fumbling, the single-handed warmup that barely hints at the skill and power of the player, the question came: *Did you forget that we were supposed to do this work together?* The song continued, along Dickinson's lines:

> Your breath has time to straighten,
>   Your brain to bubble cool,—
> Deals one imperial thunderbolt
>   That scalps your naked soul.[330]

And here, with the arresting force of "joyful captivation," God's energy coursing into my body and heart as surely as the thunderous crescendo of the virtuoso, I heard this sharp truth in its last notes: *LET. ME. IN.* The words resounded in my chest and throughout my being, with each sono-rous heartbeat speaking into otherwise perfect silence.

Stilled, quiet, stunned, I lay there. When my thoughts returned, I thought of Teresa. I was moved to say a prayer to her, speaking out directly to her for the first time. I think now I know a bit more of what she was talking about within and outside of her autobiography, the hints even in *The Interior Castle* of her awareness of her "wretchedness" that can be so off-putting to modern readers, the part of her that wanted to—and sometimes did—withdraw from God, even after receiving great favors, because she couldn't shake her own sense of inadequacy. It's a familiar scene: Door closed. Not doing well. Don't want anyone—especially you—to see me. But I was aware now; I remembered how Teresa had healed from this form of misguided humility, this self-defeating shame that can be so subtle we don't see it slowly papering over the windows.

It's a point of conversion described in her autobiography, not in *The Interior Castle.* Just before her fortieth birthday, Teresa was moved by an *ecce homo* statue of Jesus, experiencing a depth of disturbance in her spirit that she registers as the beginning of a new chapter in her life. In the statue, Jesus is a "man of sorrows," displaying his wounds: alone, abandoned, pierced, crowned with thorns, bound, and about to be killed. At first, Teresa's response is expected, typical: she feels guilt over her ingratitude to Christ given his sufferings on her behalf, on behalf of humanity. But then a perspective dawns within her that is less conventional and more lasting: Can you not help him? Does he not want—even need—your friendship, your presence, even with all your human weaknesses? Teresa felt, with a strength she could never forget, that even in her wretchedness, even in her inadequacies, Christ would want her friendship, her consolation, in this state. She began to picture Christ within her, drawing near to him in those scenes, especially Gethsemane, where he was alone and in need.[331] It helped her to approach Christ, even with all her unworthiness. After twenty years of self-described confusion, dominated by what Rowan Williams summarizes as "the longing to be acceptable to both the conventionally worldly and the conventionally pious,"[332] she discovered, with the help of this statue, a reading of Augustine's *Confessions,* and the vulnerability of God revealed in Christ, that she was "desired in her entirety, as she is;...'needed' by Christ." It was "an integrating reality for her life,"[333] and can be for ours, too: "On the awareness of that need grows the beginning of a belief in our human worth."[334] It laid the foundation for the courageous reform work of Teresa's next decades. It was the theological foundation for the catalyzing sentiment often attributed to her: "Christ has no body now on earth but yours, no hands but yours.... Yours are the feet with which he is to go about doing good."[335] Carry on, faithful ones who doubt your relevance and value.

I knew about this insight, this moment of midlife "conversion" around the suffering Jesus that Teresa had experienced, but I had found it merely interesting—not personally relevant—when I first encountered it. I had begun to seek Teresa's counsel in her texts out of the disoriented joy of being expectedly loved by Christ; I didn't need her lesson about continued partnership with Christ despite being unequally yoked until later. But, on this night, it came to me, another jewel from Teresa's box offered with her irrepressible encouragement: "Remember that Christ needs you," she was saying. "He needs your help; you are no help to Him crying against the wall about your wretchedness, or closing yourself off in your room to labor in frail solitude. You'll lose your way. *Let Him in.*"

Where Teresa goes from this moment of midlife conversion, by her own account, deserves further consideration. She becomes less unsettled by, and more steadily thankful for, the gifts that God gives her when he so desires. Again, I cannot summarize this more brilliantly than Williams does:

> Apart from any question of merit, God gives grace—compunction and repentance, but also the new and unexpected touches of intimacy that Teresa is now receiving; and when such gifts are given, it is false humility to deny or ignore them. We must acknowledge that, for all our natural poverty, we are enriched by God and are given favors in order to share them (10.4–5): and she concludes, "how can anyone benefit and share his gifts lavishly if he doesn't understand that he is rich?" (ibid., 6). Only when we are fully aware of what God is doing in us can we find courage and authority to speak for God; and only when we see ourselves as loved by God can "we desire to be despised and belittled by everyone" (ibid.). The pledge of God's love, in other words, is the only thing that can enable and authorize the life upon which Teresa has embarked… the love of God [achieves] for her what no human relationship can—a comprehensive setting free from the constraint of needing to be approved.[336]

The possibility of such long-term effects was beyond the scope of my vision on that pivotal pre-Lenten retreat. But some of the basic movements toward liberty were clear to me nevertheless. Here is my concluding journal note, written on Ash Wednesday: "Repentance is always an invitation to *freedom*, journeying to a better place, *with* God (not alone, for God)." Alone, we are deceived and constrained by false metrics at every turn, from without and from within. Under the divine scalpel, and particularly with the help of Jesus' assurance of unfathomable forgiveness through the resurrection and the gritty example of the eventually unencumbered saints, these entanglements can be cut away. We are still uneven creatures, and never forget it, but we might bear our *imago Dei* with more generosity and boldness, not allowing it to be smothered with subtle and sneaky shame.

In the middle sections of the sixth dwelling places, Teresa addresses topics of prayer and spiritual development that might seem relatively ordinary even to modern ears, more down-to-earth than raptures: the role of tears in prayer, the gift of almost-uncontainable joy and a yearning to praise God, and the need to stay close to the stories of flesh-and-blood guides, primarily the earthly Jesus but also other saints. She offers the kind of advice that, as it initially did to me, may seem commonplace because it is so reasonable and intuitive; but, upon further reflection, I realized I'd never actually heard it offered so directly: Are tears in prayer a good thing or a bad thing? Does God have anything to do with them? Are we crazy or blessed when we feel an overwhelming joy and desire to praise God, and what do we do with that movement in a society that would surely answer, "Crazy"? And, most important, once a person has received the gift(s) of such dramatic and personal encounters with God's love in prayer, should one abandon oneself to the love of God in spirit, leaving study or thoughts of the suffering Jesus behind?

The religious cultures I grew up in had implicit and fuzzy answers for the latter two questions, but tears we didn't talk about. Our culture lazily places tears in the realm of emotion and doesn't know how to overlay with complexity or mystery how they might function within spiritual processes, too. Admittedly, it's complicated. In Teresa's age, though, tears had a more favorable reputation as a sign of God's grace or movement—or at least true contrition!—and so, predictably, they also became a tempting place to either force or fake spirituality, deluding others and most of all oneself. Yearning to die and falsely fostering tears seems an obvious path to avoid from our postmodern standpoint, but, for Teresa's readers, this was a more nuanced and detached approach to tears than they might have been used to. Tears are not always as good (or honest) as they might seem, Teresa chides. She offers this warning with one of the more colorful self-disclosures of the whole text:

> I can imagine you asking me what on earth you *should* do, since I mark "danger!" everywhere. If I think there can be deception in something as good as tears, you might be wondering if maybe *I'm* the one who is deceived! Yes, of course—I might be. But, trust me, I'm not talking about this without having actually seen it in others. I've never been like this myself, because I'm not the least bit emotional. On the contrary, my hardness of heart sometimes worries me. Nevertheless, when the fire within my soul is strong, it distills, [purifies, and transforms] the heart like an alembic, no matter how hard it may be. You'll easily recognize when tears arise from *this* source, because they are comforting and calming instead of disturbing, and rarely do any harm.[337]

No false tears for the hard-hearted Teresa! Only God can melt *her* heart. But, in the end, her advice on tears also applies to so many other "phenomena" one might encounter while exploring the many dwelling places of the soul: in and of itself, not worthy of our thoughts or attention. Focusing on the tasks of "hard work and virtue" is the better course: "Let the tears come when God wants to send them; we shouldn't try to induce them ourselves."[338] Tears can be a great gift, helping to produce fruit (always that key test of authentic prayer for Teresa). But digging around for tears will lead only to muddy puddles, not true cleansing and refreshment. Her final encouragement to her sisters could apply not just to tears but also so many "effects" in prayer that we may subconsciously (or consciously) think are the markers of depth or legitimacy. Let go of any exceptions, she says: "Our best plan is to place ourselves in the Lord's presence, meditate on His mercy and grace (as well as our own lowliness), and leave Him to give us what He wills, whether water or dryness. He knows what is best for us; in this way, we'll walk in peace, and the adversary will have less opportunity to fool us."[339]

Under most paradigms, "the adversary," or "the devil," is that which leads us away from God's goodness and the works of love we're called to, no matter how the figure (or figures, including demons) might be conceived of or expressed. So, it makes sense that the devil can get caught up in tears but can't be found meddling in a gift of jubilation, characterized in Teresa's mind by "excessive joy" and a yearning to "praise our Lord." "Such interior joy in the depths of one's being, with such peace, and all this happiness stirring praises of God—this can't possibly come from the adversary," she says.[340] Abstractly, the idea of spiritual jubilation might sound rare and undesirable: fools for Christ singing praises on street corners or in the fields have had a hard time in every generation. Yet Teresa's full description is remarkably relatable and lovely, and I have a hunch that many, many people know what she is talking about, even if they have experienced it only once in their life. Such experiences of jubilation, born of unexpected grace, might well be the reason a quarter of the people in the pews still show up for church on Sundays—to praise God years or decades after the overwhelming joy came. Here is the picture she paints:

> Together with these experiences that are simultaneously painful and delectable, our Lord sometimes gives the soul some feelings of jubilation, and a strange prayer it doesn't understand.... The joy of the soul is so excessive that it doesn't want to rejoice in God alone but wants to share its joy with everyone so they might help praise our Lord. It directs all its activity and energy toward this praise. Oh, what elaborate festivals and demonstrations such a soul would organize, if possible, so that all might understand her joy! For it seems to her she has found herself, and so, like the father of the Prodigal Son, she wants to have a great party and invite everybody because she sees herself in an undoubtedly safe place, at least for now. I think this is for good reason.[341]

She turns the parable of the prodigal son delightfully on its head: instead of the father offering up a party to celebrate his lost son's arrival, we who have been lost are so happy to have been welcomed home that *we want to organize a massive festival to celebrate the father's graciousness! I have found my true self. Thanks be to God, I am home at last.* Out of sheer and excessive joy that simply must be shared, the soul desires to shout out invitations to join in a celebration of its *own* homecoming. "*I once was lost, but now I'm found!*[342] Come party and praise God with me," this soul yearns to say. It's a state that "might last for a whole day," according to Teresa, the soul being "like someone who has had a lot to drink—but not like a person so drunk as to be senseless.... These are very rough comparisons to represent something so valuable and beautiful, but I'm not clever enough to think of others," she admits.[343] Maybe it's what Saint Francis experienced when he ran through the fields shouting that he was the herald of the great King, she muses. And yet, there is a rueful acknowledgment, even for a sixteenth-century saint and religious community leader, that, most of the time, people will conceal this impulse. "While living with this great energy of joy, [we will] remain quiet and hide it," even though it pains us to hold back, wishing we might draw others into our praises but not really knowing how; intoxicated with joy and yet still aware of the ways the people around us would not understand.[344]

It is some comfort to me that even Teresa and her sisters felt circumscribed in their occasional gifts of joy. I have known the feeling of this joy and its containment, the necessary interior boundary that keeps my voice from issuing invitations to a party celebrating God's graciousness to me—and I think it's because there is a rightful caution around such individual orientation. In the Christian community, every Sunday, we throw a party, a great thanksgiving, celebrating God's graciousness to *us*. Still, it is decidedly good to have at least a few people in your life, even one person, whom you can trust to tell when this wonderful jubilation comes to you. Someone who will share in your joy and praise of God. The loving light in the eyes of my spiritual director would help me to know I wasn't crazy; there was indeed reason to rejoice; God has indeed done great things for me, as one expression of the love available to us all. Teresa expresses this goodness of an understanding cohort: "And how good He's been to you [sisters], putting you in a place where you would receive encouragement—and not the criticism you'd receive in the world—if God does give you this gift, and you show signs of it, too."[345]

It's funny and telling that when I first read *The Interior Castle*, I was very struck by the notion of being "hindered" in the praise and proclamation of God's goodness. Typing up notes and quotes from the text, I put the following sentence in bold and red type to signify a place of nearly electric synergy between what Teresa described and what I had known: "A woman in this state will be frustrated that she can't do this because she's female, and be very envious of those who are free to cry aloud and proclaim all over the world who is this great God of hosts."[346] Well, now. I am decidedly a woman in the world, dropping my kids off at school and going into work *at and for a church* in urban San Diego, living in a nation with historically unprecedented religious liberty and freedoms of speech. What, exactly, is keeping me from "proclaiming who this great God of hosts is"? Five hundred years later, Teresa still eyes the rub: "the criticism you'd receive in the world." What's the point in crying aloud about the goodness of God if you know in advance that you will be dismissed out of hand? The joy is not lost but concealed, or carefully channeled.

Still, in time, I recognized that I do have access to places where the incredible message of God's continued activity through Christ might be proclaimed—and heard. I began to see how fortunate I am to be able to preach inside a house with an understanding and caring audience, where I can tell out God's goodness in a way that, I pray, always moves from *me* to *we*. But it's not just the pastors and priests and ministers this applies to: every Christian person in community has this chance. Our churches should be places where we can tell others about personal graces as well as communal ones, right? And yet most of the churches I have known are full of natural reluctance to receive and to affirm the praises of the spiritually intoxicated ones in our midst. The prospect is scary, and Teresa—more than most—knows the dangers of "spirituality gone wild" and divorced from disciplined love in community. Yet even she ends her thoughts on "excessive joy" with a couple of pointed questions and an invitation to praise: "Why would we want to be more *sensible*? What could give us greater happiness? And may *all* the creatures join with us, forever and ever. Amen, amen, amen."[347]

Then again, maybe we should allow joy with less discretion, when it comes, because joy is not the only color of the Christian life. To be a Christian is both gift and burden, grace and task. Right on the heels of her discussions of potential "excessive joy," Teresa turns her attention to the ongoing pain of our past and present human limitations—and our awareness of them—while pivoting to a point of hard-earned wisdom that she says she will never deny: to turn away from contemplating the humanity of Jesus is a great mistake: "It's...essential not to move away on purpose from our greatest help and blessing, which is the most sacred humanity of our Lord Jesus Christ."[348] Teresa says we need to keep Jesus' earthly life and death before us, no matter how far we think we're traveling in the castle, no matter how tempting it may be to leave behind the messy realities of humanity (which are so evident in the Gospels and the church).

It's not just about individual temptation, either. Some spiritual teachers in Teresa's day were indeed teaching, just as some do in our own time, that, as we move up the ladder of spiritual maturity, we should transcend the need to contemplate the daily human existence and sufferings of Jesus. Not even maliciously: some people simply assumed—then as now—that this would be the natural progression of things. Teresa addresses this line of "progressive" thinking head-on: "It will probably also seem to you that anyone who enjoys such lofty things will no longer meditate on the mysteries of the most sacred humanity of our Lord Jesus Christ, because such a person would now be entirely engaged in love.... But [those who think so] definitely will *not* make me concede that this is a good way."[349] Teresa, the one frequently caught up in unexpected raptures, the one being taken to rooms in the castle where she enjoys glimpsing heaven's treasures, says, in effect, "No. Wrong turn. We need to keep our feet on the ground even as God gives us treasures from above. We are humans, not angels. This is where our feet belong." It doesn't matter, she says, if you feel you "can't" think about Jesus' death while being shaped by the love of the risen Christ, and you find study and meditation on other exemplary-but-still-human lives (such as Mary and the saints) less than compelling. Do your best to try, to practice keeping them in mind. Otherwise, you are cutting yourself off from a source of bread and water, and the human journey is long. Don't expect to live long on love alone. She addresses such misguided wanderers in this way:

Some souls follow prayer principles and methods where the thinking goes that when you begin to experience the prayer of quiet, and enjoy the gifts and spiritual delights given by the Lord there, it would be a very good thing to *always* be enjoying them. Well now, let them believe me when I say they shouldn't be so absorbed, as I've said. For life is long; there are many trials in it, and we *need* to look at Christ, our paragon and pattern, and His apostles and saints, reflecting on how they endured these trials, so that we might also bear them perfectly.[350]

Although angelic spirits—freed from everything physical—might stay permanently enkindled in love, this isn't possible for those of us who live in a mortal body. We *need* to engage with, and think about, and be accompanied by those who did such great things for God while having a mortal body. It's even more essential not to move away on purpose from our greatest help and blessing, which is the most sacred humanity of our Lord Jesus Christ. I can't believe that people really do this; but they just don't understand, and they bring harm to themselves and to others. At any rate, I can assure you that they won't enter these last two dwelling places: if they lose their guide, the good Jesus, they won't be able to find their way. It would be impressive if they're able to remain safely in the other dwelling places.[351]

In his unforgettable theological prose, Robert Farrar Capon echoes the image Teresa offers up of Jesus as guide. If the second person of the Trinity is like an invisible man, Capon says, Jesus is like the real, historical felt hat worn by the invisible man. If we trust that the invisible man in the hat is the one who leads us out of the perilous dark cave, then we do well to keep our eyes on the hat...and on the traditions and teachings of the church that steward essential bits of the hat for future generations, the buttons and felt that made the hat distinctive in the first place.[352]

If left to my own devices, I can't really say how far I might have traveled down this slipshod path of pursuing delights and forgetting about the trials of Jesus or other earthly trials. As it was, and is, there is no opportunity in my nine-hundred-square-foot house or bustling church campus for perpetual absorption in prayer and a continued state of prayerful delight. I have made other vows to community, in marriage and ordination, and taken on other lifelong responsibilities, in parenting, that keep me from pursuing that particular false lead. But I still smell it; it is in the air for anyone who has felt God's presence. Humans have a tendency to become spirituality junkies, seeking the high and wanting to find ways to avoid the hike. The paradox, Teresa says here, as elsewhere, is that we must indeed desire someone and something—God and faithfulness to God's ways as known through Christ—but must be indifferent to the favors. We must seek God and not His gifts, and God surely knows the difference.

Teresa's sisters may have been tempted to linger in "consolations and spiritual delights,"[353] leaving aside unpleasant realities like Jesus' suffering. On the flip side, the challenge in many non-cloistered lives, like mine, is to be disciplined enough to set time for prayer at all, not to neglect the pursuit of God amid so many other demands. We can go off the rails either way. And when we do, Teresa suggests the same tried-and-true tonic: dwell on the mysteries of Christ's life, death, and resurrection.[354] If you are floating off into the ether of sublime mysteries, chasing clouds of delight, it will be good for you to re-tether yourself to your own humanity's weight through Jesus. If you are flying around in an unfocused frenzy, wishing that you were as close to God as you once felt and hoping the peace of God will strike you like a lightning bolt, it will be good for you to connect with divine compassion and your own divine vocation, also through Jesus. I think this is what Teresa would have told me a few months before I finally took that Ash Wednesday retreat, where I found tears, joy, and a renewed closeness to Christ through the traditional stories of Jesus and the saints:

> When the fire of the will mentioned before [in 6.7.7] is not lit, and the presence of God is not felt, it's necessary that we seek it—like the bride did in the Song of Solomon. This is His Majesty's desire. He wants us to ask the creatures who it is that made them—as Saint Augustine says he did in his *Meditations* or *Confessions*—and not stupidly waste time by waiting to receive what was given to us once already. At first, it might be that the Lord will not again

give it to us for as long as a year, or even many years. His Majesty knows why; we shouldn't want to know, nor is there any reason that we should. Since we know the path to pleasing God—through the commandments and guidance [given]—let's be diligent about walking in this way, meditating on His life and death and all that we owe Him. The rest comes when the Lord wants.[355]

Read some psalms. Ponder again the gospel accounts of the crucifixion and the resurrection. Remember that the cross—obedient vulnerability to God unaffected by the world's expectations—is the gate to life itself. Spend time learning from a saint who spelled out this truth with his or her life. In Williams' words, "have companionship with those who, in the body, have served God."[356] See what happens when you look for Christ, and look to Christ, and when the Lord desires. It sounds like a pious platitude unless you have dared to trust it, and more than once: "The nature of water is soft, that of a stone is hard; but if a bottle is hung above the stone, allowing the water to fall drop by drop, it wears away the stone. So it is with the word of God; it is soft and our heart is hard," but the one who opens themselves often to the word of God opens themselves to transformation.[357]

Seeing Christ, Our Constant Companion: A Word About Visions

In the eighth and ninth chapters of the sixth dwellings, Teresa addresses the third major category of "supernatural" phenomena: visions. If, in the white mainline Protestant culture of my childhood, *locutions* was a fancy word for something that existed dangerously on the edge of town, and *raptures* might as well have been an extinct animal, then *visions* would have been found in the deep, dark woods. They were familiar-sounding, sure—found in the Bible and in the anthropologically interesting rites of passage around the world—but there was no education or conversation about them in the church. To say, "I had a vision" would surely have put you further up the psychotically suspect list than "I heard from God." Given some basic details that Teresa clears up about visions (they are almost never seen with our actual eyes, for example), part of me might wish that the whole idea had been discussed in the open air. But, then again, maybe the silence around them was unwittingly wise: more than any other "gift,"

Teresa urges discretion, even "secrecy," around visions. Tell only your confessor and/or a trusted spiritual teacher about them. She doesn't say it quite like this, but publicly discussed visions seem to be fine food for gossip and malice and misunderstanding. With appropriate discernment, they might serve plenty of good for the individual, but they don't seem to build up community.[358]

Teresa divides visions into two categories: the "intellectual" and the "imaginative." The "intellectual vision" was introduced in the section on locutions, or hearing from God, but the important—and surprising—thing to remember is that this sort "vision" actually doesn't involve "seeing" at all, even in the imagination. There is, as Williams puts it, "no visual content."[359] Why is it called a vision, then? Well, again, Teresa doesn't know,[360] but she's going to stick with the terminology she's learned, and for the time being so shall we—mostly. I think it might be helpful to think of an "intellectual vision" as an irrefutable awareness, a knowledge of Christ's presence imparted without words or visual content but nevertheless a distinct experience of God "communicat[ing] Himself to us."[361] This is not like a "sixth sense" that Jesus is near, and it is more than a hunch—it's as clear as seeing but without the seeing, by God's pure grace. Here's how Teresa introduces the concept: "The further a soul advances, the closer it is accompanied by the good Jesus—we'll consider how sometimes (when His Majesty wills it) we can't help but walk with Him constantly. This is clear from the ways and means that His Majesty communicates Himself to us, revealing His love for us through wonderful visitations and visions."[362] She doesn't want her sisters to be frightened if Jesus sometimes, even for an extended period of time, comes alongside them in unexpected "ways or means," because despite "[being] of such great majesty and power [He] would nonetheless be happy to commune in this way with a creature."[363]

This kind of "intellectual vision," this awareness of Christ's presence beside her, entered Teresa's own life unexpectedly, and at first she was uncertain and a bit fearful of this new companion. At the same time, she understood very clearly that this was the same Lord who had spoken to her in prayer (again, in an interior sense, not via her eardrums). Without seeing anything, she knew who it was "with the greatest certainty."[364] Although some of the people she asked for counsel stoked her fears ("It is probably a trick of the devil..."), she says that the strength of the Lord's own reassurance was and is enough to quiet the doubts that rise from within and from without: "Don't be afraid; it is I."[365] The clarity of this divine reassurance allows the soul to be strengthened, happy and grateful for "such good company."[366] Again, this kind of knowledge, or vision, of Christ's presence may last a long time—many days or more than a year. A logical benefit is trusting more deeply and easily that the Lord hears prayers offered (he's right here!), but, as mentioned before, this doesn't mean Christ loses any divine prerogative, that he is somehow captive or predictable or responds on demand. He remains holy and free.

The effects of such a vision, such a "knowing," are colored by the sweetness and quietness of the "[indescribably] subtle way" God is communicating himself to the person. There is "such peace,…such continuous desires to please God."[367] There is a natural bewilderment and confusion: "she didn't know why so much good had come to her." If it doesn't lead to this sort of sincere humility ("Why me?"), then the whole thing is more suspect, because "it's something clearly recognizable as a gift from God (no human effort could produce such feelings), in no way should anyone who has this think of it as their *own* good, but only a gift from the hand of God."[368] It is obviously and persistently a sheer gift, one that doesn't make the recipient feel greater but only more grateful. It is not the most spectacular favor, Teresa says, but it gives rise to a "a very tender love toward His Majesty" and increases one's desires for full surrender and service. And, of course, it's a great gift to our conscience:[369] "For although we already know that God is present in all we do, it's our nature to lose sight of that fact. But when this gift is given, a soul can't do this because the Lord, near at hand, awakens it."[370] Peace, humility, love, gratitude, increased clarity, and purity of conscience—it's easy to see why this is deemed a "precious" gift,[371] one that wouldn't be traded for any treasure on earth. But, like all spiritual delights, it is not ours to acquire, keep, or bring back. "When it's the Lord's will to withdraw [the gift of His felt presence]," it is gone, perhaps forever, or perhaps simply until the next day or time; "the Lord gives this when He wants."[372] The benefits do not disappear so quickly: this soul has been clothed with "such inward peace"[373] through the gift of Christ's quiet presence that remnants of it will remain long into the continued service rendered when one "is left with great loneliness."[374]

I generally find Teresa to be a pragmatic teacher (especially given her stereotypically sublime subject matter), but in dealing with this topic, she really breaks down the third wall. Any remnant of the detached lecturer disappears, and it's as if she looks right over her glasses at the audience, seeking out with unnerving intensity the full reckoning of her listeners: Do not be astonished if this happens to you, but it's good to have a little fear so that you walk with care. Don't be overly confident or grow careless;[375] and, whatever you do, do not take such a gift, or gifts, for granted. Not everyone is given them. If you are—or have been—given them, honor them. Strive to do more with and because of them. You are not any greater because of such experiences, and, if you rightly receive these gifts, you'll likely be more aware of how little you actually do for God.[376]

Finally, Teresa says, there's some things you should know about discretion. Only talk about this under the seal of confession with "a very educated man" or with "a very spiritual person," or both. (Try to find a confessor who is both educated and spiritual, if you can.) Don't be worried if they say your vision or experience of Christ with you is false; simply commend yourself again to God and ask not to be deceived.[377] You should be warned in advance: "If this person you confide in has not been led by the Lord along this path (even though he practices prayer), he'll immediately be alarmed and condemn it." Under any circumstances, tell your prioress. Even if you seem very stable, she will need you to speak with a confessor about this. "And, after such consultation(s)," for God's sake, calm yourself down and don't go around reporting this experience anymore," even if it is out of fear or a need for reassurance. If it's publicly known and discussed, it leads to no good and causes "many difficult trials."[378]

Some of this advice seems dated to the political and religious climate of the day (the "difficult trials" could, "given the way things currently are… affect [the soul's] religious order").[379] Much of it seems timeless, though, including her last direct word to prioresses—and anyone else listening in—who might be inclined to interpret such spiritual delights as signs of God's lasting favor. Don't get too worked up about any of this, she says, even such a wonderful gift as having Jesus as a close companion—possibly for a long period of time. It doesn't mean anything except that the person may have needed it, even out of a kind of weakness:

Don't think that because a sister has had such experiences, she's any better than the others. The Lord leads each of us as He sees we need. Such experiences, rightly used, prepare us to be better servants of God. But sometimes, God leads the weakest by this road; there's nothing here to either approve or condemn. We only need to look at the virtues, and who serves the Lord with the most self-denial, humility, and purity of conscience: this is the holiest one. However, we can't know much about this with any certainty here—until the true Judge gives each one what he or she deserves. There [in heaven], we'll be amazed to see how different His judgment is from what we understand here.[380]

Got it? Stunned by her astute authority, the students are silent. Class dismissed.

Finally, in chapter nine, Teresa touches upon the kind of visions most people are thinking of when they hear "vision": something holy seen with the inner eye, by a special allowance of God. (She doesn't have anything to say about "the exterior vision" because she "hasn't experienced this.")[381] It's as if Christ suddenly opens a door to show something precious for the benefit of the one who sees, but Teresa's assessment of such "imaginative" visions is a mixed bag. On the one hand, "the adversary interferes more often in these" than in the "unseeing" kind, and they are more fleeting; but when they are authentic, something about the way they align with our human nature makes them undeniably powerful.[382]

When our Lord is pleased to give more to this soul, He clearly shows it His most sacred humanity in the way that He wants—as He was when He walked in the world, or after the resurrection. And although He does this so quickly that we might compare it with a flash of lightning, it leaves this most glorious image so engraved in the imagination that I think it would be impossible to leave behind—until the soul sees the same where it can be enjoyed forever [in eternity].[383]

Although sometimes she uses the word "image," Teresa wants to be clear that this is not like a two-dimensional painting in a museum that is suddenly seen after a drop cloth is removed: "[The vision is] not 'painted' according to the one who sees it, but truly alive. And sometimes it's even speaking with the soul, and revealing great secrets."[384] In slightly grotesque modern terms, receiving a vision is more like being dropped into a heavenly theater than being placed in front of a Renaissance still life, but the holy brilliance of the scene does not allow for facile and placid viewership: "You can't keep staring at this any more than you can keep staring at the sun.... The brilliance of this vision is like an infused light or like a sun covered with something as thin and transparent as a diamond.... Almost every time that God grants this gift to the soul, it remains in rapture, because its lowly nature can't endure such a frightening sight."[385]

The reason Teresa is somewhat leery of "imaginative" visions, even as she testifies to their potential good, is the same reason modern skeptics are leery of visions: there are some people who have such weak imaginations, or such effective intellects, or who knows why, that they "become so absorbed in their imagination that everything they think about seems to be clearly 'seen.'"[386] It's related to the reason Teresa says one should never ask God for a vision: it shows a lack of humility, opens the door to "a thousand tricks" from the adversary, and tempts the imagination to fabricate what it desires to see.[387] If such people "[had] ever seen a true vision, they would realize their mistake."[388] Those with "true visions," or even those who are not sure, are given the same counsel as those who have been granted an intellectual vision: tell your confessor, openly and honestly, "with truth and clarity."[389] To both confessor and visionary: Proceed with caution, looking for humility and a strengthening in virtue as a sign of authenticity.[390]

There's a little historical drama couched in her lesson about visions that, at first glance, seems shockingly antiquated; but, at its heart, it is a lesson for spiritual seekers of every age. At one point, a nervous confessor advised Teresa to "give the fig"—an obscene gesture, like an American raising a middle finger—to any image of Christ that came to her in prayer, assuming it was from the devil. This greatly distressed her, and she was relieved to later take wiser counsel: whatever image of Christ comes to you, allow it to awaken devotion. It's to your benefit, then, whether or not the vision is "from Christ."[391] This kind of steadiness in the face of "extraordinary" experiences of unknown origin is wise counsel. There's an adage in contemporary spiritual direction that takes the devil out of the equation but keeps steady humility alive: "It could be the Holy Spirit...or it could be a bit of undigested beef." Either way, if the movement increases your trust in God and your love for Christ, there's no harm. No need to vehemently protest. But because such experiences are indeed tricky, once more, Teresa will conclude with this admonition: "You must never ask or want Him to lead you along this road."[392]

There is something about visions that raises Teresa's highest alarms about all the false projections and misguided desires of the spiritually hungry. Maybe visions led to the greatest personal trouble for her in community, or maybe they were the simply the most "enviable" of all spiritual delights in her time, the thing everybody seemed to want in order to bolster their own journey of faith. This response is natural, and it is not restricted to the sixteenth century. I hear it in twenty-first-century Bible studies from people who have PhDs in biochemistry and from Sudanese refugees who have leaned on God through literal desert wanderings. "It *would* just be easier if we could see, at least once...," people say wistfully. This is what we think, and what Teresa's companions thought, too. But this is a clear case of being careful what you wish for: "Do you think the works and trials suffered by those in whom the Lord does these graces are small ones?" Teresa asks. By no means. "It might be that the very thing you *think* will help you gain will bring you loss."[393] (There will be great trials.)

More to the point, Teresa reminds us that none of these favors is necessary, even the ones we think we want or need. We do not know how well-suited we are to a particular spiritual path, so, in all things, it's best to let God take the lead. She even holds up two remarkable people she knows who have asked God to stop acting upon them in these gracious ways ("If it would have been possible not to receive [spiritual delights], they would have passed"[394]) because they want to prove that they "don't serve Him for pay."[395] I do not counsel people not to ask to know God more deeply, nor do I believe Teresa would. I often tell people the advice that was so helpful to me, based on the gospel account of Doubting Thomas: Don't be afraid to ask God for more assurance, to give you what you need to believe or trust more deeply. Just don't make any claims about what that will look like or what that "needs" to be. With open hands, ask to be reassured of Christ's companionship—whether that reassurance comes in a vision or in another "delicate" way that you can no more describe than Teresa could, or nothing seems to come in that moment, for many years, or ever. How can we best be led?

> It should be left to the Lord who knows me to lead me by the path that's best, so that in everything His will be done.[396]

> In the end, sisters,...the safest thing is to not want anything but what God wants. He knows us better than we know ourselves, and He loves us. Let's put ourselves in His hands so that His will might be done in us. We can't go wrong if we remain in this posture with a determined will.

> And you must note that you won't deserve any more glory for having received a lot of these gifts; rather, those who do are more obliged to *serve* more because they've received more. The Lord doesn't take from us [any choice or action] that's actually more commendable, because those are up to us—in our own hands. So, there are many holy people who have never known what it's like to receive a gift like these, and there are others who *have* received them but aren't holy. And again, don't think that they happen continually; for each time the Lord does them, it also brings many works—and so the soul isn't thinking about receiving more but only how to serve in response.[397]

The metaphor of the spiritual "journey" might be a well-worn, even tired, one, but it remains for a reason. And, for Christians, there is a particular role for Jesus in that metaphorical landscape—as the One who draws us to God, reconciles us to God, shows us the way, and walks with us. Blissfully gazing face-to-face with Jesus is never the goal or *telos* of life, and visions as Teresa describes highlight this truth. Such experiences, as Williams explains, "are meant to show us Christ accompanying us on our fleshly journey, and ultimately for no other end.... Only in very special circumstances and for a very particular purpose would we expect to see Christ 'facing' us. The movement of our prayer is in Christ to the Father; Teresa's Christocentrism is not a cult of Jesus."[398] The truth affirmed and strengthened by the visions Teresa describes is the reality of Christ's constant companionship with us, which in no way means our journey has ended. In Scripture, this is the promise: "I am with you always, to the end of the age."[399] We still have work to do, an earthly life to live of unknown length and tenor, full of mystery and unfathomable ultimate meaning. But we're invited to partner with God in bearing more and more of the divine love into the world for as long as we're in it, to learn how to do this in whatever "little space" we're given. Blake writes,

> And we are put on earth a little space
> That we may learn to bear the beams of love.[400]

Whether we know it or not, whether we see it or not, Christ is with us as we struggle to learn to bear these "beams of love," often feeling as alone in our relatively small but still painful task as he did on the Friday when he carried the heaviest beams—cruciform ones.

On the eve of what would have been my mother's sixty-fifth birthday, I lay in bed awaiting sleep, and I felt, quite unexpectedly, Christ's presence, close. The words that came to accompany this presence were not new; they had pressed upon me at different times and in different ways, an ancient but essential promise: I *will* always *be with you.*

I was bewildered. I wasn't feeling scared or anxious about anything in particular, that I was aware of, let alone about God leaving me. I tried to explore this gift of Christ's presence with detached curiosity: was this a preparation for an end to this sort of gift? On some level, I always expect each spiritual delight to potentially be the last. But that "interpretation" didn't at all seem clear. I ended with simple gratitude for the reassurance, not knowing what it was about.

That night, I had a striking dream, the first of its sort in a long while. I was with the man who is my animus figure—again, related to Christ in a way I don't fully understand—standing in a large crowd, a community gathering. We offered one another no open affection, but there remained a deep sense of inward connection. All of the interactions between us were marked by companionship, constancy, in such a way that when someone at the party assumed he was my husband, my response was this: "Oh, no, he's not my husband [Colin was present but offstage], but I can see why you would think that" (i.e., we have been as companionable as husband and wife). There was no dialogue between us, no touching, just a working together. At the end, we were to give each other a hug goodbye. He whispered, to my surprise and relief, "I still love you." I said the same thing back to him, but he added, "I always will." The scene closed with this warm and welcome assurance that any deeper bond we had shared wasn't just all in my head, all in the past, that it was real and he recognized it, even as our actions were very chaste and almost formal.

I woke up with so many questions: How does this connect with Christ's presence and movement in my life? I thought God had been leading me to a deeper trust of partnership with Christ, but what is the newness here? What am I not yet awake to in my waking life?

Soon afterward, I entered a brief season of sadness, confusion, and frustration. I felt lonely and trapped, enmeshed in my marriage and the responsibilities of church and suffocating in what seemed to be a stagnant pool of the same old misunderstandings and miscommunications. As I loaded the clothes dryer on a hot October afternoon, fuming about a constipated family-finance conversation my husband and I were trying to have, my spirit wanted to scream. Why can I not even communicate clearly with this human whom I know and love above all others? There were practical, on-the-calendar reasons for some of these emotions (and who deals well with October heat?). But, when I finally sat down to pray, for real, I came face-to-face with the truth beneath the surface of the inscrutable pain. Glancing over my journal description of the above dream, which I'd had just three weeks earlier, I saw it again, anew, with Christ reminding me as I cried: *I did not send you out in the field to work by yourself like a worker bee, a lone laborer.* My tears were not those of shame for having forgotten this; they were tears of relief, of seeing. For a while now, that is how I had felt, how I had functioned. Christ had given me this job, this mission, these many good and holy responsibilities, but I had not been "sent out" on my own to complete them. I'd had the mentality and posture of a lone laborer, still too preoccupied with my ability to do the job, and not really trusting God or living in an intimate companionship with him in the midst of "all the world."

I know, I know. (You've already been here with me before.) Again? *Again?* The repetitive themes are not lost on the subject. But stick with me. For each spiral, God willing, there is a new depth of healing and transformation. We return to the same issues from a different vantage point, with new truths we are ready to hear. This time, it is not just that I had forgotten the essential invitation to partnership. I saw how my frustrations with my human companions was related to my forgetting the primary partnership with, and allegiance to, God. I got frustrated with Colin because he didn't really know me, even after all these years, not in the way that God can and does, and yet this idea was absurd even on the face of it: How could he? He is but human.

When I sat down to pray the Psalms, a line struck me that I'd never noticed: "I look to my right hand and find no one who knows me."[401] At first, this verse touched the pain of my feelings of aloneness, but the longer I sat with it in prayer, the more it felt like Christ was drawing me to a different perspective about it: There is no one around me who knows me, really. Not in the way that God knows me. There never will be. For every human person, there is an element of mystery, depth, selfhood, and otherness that is truly known only in relation to God. One only needs to read a Marilynne Robinson novel to remember these depths, this mystery. I am looking for too much, expecting too much, from my earthly companions. The sense of aloneness will compound if I do not allow Christ to stand close between us. I catch a glimpse of that elusive vision I seem to be drawing toward, painfully, slowly: There is comfort and peace with that essential and forever aloneness as a human, a peace that allows one to love and seek God primarily, and then to also be a truly loving companion to others, giving and receiving the variable gifts of human relationships with less attachment and neediness and insecurity. To be free and secure with oneself and God, then interact with others in a way that "cares but does not care," is the holy detachment of T. S. Eliot finally learned by heart.

If I find more and more of my joy and companionship with a God who does not "send me out" alone but goes with me, always, and sends human companions for critical junctures, too, then I can be less caught up in the imperfections and frustrations of any human relationship. It is that old invitation to freedom in Christ. "I look to my right hand and find no one who knows me" is a dark door to liberty, and even greater love, when one turns the other way and remembers there is another constant companion who will walk through it with us, knowing it's just the path we need.

Pain, Pleasure, and Peace: A Refrain

All these sufferings serve to increase her desire to enjoy the Spouse. His Majesty, knowing well our weakness, strengthens her through these challenges and others so that she might have the courage for union with such a great Lord and take Him as her Spouse.[402]

And over these years, little by little, this desire has grown in such a way that it finally comes to a point of suffering, as I'll now explain. (I'm saying "years" here to line up with the experiences of the particular person I'm speaking about. But I understand very well that we can't put limits on God, and that in one moment He could bring a soul to the highest point described here.[403]

Again, I am well aware that the "story" of personal challenges and growth I have been describing in these sections could be interpreted in many ways and live comfortably in a number of vocabularies, many of them psychological, sociological, secular. It would be possible to read my life—especially that of the past few years—as a typical journey of a woman in midlife, growing in individuation and self differentiation and basic human maturity as she learns to be in marriage and community in ways that have greater integrity and sustainability. As a friend of mine put it, "The literary scholar in me sees the cliché, but I will speak the story without shame because it is being born in my very life: woman turns forty and finds her voice." It's not a coincidence that Teresa's own moment of profound reconversion and turn toward liberation from social snares happened at age thirty-nine. There's actually a great deal written about these overlays between spiritual and psychological maturation, but I will highlight the voice of just one Carmelite priest, who wrote about the synergy between what Teresa describes in *The Interior Castle* and the work of Carl Jung. As he summarizes it:

The journey through the castle indicates a compatibility with the individuation process. The religious journey and the psychological journey are evidently one journey in Teresa's experience.

Carl Jung, too, could not separate the two developments: "Among all my patients in the second half of life—that is to say, over thirty-five—there has not been one whose problem in the last resort was not that of finding a religious outlook on life. It is safe to say that every one of them fell ill because he had lost what the living religions of every age have given to their followers, and none of them has been really healed who did not regain his religious outlook."

In Jung's estimation, religion should be the school for forty-year-olds.[404]

I do not deny the helpfulness of other, nonreligious "vocabularies," and I use them often myself, especially when they have enriched my understanding or clarified a fuzzy idea or process or experience. But there is fearsome, wondrous truth beyond all the grasping of my intellect that I can no longer deny: I am not the lone agent of my life and transformation. While I do have freedom and agency, always, to welcome and consent, there is a holy Other who acts and beckons, a God who loves and instructs, who forms and prepares, who fastens and releases, who sustains and supports. It is the basic tenet of any theism, including Christianity, but the cultural waters I was formed in were so secular that I have found myself continually *surprised* by this truth, even more than a decade into ordained ministry. I do hope I am growing in basic human maturity, the sort of compassionate moral goodness recognized by those of every faith and no faith. But I am not alone in my desire for transformation; indeed, it is a reflection (though not a simplistic facsimile) of God's desire for me. There is a final image of maturity and participation, of my potential little place in the human story, that I cannot see but God can. The mysterious alchemy of pain, pleasure, and peace that pulls me toward wholeness and right action is not an impersonal balance sheet or rule book, or a lottery of fate or biology. It is the very action and invitation of God in Christ.

On Maundy Thursday of 2020, my household, like much of the world, was isolated at home due to the coronavirus pandemic. Like many working parents who experienced their own version of this scenario, I was struggling to adapt to working at home as a pastor without physically seeing people while also guiding my children through online kindergarten and third-grade materials. There were so many online passwords to create and remember, and so little certainty about the whole next year. There was so much silent grief about the tidal wave of death that was looming, surging. I walked down to our little backyard studio, a converted garage, feeling frustrated and overwhelmed and mildly like a failure twice over, for reasons that could not seem smaller in the midst of all this: I had flaked out on my own prayer gathering at noon and then messed up the frosting on the Easter sugar cookies I was trying to make with the kids. These were comic failures (especially the second), but I sat down on the couch feeling defeated, not even necessarily intending to pray as I usually tried to do before working. I went straight to the laptop, attempting to schedule a Zoom call and instead getting sidetracked by emails, still feeling vaguely sad.

Like an inaudible buzzing, though, a call to recollection grew in intensity. More and more, I felt like I was being actively called into prayer—in a way I hadn't felt in some time. Eventually, the hum, the movement in my soul, was persistent enough that I put my computer to the side and tried to pray. I started with a basic seeking of self-knowledge: What was all this about? What were the feelings of failure, the sadness, really about? Slowly, with time, and lots of wandering thoughts about the cookies (*Forget the cookies!*), I found my way, with Christ's gentle persistence, to a place where I was forced to acknowledge how much I had closed myself off from intimacy with Christ—again. I saw the ways I was like Peter in the Maundy Thursday story, still pridefully insistent that Jesus not "wash my feet" but instead that I wash his. It had been over a year since I'd had an experience of union, and although I did not claim to understand why, entirely, I could see now that I had not made adequate space for God's action in me—I had once again prioritized my actions "for God." And so there came reminders of Christ's power and presence, at first in subdued ways that had become almost familiar. But then I experienced a depth and power I had forgotten about, developing into a new thing yet again: a pressure that gathered strength in my chest, right around my sternum, with such force I could not help but grunt when I was finally released, the discomfort shifting to my shoulders as the energy moved. I thought that if I lay down, the pain would subside; I thought I just needed more room for this energy of God to move.

But then the pressure entered invisibly through my legs and demanded that my back curl up, almost like the pull of a rope, but the pain and—in time—the heat, fire, was right in the center of my heart, my chest, and it felt like I was being pinned to the ground with a hot arrow. I was aware, even as it happened, that this arrow image was from Teresa, but it was a genuinely new experience for me, not like the general heat I had felt before, and *not* what I imagined Teresa was talking about. This felt so clearly like steel, like a fastening. And yet it did burn, it did hurt as it pressed, though not unbearably, not like the wild pain of childbirth; I did not cry out. After a few seconds, there was release, and then, in a bit, the pressing down again, the fiery steel fastening my heart. All of my energy closed in on this point. When I was able to, when there was a pause, quiet, release, I asked what this was about, what it meant, what it was *for*. (I don't know why I persist in these simple questions—the answers are never simple—but they are honest, and I do receive helpful pieces in return, holy crumbs I spend the next months and years digesting.) Without clear words, it felt like an invitation and movement toward a relationship with Christ that was more serious, that was more securely fastened—less the earnest-but-somewhat-sweetly-simplistic attachments of the engaged. It felt, somehow, like I needed to affirm that I still wanted that, and wanted this, even if it meant more potential pain and discomfort. The "fastening" did not feel like I was being bound into a lack of freedom but rather being bound to Christ, like being bound to the mast of a ship moving through varied waters: ridicule, holidays, shared suffering, breakfast on the beach.

As for what the "fiery dart" meant beyond that, it was almost comical: *Turn to Teresa*, I heard, *again*. The implication: She'll help you with and through that. It had been nearly three years since I'd read the sixth dwellings, so I honestly didn't remember what Teresa said about that particular gift in prayer. The last thing I noted in my journal was that, afterward, I was given an important reminder: *You are not special; you did not earn this.* But I was simultaneously overcome with the inherent "reward" of being acted upon in this way: a deeper assurance and knowledge of God's love even in this troubled and uneven life. I can and want to bear witness to this love. I will probably fail again to stay close to Jesus, like Peter before me, but I also trust I will be offered a chance to declare my love for all that is good and true and worthy of all praise just as often as I denied I ever knew anything of Jesus. Some people just need a beautiful sunset to maintain steadfast fidelity to the creator of heaven and earth. I seem to need more. But God is gracious beyond all measure, steadying willing-but-rocky humans in every age.

A few weeks later, I began work on the sixth dwellings section of this book. I do not claim to have known the same spiritual delight that Teresa did, and what we describe is not the same, blow by blow, but my wonder increased as I read the following:

> While the soul is walking in this way, burning on the inside,....a blow comes, as if arriving like an arrow of fire—it's not known from where it comes, or how. I'm not saying that it actually is an arrow—but whatever it is, it clearly couldn't have come from our own nature. Nor is it actually a blow, even though I use that word; it hurts more sharply, and not where pain is felt here [on earth], I think, but in the very deep and intimate part of the soul.... All at once, it binds the faculties in such a way that they don't have freedom for anything, except what will increase this pain.
>
> I wouldn't want this to seem like an exaggeration, because I'm actually beginning to see as I go on that my words fall short: it's indescribable. It's an enrapturing of the senses and faculties, except, as I've said, in ways that help us feel this affliction. For the intellect is very alive to understanding *why* the soul feels absent from God; at this time, His Majesty helps it with a lively knowledge of Himself, in such a way that it causes the pain to grow to such a degree that the one who has it begins to cry aloud.[405]
>
> Ah, God, help me! Lord, how You afflict Your lovers! But everything is small in comparison with what You give them later. It's

right that great things should cost a lot.... And more than that,...
the soul feels that this pain is *precious*.... The soul understands
well that it is so valuable that it could never deserve it.[406]

I still don't know what the fiery dart "means." I can only say what it
does: it strengthens my trust that it is not *only* me acting upon my life, my
soul, the creatures of this world. I respond to another, am acted upon by
another, One full of love and searing truth and power. I yearn to be faithful
in heart and action. I am fortified, comforted in the oldest sense of the
word. A person clearly does not need a fiery dart to trust a holy God, to
yearn to be faithful. Yet God clearly makes accommodations for weakness,
for silly humans hung up on cookies. I could not ever say, adequately, how
glad I am of it.

SEVENTH DWELLINGS:

BELONGING

"And thus, once when Jesus Christ our Lord was praying for His apostles (I don't know where this takes place), He asked that they might be one with the Father and with Him, as Jesus Christ our Lord is in the Father and the Father is in Him. I don't know what greater love there can be than this! And no one will be stopped from entering here; all of us are included, because His Majesty said, 'Not only do I pray for them but also for all those who will believe in me'; He says, 'I am in them.'"[407]

Rain to the River, Streams to the Sea

We have reached the final dwellings in the castle—the place described by Teresa through the metaphor of "divine marriage" or "spiritual marriage," the place of mutual and steadfast belonging between God and the human person. I don't know about these dwellings through experience; it is clear to me that my struggling butterfly is alive and well and still...well, struggling. Teresa is a bit nervous about claiming her own credibility on the subject,[408] but then she proceeds to offer an authoritative and compelling description of the unique kind of union found in the seventh dwellings and its effects. There can be little doubt that she speaks from experience, with the gift of her many earthly years in these final dwellings providing a depth and nuance to her description that only enhance our trust in her authenticity.

One might (stereotypically) expect *The Interior Castle* to conclude with a static vision of glorious union, all heavenly rays and blissful peace as the soul finds ultimate and lasting peace in God. Isn't this what *nirvana* looks like in any religious tradition? Thankfully—or sadly, depending on your hopes—no. This is the pop culture image of ultimate enlightenment, but it is not the testimony offered by our world's most mature souls. Specifically, for the Christian, union with God means being caught up in a larger movement upon this earth. Like a drop of rain falling into a river or a small stream flowing out into the sea—two of Teresa's images that I expand on more fully below—there is great peace in this surrender of spiritual marriage, but we still remain upon the tumultuous earth as part of God's movement, with waves and rocks an inevitable part of our existence.

The good news? The angst of the lone drop or meandering stream is almost entirely gone: "This is where the little butterfly that we've been talking about dies, and does so with great joy because Christ is now its life."[409] Here, Teresa's castle image is deployed to new effect. The seeking and throne-room power struggles have ended. The soul sits peacefully with God in its center. When we turn toward the inmost Light, we "see ourselves in this mirror that we're contemplating, where our image is engraved."[410] Yet the battles of life rage on, and it is in fact the steady holy Presence in our innermost chamber that sustains and directs our continued human activity, enabling us to love and serve those around us with greater wisdom, patience, resolve, and even effectiveness. Teresa wants us to explore our real interior castle, but she will dissuade us to the end from building "castles in the air," places of fanciful virtue that are free from mundane struggle.[411]

Her down-to-earth description of the seventh dwelling places is one of the reasons I continue to look to her as a spiritual guide at all. This relatively short final section has as many exhortations to practical love as it does descriptions of remarkable blessings and the glories of heaven. This is a spirituality that I can trust, and that I think many people do and would trust, if they saw where Teresa is trying to lead them, even with all her talk about spiritual delights and gifts and devils and unworthiness. We decide to follow leaders and teachers of all sorts because something deep within us resonates with the ultimate vision they lay out for where this whole thing is heading. If we do not want to go where someone says they are going, we will not follow them. I want to know the power of Christ's resurrection, and the healing renewal of the whole earth that our Scriptures mysteriously hold out in hope. So, I try to follow Jesus. On a smaller scale, then, whom do we trust to be our teachers of this Way? Teresa has established herself as one of those trustworthy teachers for me. In the end, I think reading the seventh dwellings section *first* is not a bad way to approach *The Interior Castle*, even for spiritual or religious beginners. We see here both the glory and the grit of Teresa's teachings, infused with the ever-surprising humility that makes her, and her faith, credible.

Let's start with how Teresa received the gift of "divine and spiritual marriage,"[412] a notion that seems so foreign even to many Christians. Although she is clear that this is not a definitive or prescriptive experience—"for other people, it will happen differently"[413]—the beginning of her life in the seventh dwellings reveals much about what it fundamentally means for her. Here's the summary:

> The Lord appeared to her just as she had finished taking Communion. He appeared in the form of great brilliance and beauty and majesty, just as after the resurrection, and told her that it was time for her to consider what belongs to Him as her own, and that He would take care of what was hers—along with other words that are more for feeling and understanding than for repeating and sharing.[414]

Do you notice the essence of the words? This is a message of trustworthy sharing, steadfast belonging: *What's mine is yours, and what's yours is mine.* There are no words about not needing to fear, but what could be more reassuring, more steadying, more centering, more grounding? *Your life belongs to me, and my life belongs to you.* You abide in me, and I abide in you, for all our days.

As usual, Teresa first shares the "glories" of this gift before turning her attention to the grit, the evident effects of this glory. The most remarkable revelation to be received as a result of being "put into this dwelling" is an intellectual vision[415] of the Holy Trinity. Remember, an intellectual vision means that there is no visual content, but still:

> Our good God now wants to remove the scales from the eyes, so that the soul might see and understand something of His merciful action, although this is done in a strange manner. The soul is put into this dwelling by an intellectual vision: a certain representation of the truth, in which the Holy Trinity is shown to him in all three persons. First, the soul's spirit is enkindled as if by a cloud of great clarity, and the soul sees these persons [of the Trinity] distinctly. Yet by an admirable knowledge given, the soul understands as a

profound truth that all three persons are one substance, one power, one knowledge, and one God.... Here all three persons communicate to the soul, speaking to the soul and making it understand those words the gospel [of John] attributes to the Lord: that He and the Father and the Holy Spirit would come to dwell with the soul who loves Him and keeps His commandments.[416]

This might sound like a perfunctory nod to the mystery of the Trinity (alignment with the creeds—check!) were it not for its lasting resonance. "Every day, this soul becomes more amazed because she feels that They have never left her. She perceives quite clearly, in the way mentioned, that They are deep inside her soul. *Very* deep inside, in the most interior depths..., she feels this divine company."[417] Teresa compares the effects of this glorious intellectual vision to being placed in a bright room with other people, after which the shutters are closed over the windows and dark shadows fall over the room (representing the end of the vision). In such a situation, in the darkness, you may not be able to see your companions, but you are just as sure that they are still present.[418] In the same way, the persons of the Trinity are ever present with the soul who has received such a vision, even though they are not "seen" in the same manner. In a way that is terribly hard for Teresa to describe (quite understandably), "the essence of her soul never moved from that dwelling place" but continues to enjoy God's company, even as she is able to attend to necessary "business worries" and the "many trials" she undergoes.[419]

Teresa anticipates this astute question from her readers: If you were talking about union before, in the fifth and sixth dwelling places, what's different about *this* union with God? As is often the case for those attempting to express mystical theology, metaphors are Teresa's best friends in explaining these distinctions. First, there's a difference in how the union comes about. "Everything that I've said and described up to this point seems to go through the senses and our natural capacities," as if God enters through these "doors" of our body and mind.[420] "Here, there's no more thought of the body than if the soul were not in it—but just spirit.... The Lord appears in the center of the soul.... It's like how He appeared to the apostles without entering the room through a door, when He said to them, '*Pax vobis*.'" In the wake of the resurrection, Jesus appeared suddenly to the apostles in the room where they were gathered, saying, *"Pax vobis,"* or "Peace be with you," no door required.[421] And, upon arrival, "what God communicates here to the soul" resists description, but it involves sublime gift, extreme delight, a glimpse of "the glory that's in heaven." She lands in the same vague place of description as have countless spiritual pilgrims: "It's impossible to say more than this: as much as we can understand, the soul—I mean the spirit of the soul—is made one with God."[422]

Okay, so we have thus far a union that in some ways sounds very similar to previous definitions of union ("[The soul] was in God, and God was in it"[423]), except in the way that it comes about (no doors!). The second difference Teresa describes is more helpful, more telling: as we might expect from the marriage metaphor, it is about a shared life, not a shared moment or moments. Here is how she explains the distinction between the union of the seventh dwellings and the kind experienced before:

> Even though union [as previously described] is the joining of two things into one, in the end they can be separated, and each remains its own thing. Indeed, as we usually see in [union], the merciful gift passes quickly, and afterward the soul is left without that companionship— or at least without an *awareness* of it. In this other merciful gift of the Lord, that is not so: the soul always remains with its God in that center.

> Let's say union [introduced in the fifth dwellings] is like two wax candles joined together [at the point of the flame] so fully that all the light was one (or at least the wicks, the wax, and light were all one), but, afterward, the one candle can be separated from the other, and they remain two candles, with two wicks. Here [in spiritual marriage], it's like rain falling from the heavens into a river or a fountain; there is nothing but water there, and you're no longer able to divide or separate the water belonging to the river from the water that fell from the sky. Or it's like a small stream flowing into the sea; there's no way it can then separate itself or "get away." Or, [put another way,] like a large amount of light coming into a single room through two windows: even though the light enters "divided," it becomes all one light inside.[424]

I take comfort in the ubiquity of these kinds of lasting spiritual-union images: like rain into a river, like streams into a sea. We have likely encountered these primordial elements before in other voices describing unity with God. It seems we cannot do better than these images to try to glimpse this sublime mystery without knowing it experientially. Yet Teresa also incorporates an image that brings liveliness and physicality and *incarnation* to a mystery that often becomes too ethereal (or too lacking in humanity) in metaphorical renderings of water and fire. If we leave off with these other (elemental) images, we might mistakenly imagine that we disappear in our union with God. Teresa allows us to remain beloved creatures, even in union. She says that with the passing of time in our union with God, one of the ways we better understand the fullness of our shared life in Christ is that we feel more and more, with greater intensity and gratitude, the truth that "God is the One who gives life to our souls."[425]

> It's clearly understood, through certain secret inspirations, that God is the One who gives life to our souls. These inspirations are often so lively and intense that they can't be doubted, because the soul feels them very strongly. Although they don't know how to explain it, this feeling is so overwhelming that sometimes they can't keep from saying some of the loving expressions that [these interior inspirations] induce: "Oh, life of my life! Strength that sustains me!" and things like this. For it seems that God is constantly sustaining the soul through those divine breasts: out of them streams of milk flow, bringing comfort to all the people in the castle.... It's...obvious that there is someone inside the soul who shoots these arrows and gives life to this life. It's clear that there's a *sun* from which this great light comes, sent to our faculties from the interior of the soul.[426]

This is a wild set of images for many of us: divine breasts sustaining the soul with flowing streams of milk, life-giving arrows, and the relatively tame sun with a brilliant light. The overall impression, though, is beautiful: there is continual nourishment, nurture, and enlightenment for the busy bodies of the castle, the many parts of ourselves that do not, cannot, rest in perfect peace with God but continue to serve. Because we are not drops of water but human beings, sustenance is needed, and sustenance is provided.

Furthermore, Teresa is quite clear that this lasting state of union with God does not mean that our "faculties and senses and passions are always in this peace."[427] It is not just that aspects of ourselves are busy; sometimes, aspects of ourselves will also be disturbed. "The other dwellings don't stop having times of conflict and work and fatigue," but, "as a general rule," these difficulties do not manage to *unseat* the soul's center point of peace.[428] Teresa tries to explain the mystery of what we might call "deep inner peace" amid trials and suffering—sketching out the picture of a king leading from the relative peace of the palace even as his kingdom is at battle; or probing physical metaphors, like the body aching while the head remains sound and pain-free. "I'm laughing at myself over these comparisons; they don't satisfy me," Teresa admits, "but I don't know others [to explain this]."[429] Go ahead and judge my metaphors, she says, but try to hold their point: "What I've said is true."[430]

After two chapters of images and descriptions of the peaceful interior life, Teresa then outlines the grit, the reality, of this life lived with and in God. "Now then," says this ever-pragmatic woman, "we're saying that this little butterfly has died, with great joy at having found rest, and Christ lives within her. Let's see what her new life is like and how it's different from her life before."[431] Here are some practical, observable effects of this blessed state, or at least how such a life might look "*ordinarily*"[432]:

1. *Forgetfulness of self.* The self is not annihilated, but it is no longer anxious and grasping. The soul "doesn't want to be anything, anywhere, except when she realizes that there may be some part for her to play that increases the glory and honor of God in some way."[433]

2. *(Still) Living a rather ordinary human life.* "Don't understand by this description, daughters, that you stop taking into account eating and sleeping (which is no small torment)." And here is that wonderful phrase again, at least for those of us outside the monastery, of many ages and states: This soul still does "everything that [she is] obligated to do, according to [her] state in life."[434] The soul is

still tending the garden, sweeping the steps, caring for the children, doing the dishes.

3. *Desiring to suffer for God, but with greater detachment than previously.* "If [the Lord] wants her to suffer, well and good; if not, she
   doesn't kill herself over it like she used to."[435]

4. *Peace and joy in the face of persecution, and compassion for persecutors.*
   This soul has the magnanimity to pray that the ones who mock
   and persecute it would receive any spiritual delights it currently
   has or has had (even to its own loss of these gifts) "and thus prevent
   them from offending our Lord."[436]

5. *Desiring to serve God by benefiting others.* No longer does this soul
   want to die to be with God more quickly; instead, it wants "to *live*
   for many years" if, through its struggles and sacrifices, however
   small, it might help God to be known and praised.[437]

6. *No fear of death.* The soul would no more fear death than it would
   "a gentle rapture."[438]

7. *Great detachment and quietness of spirit.* The hunger for spiritual
   delight and other consolations is gone; raptures have faded or
   ceased; the soul is silent[439] and content, rich in remembrance and
   with "great tenderness for our Lord."[440] The soul "has found her
   rest."[441] Generally, such a soul desires to be either alone or of loving
   service to others.[442]

8. *Gentle "enkindling" from God when needed.* When the soul is pulled
   away from God through distractions, God draws it back to Him in
   a frequently occurring, "ordinary"[443] way, as if stoking a fire from
   within the soul. These "touches of [God's] love, so gentle and penetrating," become a way that God communicates with and recol-
   lects the mind and soul through day-to-day life.[444]

So, Teresa says, add these effects to the others I've mentioned from
the other degrees of prayer and spiritual growth, and they should give
you a pretty good picture of what emerges from this gift of "peace of the
soul."[445] She searches Scripture for images that match this great gift: the
kiss sought by the bride; an abundance of water for the thirsting, wounded
deer; the soul delighting in God's tabernacle; the dove's return to Noah's

ark with the olive branch in its beak.[446] The images are all of fulfillment and rest and healing, but not of life's end.

Indeed, "life is long,"[447] and, again, it is her humble description of the continued *humanity* of even souls who have reached this deepest place of spiritual maturity that clenched my trust in her guidance. "Sisters, you must not think that the effects I've described in these souls are *always* there. That's why I say 'ordinarily' or 'usually,' at least when I remember to."[448] Sometimes, for "a day at most, or a little longer," the shadow side, full of fear or anxiety or anger or inordinate desires, seems to reign again, even in these enlightened souls; this is rightfully humbling.[449] Also, it would be a mistake to think of this person as having achieved a sort of blemish-free perfection, even on the majority of days when they are not unduly disturbed. Although characterized by a strong *desire* not to sin—a desire to love God and others well—inadvertently, they will commit "many imperfections, and even sins."[450] Even with this great gift of peace, this great awareness of a life shared with God, we could still fall again, like so many favored ones before us have done, if we lose our humility, our awareness of the ways in which we love imperfectly and unevenly as human beings.[451]

Tellingly, Teresa insists that humans still retain the freedom to abandon God: even in this "divine marriage," we are not "trapped" or "fulfilled *perfectly* in our lifetime." This remarkable blessing of unity, constant company, and shared responsibility with him can be lost if we "turn away from God."[452] Teresa is likely speaking of herself when she says, "I know for sure that, even when the soul seems to be in this state, and has been for many years, she doesn't consider herself safe."[453] It would be a mistake to think of this perspective as an anxious neurosis; instead, it is a simple awareness of the difference between human beings and God. She never suggests that God will take away this "peace of the soul,"[454] once given, but we might always "turn away." Love is squelched by force; we remain free to wander from God, and also to love him, to our last breath.

I would not trust Teresa without this sober assessment of even the most enlightened souls. I think it is a beautiful image of a person resting in, relying on, and working out of God's sustaining love yet never claiming to be anything but a living human being, beholding God and bearing as much of their shared love into the world as possible. It might not be much, but it's still a glorious life for that drop of water, that struggling stream that finds freedom and wholeness when it is knowingly and willingly submerged into a greater current. Who knows where that life will go? Here, even Teresa is reassuring, not dire: Fear not, sisters. Go forth when beckoned. "You have no lack of crosses in this state," but they will not steal your peace. "These storms pass quickly, like a wave."[455] You will not regret belonging so fully to God, for he also shares generously with you. "My [own] peace I give you," says the Lord. It is love's fulfillment, the mantle over this soul that has abandoned itself to God's purposes. "I do not give to you as the world gives. Do not let your hearts be troubled, and do not let them be afraid."[456]

"Don't Tell Me Who I Am Yet": Strength to Serve, Resist, and Reform

> It will be good, sisters, to tell you *why* the Lord gives so many merciful gifts in this world—the point of these "favors." Although you'll have understood this if you've paid attention to the effects they produce, I want to tell you again here so that no one thinks it's only to give pleasure to these souls. Such thinking would be a great mistake. For His Majesty can't do a greater "favor" than to give us a life that might imitate the life of the Son He so loved. And so I'm certain that these gifts or favors are for strengthening our weakness,…enabling us to imitate Him in His great sufferings.[457]

Although that which lies within and between the soul and God is the primary focus of her text, Teresa is not content to end her work with a vision of personal transformation. Peace in our hearts is not the end game, friends. She wants to remind us, one last time, what all of this is *for*, why God grants gifts in prayer and beckons and pulls people toward peace and wholeness in so many different ways: it is all so that we might be stronger, steadier servants of God's love, liberated from the false attachments of this world and empowered to walk courageously wherever God leads. "Let us desire and occupy ourselves in prayer, not for our own enjoyment but to have this kind of strength to serve,"[458] she says bluntly.

A life of prayer is empowerment for a vocation always greater than ourselves, and always related to God's kingdom: the struggle for greater justice, love, wholeness, beauty. "This is the point of prayer, my daughters," she writes. "*This* is what spiritual marriage is for: works, the continual birth of good works."[459] The apostle Paul is her prime example: "Through Paul's life, we can see the effects of true visions and contemplation, when they're from our Lord…. Did Paul happen to hide away with these gifts, enjoying them and not engaging with anything else?"[460] No, her faithful sisters know; no, he did not. In fact, he went on to take a radical, grueling role that could not have been more surprising or that he could not have been more ill-suited for, in the world's eyes: the Jewish man who was unparalleled (at least in his own estimation) in his zeal for the Hebrew *Torah* and his rejection of Christ-followers became the apostle of Jesus—and not to the Jews, but to the Gentiles. Apostle to the Jews would have been a big, holy surprise but would have made some sense. Apostle to the Gentiles? Who *is* this man?

An octogenarian monk recently wrote the following, which I can't get out of my head:

> Time, as I bear it daily, is weighted with eternity. The God who resists being named has a name for me. Throughout my time on earth, every day is a letter in the spelling out of that name for me: a slow revelation of who I am. It is a name that cannot be pronounced until the end of life. That pronunciation, I suggest, is what is meant by "the judgment." Judgment is the clarification and truth of each person. *I am.*
>
> I am what I live. Don't tell me who I am yet. It is still being spelled out.[461]

Don't tell me who I am. The God who resists being named has a name for me. Every day is a letter in the spelling out of that name. The social order of any era or nation has its own standards for who a human being is, what they are worth, what they are suited and not suited to do, what their "real" name is. Even the language of "suited" is telling: if, like cards, your "suit" tells which category or group you belong to; if, like clothes, your exterior garment tells the eyes of others where you fit economically, and thus where there will be a flow of good things toward you and where there will be resistance against you. To be transformed by God's love is to allow another voice to speak into your heart about who you are and what you are meant to do. When a person hears this holy voice long enough or loudly enough, they will be strengthened to say to those who would impose limitations on them, "No, you're wrong. That's not who I am." And, when the Spirit presses on that person's heart to speak out for other grossly misplaced and misrepresented people—or when others hear the same urgent correction speaking *beloved* to the ones the world is oppressing and grinding to the ground, ignoring the image of God gifted to them in the very act of creation—the words shift, but the power remains: *That's not who we are.*

Teresa lived out this radical, God-given strength of identity in her own way, defying almost all of the social scripts of her day (though not the church rules) about female authority and leadership. Because she knew she was called and empowered by God, she forged through innumerable bureaucratic, logistical, and financial barriers to establish fourteen new convents, the first opening when she was forty-seven and the last in her final year of life, when she was sixty-seven. But today, as I write this, there is a different Holy Spirit-inspired reform on the move. The country of my birth, rooted in systemic racism since its founding, is again roiled with voices courageously speaking God's truth about who they are to a society that has always devalued them. Voices fill the streets with this message: *Black lives matter.* The message is modified to accommodate the weakness of white America. The truth is, *Black lives are beloved.* Every life snuffed out by police brutality and the other symptoms of systemic racism was a beloved life—the child of human persons, yes, but also weighted with more value in God's sight than we can comprehend. Where does the strength come from in these leaders, in this community, in all those forced to fight for dignity for way, way too long? It is God-given. *Deep calls to deep.*[462]

God speaks this truth of our real identity into listening hearts in many ways—contemplative prayer or "experiences of God" through the Spirit is but one of them. Still, the role of religious experience in activism is often left out of public discourse even as it remains part of the picture, part of the feeding and strengthening happening behind the scenes.[463] I mentioned them briefly in "Fifth Dwellings," but it's time to share more about four women from another era who paint this truth so dramatically with their lives of "holy boldness, rooted in their unshakable belief that God gave them the authority and power to live out their vocations."[464] They speak to us through their own words, penned in an even bleaker chapter of American racism, as nineteenth-century Black women who were brutalized and dehumanized from their births and at every turn. While living in a society that thought of them as "objects," they experienced a deep shift in their minds and hearts—recognizing themselves as honored subjects and then becoming activists and reformers through God's presence to them and in them. Joy R. Bostic summarizes their remarkable stories thus:

> In the spiritual autobiographies of Jarena Lee, Sojourner Truth, Zilpha Elaw, and Rebecca Cox Jackson, we hear testimonies of women who broke the grip of anxiety and fear caused by the uncertainty of their spiritual and material lives within the web of the matrix of domination. Through her religious experiences, Jarena Lee conquered the demonic forces that would have destroyed her life, was transformed into a new being, and went on in her religious activism to bring about healing for many converts. Sojourner Truth evolved in her understanding of God, developed a critical consciousness concerning race and gender oppression, and became an advocate for justice. Zilpha Elaw believed she was instructed and set apart by God in spite of societal pressures and role expectations, and thus pursued a public ministry in the deep South as well as among Whites in Europe. In response to God's call, she risked physical harm and endured sexist and racist opposition to her religious work. And Rebecca Cox Jackson, whose radical obedience to her inner voice led to her religious activism, established a Black Shaker community.[465]

In these women's lives, one sees the truth of an insight Teresa insists upon as she closes: We are given peace inside so that we might endure "less and less peace" on the outside, and even so that we might come to the point of not even desiring peace in our external lives.[466] Do you see, do you hear, the great power of this peace? The women Bostic describes all denied what their societies, cultures, and families told them about who they were, even though it came at great cost. The principalities and powers of this world will never easily accept such revolutionary claims of worth and belonging. "The soul wages more war from the center than it did when it was outside the center with the others, suffering—so that the faculties and senses and everything to do with the body won't be idle,"[467] Teresa says. I may not like her battle imagery, but I have had a soft life, and not much fighting has been required of me yet. Still, I have seen this strength up close in the lives of my parishioners, women and men who have lived through actual wars and have taught me up close what it looks like to let God define who you are: "If we are made one with the Strong, we will be strengthened through such a full union of spirit with spirit."[468] And, lest we forget, lest we neglect to spend time alone with God, Teresa draws us back to an image of intimate love: "The soul is strengthened," she says, "by drinking the wine of this wine cellar where the Spouse has brought it (and doesn't let it go)," where the banner overhead is love.[469]

It is not just God, in general terms, who gives us strength to be who we really are, who we are called to be. It is God's *love*—in its various manifestations—close at hand even when the world deceitfully insists we are unlovable, or when we have trouble trusting that love for inscrutable reasons. Mary, the one who sits at Jesus' feet, and Martha, the one who serves Jesus, must come together and both be manifest continually in the mature life of faith.[470] Teresa implores,

> Fix your eyes on the Crucified, and everything else will seem small to you. If His Majesty showed His love for us through such horrifying works and sufferings, how can you want to satisfy Him with words alone? Do you know what it means to be truly spiritual? It means becoming slaves of God…. For the foundation of this whole building is humility, as I've said.[471]

To be a slave of God sounds terrible unless we remember God's own humility and goodness, unless we know that this bond is the only one that actually matters and is forged in love for us and the world.

Well. Things have gotten a bit grand around here, and we seem to have lost sight of the simple acts of love required in day-to-day community life that shape and fortify our souls, too. Teresa will not allow that, especially as a closing note, even though she is clearly not opposed to grand acts of radical resistance and reform inspired by God's love. We cannot forget that she was no lone spiritual superstar: her whole life was spent in communities—participating in them, leading them, and founding them. Through this lifetime of formation with and through others, she knows profoundly that we cannot progress and mature "alone with God." As Carmelite priest John Welch summarizes: "The individuation process should take place within a community for a community.... Our development is a precarious journey as it is, without the additional problem of having no companions on the journey."[472] Although we cannot allow others to define us in the deep way that God can, has, and does, the parallel truth is expressed by Carl Jung—God made us as social creatures, and essential work *also* happens in and through human relationships:

> As nobody can become aware of his individuality unless he is closely and responsibly related to his fellow beings, he is not withdrawing to an egoistic desert when he tries to find himself. He can only discover himself when he is deeply and unconditionally related to some, and generally related to a great many, individuals with whom he has a chance to compare and from whom he is able to discriminate himself.[473]

Teresa was deeply and unconditionally related to the sisters in her convents and generally related to a broader network of people in her society and in the Church. Although not highlighted in *The Interior Castle*, the sanctifying role of these relationships gets more attention in her other writings. Even here, she wants to conclude not with "castles in the air" but with the small sacrifices of service we can make *where possible* to the people in our lives, right now.[474] Promising in prayer to "do wonders" for God is worthless "if then, when I leave and I have the chance, I do everything just the opposite."[475] To the end, the pragmatic and wise prioress encourages those of us who feel cosmically insignificant, asking us to love those in our own households, our own neighbors:

> Strive after the virtues, practicing and exercising them.[476]

> What can't be done all at once *can* be done little by little.[477]

And perhaps expressed most powerfully:

> Sometimes the adversary gives us grandiose desires and ambitions, so that instead of using what we have at hand to serve our Lord in

possible things, we are content with having *desired* the impossible. Don't try to help everybody, but instead focus on those who are actually in your company.... Do you think that your deep humility and subjugation—serving everyone with great love toward them— alongside your contagious love of the Lord—kindling the fire of faith in those around you—is of little benefit? You awaken them with these and the other virtues you always follow. This service is not small but great, and very pleasing to the Lord. By your doing the work that you *can* do, His Majesty will understand that you *would* do much more [if you could].[478]

When I came to St. Luke's in 2016, I met many former refugees from Sudan and recent refugees from the Democratic Republic of the Congo, men and women so steeped in the practice of virtues that they were able to graciously accept two young white strangers into their midst. Over the years, more than a few of them have repeatedly awed me with their hospitality and generosity, welcoming me into their homes and hospital rooms, and sending me home with pounds and pounds of Sudanese comfort food that I have come to crave: greens with peanut butter, anjira, zalabia fried bread, and cardamom-spiced black tea laden with sugar. I lead them in prayers and steward the sacraments among them as best I can, but I know I make mistakes, cultural and otherwise. I love and serve them imperfectly. When Colin and I embarked on the venture of restarting this church, I had so many unspoken doubts that even the Holy Spirit could knit together a body so diverse, so fractured in experience and material privilege by flagrant injustice. What boundary is too wide for God to bridge? Can a white girl from Oregon with slave-holding ancestors and no Arabic-language skills serve as a pastor to Lost Boys who are now men, and their families? How far away is too far for communion, let alone leading it? But then two things happened simultaneously. I started being loved by Christ in prayer, undeniably and unexpectedly, and I started being loved by the people of St. Luke's, undeniably and unexpectedly.

One evening, I went to Suzy's house to go over church retreat registrations. I was tired. I sat on the couch on her porch, the same couch where she had told me about walking through the Egyptian desert while pregnant, in the same home where I had once left too soon because I didn't understand the cultural customs around visiting—returning to my own house long before I should have, and really needed to, in order tuck my three-year-old into his queen bed. On this night, though, I continued to sit. Suzy brought me tea and cookies—and then a tray of warm sambusas, microwaved and perfect. Although I felt weary, as I ate and drank, a warm peace spread over me. I looked at Suzy, sitting on my left, saying, "Eat," mothering me. It was a place of deep, undeserved rest. Pure grace. In the blessed silence between us, in the dim light of her closed-in porch, I heard an unspoken question and an answer. *Do you know who you are? You are a beloved daughter of God. Your name is still being spelled out.*

EPILOGUE

One evening, at the dinner table, my nine-year-old daughter said, "So you're trying to finish your book tonight, huh? Don't mess up the ending. A bad ending is so disappointing after a good book." She also said, "I probably won't read it. I don't really find books about prayer interesting, except maybe the Bible." My son implored me to finish so that we could go get slushies.

If my children ever do read this text, no matter what their current understanding of God, I hope they will know why I wrote it. I did not write under obedience to an ecclesiastical authority, as Teresa of Ávila did when she wrote *The Interior Castle*. But I felt quite clearly that I was asked to offer my own "story of God" for the potential benefit of others. I prayed as I wrote that what I gave would be like the trees of Ezekiel 47:12: "On the banks, on both sides of the river, there will grow all kinds of trees for food. Their leaves will not wither, nor their fruit fail, but they will bear fresh fruit every month, because the water for them flows from the sanctuary. Their fruit will be for food, and their leaves for healing."[479] By God's grace, with water I cannot draw nor direct, I hope these words are food for others struggling to keep praying, and healing for others wounded in life and faith. Teresa served me in this way. I hope I have served the reader by opening up Teresa's castle and trying to present her teachings in a way that is identifiable to the modern reader and yet authentic to her inimitable personality and wisdom.

My one fear is that this text is false in the sense that a nature documentary is false: you get a badly distorted idea of how often something "exciting" happens. To my beloved children and all other readers: most prayer is like bird-watching. There will be many times when you see or feel nothing, but you are still glad you went out. I think most people would be surprised at how "little" of God's (powerful) grace it takes to sustain a rich life of faith, a steady walk in the good ways of God; it doesn't require constantly "hearing from God" directly, and yet we are sustained and nourished as we need, often in quiet and indirect ways, and sometimes by the intentional remembrance of our most meaningful encounters with the holy. I also hope you know clearly that Teresa's "castle" is nowhere near exhaustive. There are "many more" dwelling places she doesn't mention, "below and above and all around, with beautiful gardens and fountains and labyrinths and things so delightful...."[480] I don't know the path by which the Lord will lead you. It may not be anything like mine. I hope I get to catch glimpses of it with my earthly eyes, or through what you choose to share, and thus learn new depths of this holy mystery. I hope to hear more about how the Lord has led others, from faces I've yet to meet.

> There are many ways the Lord communicates Himself to the soul through these visions or visitations. Some of them come when the soul is troubled; others when a great trial or work is on the way; others so that His Majesty might enjoy the soul, and also share His enjoyment with it.... Yet I don't want it to seem to you that *everything* you imagine is a vision...but also so that, when it *is* a vision, you don't go around agitated or distressed.[481]

Through this book, I wanted to tell out something of the many ways the Lord communicates to the soul so that others might not be so disturbed or afflicted if a *gusto* blows down the door in their own life and psyche, where they were so sure that God—if God even existed—would never deign to tread. This has been Teresa's gift to me, diminishing my disturbance at being led by a path with some similarities to hers, and thereby increasing my praise for the God of every age. Those who have been touched by a conscious awareness of God's action in their lives, unforgettable and undeniable, share a kinship that is all too often silent. Maybe it is sweeter that way because it allows us to stumble upon kindred spirits who know the "strange loneliness"[482] of being caught between the wonders of God's love and the need to walk in love upon the heavy earth—pilgrims still dangling in the vicissitudes of fulfillment and yearning.

> There's not a creature on the whole earth who can keep [the soul] company—in fact, I don't think even any heavenly creatures could; only the One she loves [would be able].... But she sees that she's like a person hanging, who can't settle and rest on any earthly thing *or* go up to heaven. Parched with this thirst, she can't reach the water. And I don't know that she can bear it; it's a thirst that nothing will quench—and she doesn't want it to be quenched, *unless* it's with that water our Lord spoke of to the Samaritan woman, but that's not given to her.[483]

I know that Teresa is referring to spiritual longing here, the kind that only God can fulfill and that sometimes God withholds, but I still want to pick up her definitive conclusion and take it to a softer place. (I must admit that I am not as steely as she; she is a master of willful definitives, and I am a master of uncertain equivocation.) Such water is not given to the soul? True, no one gives *such* water as God can give, but I have been given life-giving water by fellow pilgrims countless times when "hanging," when weary: books, songs, hymns, art, observations offered up from unseen historical and contemporary soul friends, sojourners like Teresa along this same strange journey that has mostly faded from public view and discussion. This is why we offer our stories of God at all, leaving scuffed but fiery footprints upon the earth, trusting that another soul's thirst might be slaked by their sight in ways we know not. At the very least, their strange loneliness will be diminished. They will know that another traveler was led by God along this path. Our praises increase.

This writing was finished on the Feast of the Holy Trinity, for the glory of God, who lives and reigns forever and ever, amen.

ACKNOWLEDGMENTS

If it is not already clear that I could not have persevered in—much less completed—this particular work without the mysterious help of God, in ways recognized *and* utterly unknown to me, I have failed to communicate an essential truth. Thus, once more, I acknowledge the truth of this ancient deflection of credit: "Glory to God whose power, working in us, can do infinitely more than we can ask or imagine...."[484]

Andrea Heinecke and the team at the Bindery Agency first believed in this sprawling book on prayer and steadfastly sought to find a publishing partner who would bring it to light, even after I had accepted its future as a treasured personal memoir living in my desk drawer alone.

Christine Whitaker understood my essential aim of bearing witness to the ineffable goodness of the God who communicates with us in ways that cannot really be spoken about but might, at times and imperfectly, be written about. Her encouragement and trust, along with the enthusiasm of Amy Bartlett, was its own delightful and unexpected gift.

Lois Puglisi surpassed any imaginings I might have had of a publishing house editor: her kindness, respectful care, intelligence, and razor-sharp eye were a blessing to me and every reader of this book.

Jim Wallis and the Sojourners community provided the richly formative environment that proved to be the seedbed of my vocations to both ordained ministry and writing. My faith and my writing matured due to the mentorship and example of so many there, both in that formative year and well beyond.

The RSCJ sisters of the Spiritual Ministry Center in San Diego provided hospitality that has made space for growth in my soul for nearly fifteen years now. Their prayers and faithfulness seem to infuse the walls of the comfortable retreat house they run.

The people of St. Paul's Cathedral sponsored me for ordained ministry and supported my corporate prayer life when I was still learning to pray on my own, and then welcomed me back again as a curate for more foundational learning. The community at the University of the South's School of Theology (Sewanee) shaped and prepared me for leadership in enduring ways while the marvelousness of God was still very much in question for me. The congregation of St. Luke's Episcopal Church in North Park has strengthened my faith beyond measure, demonstrating and celebrating the work of the Spirit around the globe and in our midst—and always with the virtue Teresa prized most: humility.

A Collegeville Institute writing workshop provided incisive writing instruction (thank you, Lauren Winner), as well as a lovely community of women who encouraged, inspired, and supported me in various ways for years after our week together ended.

An armchair psychologist might naively assume that this book is the work of someone who has not been well-loved and thus sought divine reassurance of her lovability. Such an imagined figure couldn't be more wrong: My mother, Elizabeth Shaw, rejoiced in her children's lives far beyond reason. My father, Reed Stewart, has always let me know he is proud of what I do and who I am, and has shown me what layers of healing transformation look like. In addition to this foundation, the loving support of my siblings—Larz Stewart and Lana Anderson—grandparents, aunts, uncles, and cousins has surrounded me from infancy and continues into adulthood. Thank you *all* for loving me with such constancy, both within and outside of a religious framework; I know so much of God's goodness through—and thanks to—you, and you encouraged me in this project even without understanding what I was writing about!

A few friends celebrated milestones in this writing even across (literal) pandemic fences—Matt and Brooke Gonzales—and oceans—Paige Beckley Biggs. Jessie Chatigny was simultaneously coach and cheerleader through the publishing process. And I could not have birthed this book without the aid of the (St. John of the Cross) midwives: Anastasia Brewster, Lisa Kemble, Kim Dawsey-Richardson, Annie Day, Amy Reams, and Sarah Carter. Breanna Chia was my first and forever favorite reader, responding with a depth of affirmation that gave me a large dose of the courage I needed to continue.

Elisabeth Koenig gave me the wisest counsel, almost all the books I value most, and the strongest human conviction I've encountered that there is joy, wonder, and, above all, *love* at work in the mysterious ways of God.

Pete and Penny Mathewson have cared for me and my children in countless ways and for innumerable hours during the nearly seven years this project has been in process. I could not have had the space necessary to write—physically or psychologically, especially as a mother—without their devotion to our growing kids.

Those same children were my primary inspiration for writing down any of this at all, and they have helped over the years in ways they may not have recognized. Robin asked the best questions, and her keen sense of realism kept me more honest; Jem's sweet and steady appreciation of who I am, with all my flaws, mirrored God's unchanging love when I doubted it; and Nan insisted I not forget one of the central lessons of this process—we can say yes to "swimming deeper" than we think is possible or reasonable when it is God who calls us, and there is joy in those fearsome waters.

Finally, I give thanks to the one who shouldered *much* more domestic and ecclesial work than he signed up for due to this ever-expanding "castle book" project, and yet fought for the completion of the work even before I learned to fight for it myself. Without Colin, I simply couldn't have written more than a short essay in this life I've been given, and I wouldn't know much about what it *actually* means and looks like to have a loving partnership. You make my life better, every day.

NOTES

Note from the Author

1. See Dana Greene, "Evelyn Underhill (1875–1941), *Mysticism*" in *Christian Spirituality: The Classics*, ed. Arthur Holder (London and New York: Routledge, 2010), 325–327.

Prologue

2. Romans 10:14 (TLV).

Introductions

3. Deuteronomy 1:31 (NASB95). The poetic formatting of this verse is an intentional departure from the original paragraph form for the purpose of creating reflective pauses, similar to what is found in prayer books/liturgies.

4. Christena Cleveland, "God Our Mother—Live from Boston," October 17, 2017, *The Liturgists*, podcast, 3:31, 4:46, https://theliturgists.com/season-3/. Emphasis added.

5. For those unfamiliar with Roman Catholic religious orders, the Carmelites are a branch of the church family known for their commitment to a deep contemplative prayer practice, although, as with all organizations, the expression of this initial (founding) commitment can be unsteady, which is precisely what Teresa tried to address in her day through her reform work.

6. Since 1622, just forty years after her death.

7. Raimundo Panikkar, "Preface," in *The Interior Castle* by Teresa of Avila, trans. Kieran Kavanaugh, O.C.D. and Otilio Rodriguez, O.C.D. (New York: Paulist Press, 1979), xiii.

8. Rowan Williams, *Teresa of Avila* (London and New York: Continuum, 2000), 42. This quotation and all subsequent quotations from this work are used by permission of Bloomsbury Publishing Plc.

9. "Introduction," *The Interior Castle* by Teresa of Avila, trans. Kieran Kavanaugh, O.C.D., and Otilio Rodriguez, O.C.D. (New York: Paulist Press, 1979),15–16.

10. "Introduction," *Interior Castle*, trans. Kieran Kavanaugh, O.C.D., and Otilio Rodriguez, O.C.D., 17–18. The Monastery of the Incarnation was also Teresa's initial home as a nun.

11. There are many and various accounts of this exchange, with slightly different wording, but I first encountered this story in Raimundo Pannikar's preface to the 1979 Kavanaugh and Rodriguez translation of *The Interior Castle*, page xvii.

First Dwellings: Turning In

12. Unless otherwise indicated, all quotations from *The Interior Castle* in *An Intimate Good* are taken from Teresa of Ávila, *The Interior Castle: Exploring a Spiritual Classic as a Modern Reader*, ed. Laurel Mathewson (New Kensington, PA: Whitaker House, 2024). Abbreviations identifying the location of quotes from the "Dwelling Places" sections of *The Interior Castle* will be used throughout this book in the endnotes. For example, "1.1.1." refers to "First Dwelling Places," chapter 1, section 1.

13. Unless otherwise indicated, all quotations from Teresa's prologue to *The Interior Castle* cited in the section "Concerned with and for Souls" of *An Intimate Good* are from the Mathewson edition.

14. Teresa of Ávila, *The Interior Castle*, trans. Kieran Kavanaugh, O.C.D., and Otilio Rodriguez, O.C.D. (New York: Paulist Press, 1979), 34.

15. The terms *soul* and *spirit* are often used interchangeably in general conversation and idioms ("How are your spirits?"; "It was good for my soul"), and Teresa's work reflects this ambiguity (especially in the section "Flight of the Spirit" in chapter 5 of "Sixth Dwellings"). Still, I think the comparative images she uses to describe the soul (including, of course, that of a vast castle with many apartments, or dwellings) move the notion beyond a synonym for "spirit," which is often thought of as one of three "subsets" of the whole person (body, soul [defined as the mind, the will, and the emotions], and spirit). In fact, as noted, for Teresa, the word *soul* is often used as we do the word *person*. Nevertheless, in this work, to discuss the soul, or to *be* a soul, is to be concerned and engaged with matters of the spirit, which is to say with the reality of God that includes but also encompasses and surpasses the material world as we perceive it.

16. 1.1.1.

17. 1.2.3.

18. 1.2.1; 1.2.2.

19. 1.1.1.

20. 1.1.2.

21. 1.1.2.

22. 1.1.3.

23. 1.2.8.

24. 1.1.5.

25. 1.1.3. Other editions of *The Interior Castle* use the words *favor* and *favors* (translated from the Spanish *merced* and *mercedes*) rather than *gift* or *gifts*, but I tend to avoid the term *favor* because, in English, *favored* has developed connotations of triviality and even sordidness. Moreover, the meaning of the Spanish word is more like "gift" or "mercy." There is an inherent power difference assumed by *merced* (as with "mercy") that is not necessarily captured by *gift*; but, in the end, I still prefer *gift* as a modern translation. However, I do sometimes use the words *favor* and *favors* as a synonym. Later in "First Dwellings," I explain more about the meaning of *favor* in the context of God granting us His favors, or gifts, and how this word reflects our receiving from God what He alone has the power to give. Note that there is another word for "gifts" in Spanish (*regalo*) that Teresa sometimes uses, which

can make the translation of her work challenging in places. I have also tried to note where Teresa uses the more direct Spanish word for "favored," which she does at least once in referring to a "favored one," and which is a bit different from calling someone a "gifted one."

26. 1.1.2.

27. 1.1.5.

28. 1.1.3.

29. *WordReference.com*, s.v. "mercedes," accessed November 20, 2023, https://www.wordreference.com/es/en/translation.asp?spen=mercedes.

30. 1.1.3.

31. 1.1.3.

32. 1.1.3.

33. 1.1.4.

34. 1.1.4.

35. 1.1.4.

36. 1.1.4.

37. 1.1.3; Teresa seems to be referring to Saint Paul receiving the gift of a "supernatural" encounter with the risen Christ on the road to Damascus, which is the catalyst for his ministry of proclaiming the gospel of Jesus for the remainder of his life. In the case of Mary Magdalene, she's possibly referring to Mary similarly receiving the gift of an encounter with the risen Christ and then running to tell the disciples, a role that has led some to refer to Mary as the "Apostle of the Resurrection."

38. 1.1.7.

39. 1.1.6.

40. 1.1.6.

41. 1.1.6; see Genesis 19:1–26.

42. Francis Spufford, *Unapologetic: Why, Despite Everything, Christianity Can Still Make Surprising Emotional Sense* (New York: HarperOne, 2014), 27.

43. 1.2.8.

44. 1.2.9.

45. 1.2.3.

46. 1.2.4.

47. Anne Lamott, *Help, Thanks, Wow: The Three Essential Prayers* (New York: Riverhead Books, 2012).

48. 1.2.8.

49. 1.1.5.

50. 1.1.8.

51. By "reptiles," Teresa is speaking metaphorically of all the unhelpful, dangerous, distracting elements and values from the world that slip into our prayers.

Second Dwellings: Seeking

52. 2.1.2.

53. I recognize, with great sadness and humility, that it is just this formula of vulnerability, trust, and representation of God that makes harm done in or through the church so painful and damaging. I was fortunate to find myself in emotionally and spiritually healthy hands; many other vulnerable people are not so fortunate, and my present commitment as a pastor is to be part of a generation that acknowledges the deep imperfections of our communities and remains ever mindful of the possibilities of such abuses of power and trust.

54. 2.1.2.

55. 2.1.2.
56. 2.1.3.
57. 2.1.4.
58. 2.1.4.
59. 2.1.2.
60. 2.1.2.
61. Williams, *Teresa of Avila*, 117–18. Emphasis is in the original.
62. 2.1.4.
63. 2.1.4–5. Emphasis added.
64. 2.1.3.
65. 2.1.3.
66. 2.1.6.
67. 2.1.9.
68. 2.1.10.
69. As Teresa described such a state years later in *The Interior Castle*, 2.1.9.
70. 2.1.10.
71. Some journal excerpts have been lightly edited to conform to the overall style of this book.
72. 2.1.7.
73. 2.1.11.
74. 2.1.8.
75. 2.1.8.

Third Dwellings: Commitment

76. 3.1.5.
77. 3.1.1.
78. 3.1.1
79. This Latin phrase, which means "Happy are those who fear the Lord," is central to Teresa's conceptualization of those who are in the third dwellings. It is a reference to Psalm 112:1: "Praise the LORD! Happy are those who fear the LORD, who greatly delight in his commandments."
80. 3.1.3.
81. 3.1.4.
82. Ruth Burrows, *Interior Castle Explored* (Mahwah, NJ: HiddenSpring, 2007), 28.
83. 3.1.5.
84. 3.1.5.
85. 3.1.5.
86. See Mark 10:17–31; Matthew 19:16–30; Luke 18:18–30.
87. 3.1.6.
88. Mark 10:17–22
89. 3.1.6.
90. 3.1.6.
91. 3.2.1.
92. Williams, *Teresa of Avila*,118.
93. Williams, 118.
94. 3.1.6.
95. 3.1.6.
96. Ysaye M. Barnwell, "Wanting Memories," 1993.

97. Williams, *Teresa of Avila*, 119.

98. Williams, 118.

99. Teresa of Avila, *The Interior Castle*, trans. Kavanaugh and Rodriguez, 3.2.10; my formatting.

100. 3.2.12.

101 Karl Rahner, *The Need and the Blessing of Prayer*, trans. Bruce W. Gillette (Collegeville, MN: The Liturgical Press, 1997), 3.

102. Kathleen Norris, *Acedia & me: A Marriage, Monks, and a Writer's Life* (New York: Riverhead Books, 2008), 260.

103. Ivan Goncharov, *Oblomov* (New York: Penguin Books, 1954), 101, quoted in *Acedia & me: A Marriage, Monks, and a Writer's Life* (New York: Riverhead Books, 2008), 298.

104. This quote and subsequent quotes in this section are from a speech by Dr. Vincent G. Harding given at *Sojourners* magazine in Washington, DC, in 2006. Used with permission of Sojourners.

105. Psalm 71:20 (ESV).

106. 3.2.6.

107. Williams, *Teresa of Avila*, 119–120.

108. Theodore Parker. See "The Arc of the Moral Universe Is Long, but It Bends Toward Justice," QuoteInvestigator, November 15, 2012, https://quoteinvestigator.com/2012/11/15/arc-of-universe/.

109. Often attributed to Aboriginal activist Lilla Watson. May have been jointly composed by Watson and others from an Aboriginal activists group in Queensland in the 1970s. See "Attributing Words," *Unnecessary Evils* blog, November 3, 2008, http://unnecessaryevils.blogspot.com/2008/11/attributing-words.html.

110. See Micah 6:8.

111. 3.1.8. Emphasis is in the original.

112. 3.1.9.

113. Williams, *Teresa of Avila*, 120.

114. 3.1.9.

115. 3.1.9.

Fourth Dwellings: Awe

116. 4.1.1.

117. In *The Interior Castle*, Teresa refers to "the prayer of quiet" as a form of or synonym for *gustos*, or spiritual delights. For example, she writes, "The experiences I call 'spiritual delights of God'—which, in other places, I've called 'the prayer of quiet'—are of a very different kind" (4.22). She is not always consistent with her terminology, but this association of the two terms (given by Teresa herself) might help us better understand both terms.

118. 4.1.2.

119. NRSV.

120. NASB.

121. The all-caps emphasis here and in other quoted excerpts comes straight from the journal.

122. NAB2010.

123. NASB.

124. NASB.

125. Douglas John Hall, *Collected Readings*, ed. David B. Lott (Minneapolis: Fortress, 2013), 249.

126. NAB2010. The section designations for this psalm in the NAB have been removed for flow and readability.

127. NAB2002.

128. 4.3.5.

129. Kieran Kavanaugh, O.C.D., and Otilio Rodriguez, O.C.D., trans., *The Interior Castle* (New York: Paulist Press, 1979), 204n1.

130. 4.3.1.

131. 4.3.2.

132. 4.3.3.

133. 4.3.4.

134. 4.3.8.

135. Psalm 139:1–5.

136. 4.1.4.

137. Psalm 139:6–7, 10–13.

138. Psalm 139:13 (NRSV). I do not remember which Bible translation was printed on my leaflet, but I do know that verse 13 (verse 12 in the *Book of Common Prayer* psalter), which caught my attention and my prayer, was phrased as it is in the *New Revised Standard Version*, because these are the words I reprinted in my journal more than once: "For it was you who formed my inward parts." I have retained the *Book of Common Prayer* version in the other sections simply because I find it more beautifully translated.

139. Sarah Coakley, *God, Sexuality, and the Self: An Essay "On the Trinity"* (Cambridge, UK: Cambridge University Press, 2013), 43.

140. 4.1.5—referencing Psalm 119:32 (YLT): "Thou dost enlarge my heart!" Prime is the office—or daily time—of community prayer, typically said at 6:00 a.m. Teresa only includes the Latin; the translation has been added for understanding.

141. John Keats, letter to John Hamilton Reynolds, May 3, 1818, "Letters," JohnKeats.com, http://www.john-keats.com/briefe/030518.htm.

142. 4.2.8.

143. 4.1.2.

144. 4.2.9.

145. 4.2.9.

146. 4.2.9.

147. 4.2.9.

148. John 4:1–29.

149. Luke 8:43–48.

150. Luke 4:40.

151. Luke 3:10 (ESV).

152. 4.2.9.

153. 4.2.8.

154. 4.3.9.

155. 4.3.13.

156. 4.3.9.

157. 4.3.10.

158. 4.3.10.

159. 4.1.3.

160. Although Robinson may also have written about this topic, I heard her say this most succinctly at an informal gathering with students and faculty at the University of the South's (Sewanee, TN) School of Theology when I was a student there.

161. Spufford, *Unapologetic*, 103–05.

162. Job 38:2–7; 40:3–4.

163. 4.1.7.

164. Kahlil Gibran, *The Prophet* (Hertfordshire, UK: Wordsworth, 1996), 4.

165. Luke 3:7–14.

166. 4.2.8.

167. Matthew 19:29 (NASB).

168. T. S. Eliot, *The Longer Poems: The Waste Land, Ash Wednesday, Four Quartets*, trans. Derek Traversi (London: Bodley Head, 1976), 83.

169. 4.2.10.

170. Richard Rohr, "Friday After Ash Wednesday," in *God for Us: Rediscovering the Meaning of Lent and Easter*, ed. Greg Pennoyer and Gregory Wolfe (Brewster, MA: Paraclete Press, 2014), 17. In this essay, Rohr discusses two of the three passages designated for the day—Isaiah 58 and Matthew 9.

Fifth Dwellings: Beloved

171. 5.1.1. The word Teresa uses here for "joys" is *gozos*, which is a bit different from *gustos*. She seems to be using it as a synonym for *gustos*, just as we might use *joys* as a synonym for *delights*.

172. Kavanaugh and Rodriguez, *Interior Castle*, 85.

173. 5.1.6.

174. 5.1.4.

175. 5.1.8–10.

176. 5.1.10.

177. 5.1.3. Both of these adjectives are used: *deleitosa* and *sabrosa*.

178. 5.1.5.

179. 5.1.7.

180. 5.1.7.

181. 5.1.9.

182. 5.1.9.

183. Joy R. Bostic discusses the spiritual biographies and legacies of these four women in her essay "Mystical Experience, Radical Subjectification, and Activism in the Religious Traditions of African American Women," in Janet Ruffing, *Mysticism and Social Transformation* (Syracuse, NY: Syracuse University Press, 2001), 143–60. I refer to this essay further in "Seventh Dwellings."

184. 5.1.3.

185. Psalm 45:3–9.

186. Richard Rohr, "First Tuesday of Lent," in *God for Us: Rediscovering the Meaning of Lent and Easter,*" ed. Greg Pennoyer (Brewster, MA: Paraclete Press, 2014), 33. My formatting.

187. 5.1.11.

188. NASB95.

189. 5.4.3.

190. 5.4.4.

191. Williams, *Teresa of Avila*, 129. Emphasis added.

192. Colossians 3:3.

193. Marie Howe, "Annunciation," in *A Kingdom of Ordinary Time: Poems* (New York: Norton, 2008), 43. All quotations from "Annunciation" used by permission.

194. 5.2.12.

195. Ephesians 3:16–19 (ESV), my formatting.

196. Howe, "Annunciation," 43.

197. 5.2.12.

198. Eugene Peterson, *The Contemplative Pastor* (Grand Rapids, MI: William B. Eerdmans Publishing Co., 1989,) 103–5. Used by permission.

199. Peterson, 105.

200. 5.2.1.

201. 5.2.7–8.

202. Martin L. Smith, *The Word Is Very Near You: A Guide to Praying with Scripture* (Cambridge, MA: Cowley Publications, 1989), 188.

203. 5.3.3: "For true union can be reached, with God's help, if we try to attain it by keeping our wills fixed on whatever is God's will.... Because the most valuable thing about [the other gracious union] actually *comes in and through this union* I'm now describing." Emphasis is in the original.

204. 5.1.3.

205. 5.1.8.

206. 5.3.1.

207. 5.3.2. Emphasis is in the original.

208. 5.4.6.

209. 5.3.2.

210. 5.3.3. Emphasis is in the original.

211. 5.1.2.

212. 5.1.2.

213. 5.3.5.

214. 5.3.7.

215. 5.3.9–10.

216. 5.3.8.

217. 5.3.9.

218. The case of those in solitary hermitages might be considered differently.

219. 5.3.11. Emphasis is in the original.

220. 5.3.9.

221. Teresa of Avila, *Interior Castle*, trans. Kavanaugh and Rodriguez, 5.3.9.

222. 5.3.9.

223. Frederick Buechner: "The place God calls you to is the place where your deep gladness and the world's deep hunger meet." Buechner, *Wishful Thinking: A Seeker's ABC* (San Francisco: HarperOne, 1993), 119.

224. 5.4.8.

225. 5.4.8. Emphasis added.

226. See John 15:12–17.

227. See Luke 1:30–38.

228. For a beautiful exploration of this moment when Mary consents to bear Christ into the world, see the poem "Annunciation" by Denise Levertov in her book *The Sapphire & the Stream: Selected Poems on Religious Themes* (New York: New Directions, 1997), 59–61.

229. Luke 1:34 (KJV).

Sixth Dwellings: Partnership

230. 6.1.1.

231. See Matthew 26:41.

232. The words to this second- or third-century hymn, as found in the *Book of Common*

Prayer (the form I recite or sing): "Glory to God in the highest, and peace to his people on earth. Lord God, heavenly King, almighty God and Father, we worship you, we give you thanks, we praise you for your glory. Lord Jesus Christ, only Son of the Father Lord God, Lamb of God, you take away the sin of the world: have mercy on us: you are seated at the right hand of the Father: receive our prayer. For you alone are the Holy One, you alone are the Lord, you alone are the Most High, Jesus Christ, with the Holy Spirit, in the glory of God the Father. Amen."

233. Williams, *Teresa of Avila*, 130.

234. See Psalm 8:5.

235. Teresa's introduction to chapter 1, as translated by E. Allison Peers, reads, in part, "Shows how, when the Lord begins to grant the soul greater favours, it has also to endure greater trials."

236. Williams, *Teresa of Avila*, 130.

237. 6.1.1.

238. 6.1.1.

239. Williams, *Teresa of Avila*, 130.

240. 6.1.1. Interestingly, Teresa does also say just a bit later that "perhaps not all souls will be led along this [painful] path, though I sincerely doubt that souls that truly have a taste of heavenly things—even from time to time—can live in freedom from earthly trials, in one way or another" (6.1.2).

241. "It is a stage in which the conscious, planning ego has completely lost control.... Those who have assimilated the sixth mansions to St. John's 'Passive night of the spirit' are surely right" (Williams, 136).

242. 6.1.11.

243. 6.1.12.

244. 6.1.13.

245. 6.1.13.

246. 6.1.3.

247. 6.1.4.

248. 6.1.5.

249. 6.1.4.

250. 6.1.5.

251. 6.3.1.

252. 6.3.1. I deeply appreciate Teresa's pastoral wisdom in dealing with such cases, however—she basically says not to pay attention to them, but also not to further disturb people by telling them their locutions are from the devil: "One should listen to them, as one would to any sick person," with compassion but also potentially with the advice to give up contemplative prayer for a time (6.3.3).

253. 6.3.4.

254. 6.3.4.

255. 6.3.5.

256. 6.3.5.

257. 6.3.6.

258. 6.3.7.

259. 6.3.7–8.

260. 6.3.11.

261. 6.3.11.

262. 6.3.11.

263. Paul Quenon, *In Praise of the Useless Life: A Monk's Memoir* (Notre Dame, IN: Ave

Maria Press, 2018), 29.

264. 6.3.12.

265. 6.3.12.

266. 6.8.2.

267. 6.8.2.

268. 6.8.1.

269. 6.8.3.

270. 6.8.5.

271. 6.3.12.

272. 6.3.12.

273. 6.3.13–16.

274. 6.8.3.

275. Excerpt from Richard Crashaw's 1628 Baroque poem "The Flaming Heart Upon the Book and Picture of the Seraphicall Saint Teresa (as She Is Usually Expressed with a Seraphim Beside Her)," *Carmen Deo Nostro*, in *Steps to the Temple, Delights of the Muses, and Other Poems*, ed. A. R. Waller (Cambridge: Cambridge University Press, 1904), 276, https://books.google.com/books?id=6ns6AAAAMAAJ&q=His+be+the+bravery#v. The excerpt has been lightly edited to modernize the spelling.

276. Williams, *Teresa of Avila*, 130.

277. Teresa of Avila, *The Book of Her Life*, in *The Collected Works of St. Teresa of Avila*, vol. 1, trans. Kieran Kavanaugh, O.C.D., and Otilio Rodriguez, O.C.D. (Washington, DC: ICS Publications, 1976), 193–194.

278. Her caution is evident: "These impulses are so refined and subtle, coming from very deep within the soul; I don't know of a comparison I can make that will fit" (6.2.1).

279. Teresa of Avila, *Interior Castle*, trans. Kavanaugh and Rodriguez, 6.2, introductory summary.

280. 6.2.1.

281. 6.2.1.

282. Williams, *Teresa of Avila*, 130.

283. 6.2.5. By any measure, Teresa knew the gifts of the sixth dwellings firsthand for decades before what most consider her experience of "spiritual marriage" or arrival in the seventh dwellings.

284. 6.2.2.

285. 6.2.5.

286. 6.2.5. "One person who was granted this favor spent several years enjoying it, and it satisfied her so completely that, even if she had served the Lord for many years by suffering through great trials, she would have felt well-rewarded" (6.2.5).

287. 6.2.6.

288. 6.2.7.

289. 6.2.7.

290. 6.2.3.

291. Williams, *Teresa of Avila*, 136.

292. 6.2.3.

293. 6.2.4.

294. 6.2.4.

295. 6.2.4. Emphasis added.

296. 6.2.4.

297. In the Spanish text, Teresa identifies God with "the fire" very directly. She writes, "*De este fuego del brasero encendido que es mi Dios…*," which might be translated as "This fire of

the lit brazier, which is my God..." (6.2.4).

298. 6.2.1. See also 6.2.3, 6.2.5.

299. 6.2.8.

300. Saint Augustine, *The Confessions of St. Augustine* (Whitaker House, 2018), 11.

301. Psalm 51:13.

302. Psalm 119:176.

303. 6.1.1.

304. 1.2.14.

305. Williams, *Teresa of Avila*, 136.

306. 6.6.4.

307. Teresa of Avila, *Interior Castle*, trans. Kavanaugh and Rodriguez, 6.4, introductory summary.

308. 6.5.1.

309. Williams, *Teresa of Avila*, 68.

310. See Matthew 16:4.

311. See, for example, Matthew 4:5–7.

312. 6.4.2.

313. 6.4.3.

314. 6.4.3.

315. 6.5.1.

316. 6.5.9.

317. 6.5.2–3.

318. 6.4.5.

319. 6.4.6.

320. 6.4.7.

321. 6.5.10.

322. 6.7.8.

323. David Whyte, *Crossing the Unknown Sea: Work as a Pilgrimage of Identity* (New York: Riverhead Books, 2001), 132.

324. Psalm 113:5–8.

325. 6.7.1.

326. 6.6.2.

327. "The Song of Zechariah," *The Book of Common Prayer and Administration of the Sacraments and Other Rites and Ceremonies of the Church: Together with the Psalter or Psalms of David According to the Use of the Episcopal Church* (New York: Seabury Press, 1979), 92–93.

328. Johann Olearius, "Comfort, Comfort Ye My People" (1671), trans. Catherine Winkworth, https://hymnary.org/hymn/EH1982/67.

329. Emily Dickinson, "XLVI," *The Complete Poems of Emily Dickinson*, ed. Martha Dickinson Bianchi (Boston: Little, Brown and Company, 1924), 171, https://books.google.com/books?id=xRmeuwEACAAJ&q=fumbles+at#v=snippet&q.

330. Dickinson, "XLVI," 172.

331. *The Book of Her Life*, vol. 1, ed. Kavanaugh and Rodriguez, 71.

332. Williams, *Teresa of Avila*, 54.

333. Williams, 54.

334. Williams, 133.

335. This quote is not found in her writings, but it does seem generally reflective of Teresa's radical insistence that Christ needs friends on this earth.

336. Williams, *Teresa of Avila*, 53–54.

337. 6.6.8.

338. 6.6.9.

339. 6.6.9.

340. 6.6.10.

341. 6.6.10.

342. Reference to "Amazing Grace" (1772) written by John Newton.

343. 6.6.13.

344. 6.6.11.

345. 6.6.11.

346. 6.6.3.

347. 6.6.13.

348. 6.7.6.

349. 6.7.5.

350. 6.7.13.

351. 6.7.6.

352. See Robert Farrar Capon, *The Third Peacock: The Problem of Good and Evil* (San Francisco: Harper and Row, 1986), chapter 7, "The Hat on the Invisible Man," 67–78.

353. 6.7.13.

354. 6.7.9–12.

355. 6.7.9.

356. Williams, *Teresa of Avila*, 133.

357. Attributed to desert father Abba Poemen. Cited in Michael Casey, *Sacred Reading: The Ancient Art of Lectio Divina* (Liguori, MO: Liguori/Triumph, 1995), 10. Casey phrases the end of the teaching in this way: "So it is with the word of God; it is soft and our heart is hard, but the [one] who hears the word of God often, opens his heart to the fear of God."

358. 6.8.7–9.

359. Williams, *Teresa of Avila*, 134.

360. 6.8.2.

361. 6.8.1.

362. 6.8.1.

363. 6.8.1.

364. 6.8.6.

365. 6.8.3.

366. 6.8.3.

367. 6.8.3.

368. 6.8.4.

369. 6.8.4. Later in the sixth dwellings, Teresa addresses another spiritual delight that has a similar effect of heightened conscience, born of a different experience: "When the Lord wills, this might happen: while the soul is in prayer, and fully in possession of its senses, it suddenly experiences a suspension in which the Lord leads it to understand great secrets [an intellectual vision].... In this [vision], the soul discovers how all things are seen in God, and how He contains all things within Himself. This is of great benefit because, even though it only lasts a moment, it remains engraved upon the soul. And it also causes great confusion in showing us more clearly the wrongness of offending God, because it's *in* God Himself—I mean, while dwelling within Him—that we do all this wrong" (6.10.2). "It's very clearly understood that God alone is truth" (6.10.5).

370. 6.8.4.

371. 6.8.5.

372. 6.8.5.

373. 6.8.7.
374. 6.8.5.
375. 6.8.8.
376. 6.8.6.
377. "If the confessor tells you that it's the adversary, this will be harder for you (though no truly educated man would say such a thing if you've experienced the *effects* described). But, if he does say it, I know that the Lord Himself will console you and reassure you—He who is walking at your side. The Lord will continue to enlighten your confessor so that he might in turn give light to you" (6.8.8).
378. 6.8.9.
379. 6.8.9.
380. 6.8.10.
381. 6.9.4.
382. 6.9.1.
383. 6.9.3.
384. 6.8.4.
385. 6.8.4.
386. 6.9.9.
387. 6.9.15.
388. 6.9.9.
389. 6.9.12.
390. 6.9.11.
391. 6.9.12–13.
392. 6.9.14.
393. 6.9.15.
394. 6.9.17.
395. 6.9.18.
396. 6.9.15.
397. 6.9.16.
398. Williams, *Teresa of Avila*, 134.
399. Matthew 28:20.
400. William Blake, "The Little Black Boy," in *Songs of Innocence and of Experience*, The William Blake Archive, https://blakearchive.org/copy/songsie.b?descId=songsie.b.illbk.08.
401. Psalm 142:4.
402. 6.4.1.
403. 6.11.1.
404. John Welch, O.Carm., *Spiritual Pilgrims: Carl Jung and Teresa of Avila* (New York: Paulist Press, 1982), 104.
405. 6.11.2–3.
406. 6.11.6.

Seventh Dwellings: Belonging

407. 7.2.7. Emphasis is in the original.
408. 7.1.2: "For it seems that others will think that I know it from experience."
409. 7.2.5.
410. 7.2.8.
411. 7.4.15.
412. 7.2.1.

413. 7.2.1.
414. 7.2.1.
415. 7.1.6.
416. 7.1.6.
417. 7.1.7. Emphasis is in the original.
418. 7.1.9.
419. 7.1.10.
420. 7.2.3.
421. 7.2.3.
422. 7.2.3.
423. 5.1.8.
424. 7.2.4. Emphasis is in the original.
425. 7.2.6.
426. 7.2.6.
427. 7.2.10.
428. 7.2.10.
429. 7.2.11.
430. 7.2.11.
431. 7.3.1.
432. 7.4.1. Emphasis added.
433. 7.3.2.
434. 7.3.3.
435. 7.3.4.
436. 7.3.5. Emphasis is in the original.
437. 7.3.6. Emphasis is in the original.
438. 7.3.7.
439. "Every way that the Lord helps and teaches the soul here is in such peace and quiet. It seems to me to be like the building of Solomon's temple, during which no noise could be heard.... He alone and the soul rejoice together in deep silence" (7.3.11).
440. 7.3.8, 10.
441. 7.3.12.
442. 7.3.8.
443. 7.3.8.
444. 7.3.8–9. I love this description of how one is to respond to such "enkindling": "When this happens to you, remember that it belongs to this innermost dwelling place, where God is in our soul.... Don't fail to respond to His Majesty for any reason, even if you're busy outwardly and in the middle of a conversation with people. It will often happen in public that our Lord wants to give you this secret gift, and it's very easy to make a response inwardly: you can respond with an act or expression of love, as I've said, or say what Saint Paul did: 'Lord, what do you want me to do?' He will teach you there in many ways what pleases Him, and the acceptable time. Because it seems to be understood that He hears us, is listening—and this delicate touch almost always gives the soul the ability to do what was said, with determination" (7.3.9).
445. 7.3.13.
446. 7.3.13.
447. 6.7.13.
448. 7.4.1.
449. 7.4.2.
450. 7.4.3.

451. 7.3.14; 7.4.3.
452. 7.2.1.
453. 7.2.9.
454. 7.3.13.
455. 7.3.15.
456. John 14:27.
457. 7.4.4.
458. 7.4.12.
459. 7.4.6.
460. 7.4.5.
461. Paul Quenon, *In Praise of the Useless Life*, 52. Emphasis is in the original.
462. Psalm 42:7: "Deep calls to deep in the roar of your waterfalls; all your waves and breakers have swept over me" (NIV).
463. This dynamic of essential strength drawn from pivotal spiritual experiences is evident in James Cone's *The Cross and the Lynching Tree* (Orbis Books, 2013), particularly in chapter 3, "Bearing the Cross and Staring Down the Lynching Tree: Martin Luther King Jr.'s Struggle to Redeem the Soul of America." In this chapter, Cone recounts the conviction and courage given to both Martin Luther King Jr. and Mamie Till through divine communications of presence and redeeming purpose.
464. Joy R. Bostic, "Mystical Experience, Radical Subjectification, and Activism in the Religious Traditions of African American Women," in Janet Ruffing, ed., *Mysticism and Social Transformation* (Syracuse, NY: Syracuse University Press, 2001), 157.
465. Bostic, "Mystical Experience," 156.
466. 7.4.10.
467. 7.4.10.
468. 7.4.10.
469. 7.4.11. See Song of Solomon 2:4.
470. 7.4.12.
471. 7.4.8.
472. Welch, *Spiritual Pilgrims*, 107.
473. Carl Jung, in Welch, *Spiritual Pilgrims*, 106.
474. 7.4.15.
475. 7.4.7.
476. 7.4.9.
477. 7.4.7.
478. 7.4.14.

Epilogue

479. ESV.
480. Epilogue to *Interior Castle*, ed. Mathewson, point 3.
481. 6.10.1.
482. 6.11.5.
483. 6.11.5.

Acknowledgments

484. Ephesians 3:20, as used in the *Book of Common Prayer* for morning and evening prayers.

RECOMMENDED READINGS

The books that have informed my faith and my understanding of Teresa's work are too numerous to list, and some of those are reflected in the endnotes for each chapter. This brief recommended readings list aims to point interested readers toward a few gems that center either on prayer practice or Teresa's life and work in an accessible (not *primarily* academic) way.

Prayer and Christian Spirituality

Bondi, Roberta C. *To Love as God Loves: Conversations with the Early Church*. Philadelphia: Fortress Press, 1987.

Holder, Arthur, ed. *Christian Spirituality: The Classics*. London and New York: Routledge, 2009.

Martin, James, S.J. *Learning to Pray: A Guide for Everyone*. San Francisco: HarperOne, 2021.

Smith, Martin, L. *The Word Is Very Near You: A Guide to Praying with Scripture*. Cambridge, MA: Cowley Publications, 1989.

Underhill, Evelyn. *The Spiritual Life: Four Broadcast Talks.* London: Hodder & Stoughton, 1937. Facsimile of the first edition. Eastford, CT: Martino Fine Books, 2013.

Teresa of Ávila and The Interior Castle

Ahlgren, Gillian T. W. *Entering Teresa of Avila's Interior Castle: A Reader's Companion.* Mahwah, NJ: Paulist Press, 2005.

Burrows, Ruth, O.C.D. *The Interior Castle Explored: St. Teresa's Teaching on the Life of Deep Union with God.* Mahwah, NJ: HiddenSpring, 2007.

Medwick, Cathleen. *Teresa of Avila: The Progress of a Soul.* New York: Doubleday, 1999.

Teresa of Avila. *The Collected Works of St. Teresa of Avila.* Translated by Kieran Kavanaugh, O.C.D., and Otilio Rodriguez, O.C.D. 3 vols. Washington, DC: ICS Publications, 1976.

———. *The Interior Castle.* Translated by Kieran Kavanaugh, O.C.D., and Otilio Rodriguez, O.C.D. New York: Paulist Press, 1979.

———. *The Interior Castle: Exploring a Spiritual Classic as a Modern Reader.* Edited by Laurel Mathewson. New Kensington, PA: Whitaker House, 2024.

———. *The Life of Saint Teresa of Avila by Herself.* Translated by J. M. Cohen. New York: Penguin Classics, 1988.

Williams, Rowan, *Teresa of Avila.* New York: Continuum, 2000.

ABOUT THE AUTHOR

Laurel Mathewson was born and raised in Oregon, where she received a lasting love for the natural world, rural communities, and social justice. She graduated with honors from Stanford University, where she found her intellectual passion in the intersections of literature and landscape, faith and politics, and social transformation—as well as a life partner in her now husband, Colin. In her existential and vocational quest after losing her mother to cancer at the age of twenty-one, Laurel worked in academia, in media (as an editorial assistant at Sojourners in Washington, DC, with founder Jim Wallis), and in ministry. Finally landing in a dual vocation as a writer and a Christian minister, Laurel, along with her husband, headed to seminary, and both were ordained as priests in the Episcopal Church in 2013. Their current church, St. Luke's, is a multicultural community in San Diego where the Lord's prayer might be heard in English, Arabic, or Swahili, depending on the Sunday.

Laurel is the editor of *The Interior Castle: Exploring a Spiritual Classic as a Modern Reader*. She has written award-winning work for *Sojourners* magazine, *Geez* magazine, and *The Christian Century*. As an "elder millennial" mother and pastor, Laurel is passionate about preaching, teaching, pondering the ever-surprising love of God with a diverse and multigenerational audience of serious skeptics and serious believers, parenting her three children, ocean swimming, and well-made cookies. Her essential vocation, in the end, is as an interpreter: of texts, traditions, and contemporary experience; between Catholic and Protestant strands of Christianity; and between seemingly incongruous or unintelligible perspectives, even across the centuries.